TITO'S
PROMISED LAND
Yugoslavia

TITO'S
PROMISED LAND

Yugoslavia

Alex N. Dragnich
Professor of Political Science

VANDERBILT UNIVERSITY

RUTGERS UNIVERSITY PRESS

NEW BRUNSWICK, NEW JERSEY

1954

To ALL those courageous souls
who, like my father and mother,
came to these shores and thereby
bestowed upon their children
the priceless heritage of freedom

Preface

THIS BOOK is about Communism in Yugoslavia. It is a study of how the Communists came to power, of the ways in which they govern and of the consequences for the Yugoslav people. It seeks to present a descriptive analysis of the Tito regime and to appraise the prospects for the future.

I should like to introduce a personal note on my approach to the writing of this book. Those who are familiar with Communist-controlled countries know how difficult it is to gather reliable data about them. Fortunately, several circumstances combined to accord me some advantage. In addition to a brief stay in Yugoslavia in 1939, I had the invaluable experience of spending three years (1947–1950, and several months in 1952) in Tito's Yugoslavia, where I was able to observe at firsthand how the Communist system operates in practice. Moreover, during my sojourn there I was able to take advantage of my facility in the Serbo-Croatian language, both in following Yugoslav publications and in talking with countless Yugoslav citizens. The result was a vast accumulation of information, supplemented by recent items from the Yugoslav press. It is primarily out of this data that the book is made.

Throughout the book numerous concrete examples are cited to illustrate this or that point, but I have been on guard against generalizing from isolated instances. I have employed examples in the interests of a more vivid portrayal, but only when I was convinced on the basis of other information that they were the rule rather than the exception. The source of many of them is the official Yugoslav press. It was my experience that almost invariably the reporting and discussion of certain occurrences in the government press were an indication that they were anything but isolated.

Although the official name of the Yugoslav Communist Party was changed late in 1952 to the League of Yugoslav Communists, I have preferred for the sake of clarity to speak of it as the "party." A "party" is more universally understood as an instrument of political power, which in fact the "league" remains. The word Communism (or Communist), unless otherwise indicated in the context, is used to depict the political, economic and social system that Communist-controlled states have actually brought into being, rather than the society envisioned by Marxian theorists.

The purge in January 1954 of one of Yugoslavia's top Communists, Milovan Djilas, came after this book went to press. His expulsion, to be followed no doubt by the purging of other party members, does not alter the basic conclusions about the Tito regime set forth in these pages. Rather, it serves to reinforce them. It does illustrate, however, that events move rapidly and that consequently no study of this type can be completely up to date in every detail.

The debts of gratitude I owe are many. Unfortunately, only a few can be acknowledged here. I am greatly indebted to the Social Science Research Council and to the Penrose Fund of the American Philosophical Society for grants which enabled me to pursue my research in Yugoslavia for several months in 1952. I am also grateful for summer research grants made available jointly by the Carnegie Foundation and Vanderbilt University, as well as by the latter's Institute of Research and Training in the Social Sciences. I owe Vanderbilt an additional debt because it freed me from teaching duties for several months at a crucial period of my writing. I owe much to many individuals, and to none more than to my wife, who has helped me in more ways than even she knows. I am also indebted to many Yugoslav friends, who for obvious reasons must remain unnamed. To a number of officers in our Foreign Service I am indebted in various ways, but I refrain from mentioning them by name for fear perhaps of doing them a disservice in their present or future posts. I am grateful to Professor Avery Leiserson, chairman of our department of political science, for his encouragement and for his reading of several chapters of the manuscript. The ultimate responsibility for statements of fact and opinion is, of course, my own.

ALEX N. DRAGNICH

Nashville, Tennessee
April, 1954

A Note on Pronunciation

While Yugoslav words are pronounced just as they are written, there being no silent letters, the reader may find the following guide helpful in the pronunciation of certain letters.

a	as *a* in father
e	*e* in pet
i	*i* in machine
o	*o* in over
c	*ts* in lets
j	*y* in yet
dj	*g* in George
u	*u* in rule

Instead of employing different diacritical marks over the letters *c, s* or *z,* which is frequently required in the language when the Latin alphabet is used, the author has added the letter *h* in such instances to facilitate an easy approximation of the correct pronunciation.

Contents

TITO'S
PROMISED LAND
Yugoslavia

PART ONE

HOW COMMUNISM
CAME
TO YUGOSLAVIA

THE history of the coming of Communism to Yugoslavia is largely the history of World War II. It is the history of war-bred or war-aggravated conditions and circumstances, of the Yugoslav Communists' unswerving determination to seize power, and of Allied (American, British and Russian) military and political decisions. Seeing these in meaningful perspective, however, requires at least a limited acquaintance with pre-World War II Yugoslav history.

Chapter 1:

The Yugoslav State in the Making

THE Yugoslavs (literally South Slavs) are the descendants of the Slavic tribes that settled in the Balkan peninsula about the sixth century. Ethnically they were one people, but the intervening fourteen centuries have brought important changes. Geographic separation and differing modes of earning a living (largely imposed by physical terrain), the impact of political division and subjugation to different foreign foes, the influence of Islam and the two branches of the Christian church (Eastern Orthodox and Roman Catholic) – all have left their imprint.

Notwithstanding these historically divergent influences, racial kinship has by and large survived. Yugoslavs have retained their Slavic character, and a language common to the overwhelming majority of them has been evolved. But it would be erroneous to assume that differing political, cultural and religious experiences have not left lasting impressions which have been responsible for no little dissension among them.

The Slav population may be divided into three reasonably well-defined groups, and perhaps a fourth which is less clearly distinguishable. The Serbs are the most numerous, constituting more or less a majority of the population of approximately sixteen million. Included as part of the Serb group are the Montenegrins (totaling a third of a million) who, although for many years they enjoyed a separate national existence, are really Serbs. Located for the most part in the southeastern half of the country, the Serbs were geographically nearer to the cultural and other influences of the East. Their religion is Serbian Orthodox. The Croatians, occupying roughly the north-central area, make up the second largest group, numbering a bit over three and one-half million. They have been subjected to the influences of Central Europe far more than have the Serbs. Unlike the Serbs, they are Roman Catholics. Although using different alphabets, Croats and Serbs have a common language, usually designated as Serbo-Croatian. The third group, the Slovenes, numbering about one and one-half million, are located in the northwestern part of the nation. They have been subjected to Western influences more than any other group among the Yugoslavs, and are, like the Croats, Roman Catholic in religious persuasion. Their language, Slovene, although similar to Serbo-Croatian is sufficiently different to constitute a separate tongue.

The Macedonian Slavs, occupying what was once the center of the Serbian kingdom of the Middle Ages, are a less clearly defined group. Serbs have contended that they were essentially Serb, and Bulgarians that they were Bulgarian. But a sizable portion of the actual inhabitants of this most southeasterly tip of Yugoslavia like to call themselves Macedonians. Their spoken tongue is perhaps as akin to the Serbo-Croatian as it is to Bulgarian. They are of Orthodox religion, and the area which they inhabit has a population of approximately one million, but this figure includes a sizable Albanian minority.

Non-Slav minorities in Yugoslavia number nearly one million persons. These are chiefly Albanians, Hungarians, Italians and Rumanians. The prewar German (Volksdeutsche) minority, which had numbered nearly one-half million, has disappeared. Some fled with the Nazi armies in 1945, and most of those who remained were shipped off to Russian slave-labor camps.

Struggle for Independence

The struggle for Yugoslav independence, broadly speaking, dates back to the breakup of the Serbian and Croatian medieval kingdoms. Serbia was defeated by the Turks in 1389 and continued under Turkish domination until the nineteenth century. Considerably prior to the Turkish conquest of Serbia, however, Croatia was overcome by central European masters. Eventually falling under the control of the Austro-Hungarian Empire, she was not to realize liberation until the defeat of the Central Powers in World War I. Other Yugoslav lands, notably Slovenia, had at varying times come under Austrian and Italian rule.

The struggle for Yugoslav independence in a more concrete sense dates from 1804, the year of the first, at least partially successful, revolt of the Serbs against Ottoman rule. Earlier there had been a number of rebellions, but these were ruthlessly suppressed. Some, like the uprising led by Matija Gubec in Croatia, received considerable publicity, while others of even greater proportions were scarcely recorded. And it should be noted in passing that Montenegro was never successfully subdued by the Turks.

The fires of the Serbian revolution of 1804, briefly smothered for a time, broke out anew in 1815, and were never extinguished thereafter. Step by step, the Serbs gained more and more power over their domain, particularly in the '50's and '60's, until in 1869 they were in a position to draft their own constitution.

Serbia as Symbol of Unity

First a principality and then a kingdom, Serbia evolved into a constitutional monarchy in which political democracy flourished. Most of the remaining Yugoslavs (Croats, Slovenes and Serbs) were, by contrast, under dictatorial Austro-Hungarian rule, and increasingly suffering from its denationalization policies. As late as 1907 other Yugoslavs were added to the Habsburg Empire when Austria-Hungary, conscious that Turkish control in the Balkans was on the decline, annexed the formerly Turkish-controlled provinces of Bosnia and Herzegovina. Both provinces were almost entirely populated by Serbs and Croats.

To Yugoslavs in these and other areas of the Habsburg Empire, Serbia was becoming more and more a symbol of unity. More and more Yugoslavs outside Serbia viewed her as their future liberator. They saw in her the realization of their own aspirations for freedom and independence.

The self-styled "experts" of today who seek to explain contemporary developments in Yugoslavia on the ground that the Yugoslavs have never really known democracy have seemingly never heard of this chapter in Yugoslav history. As early as 1874, for example, Serbian prime ministers recognized, in the best par-

liamentary tradition, that they and their colleagues must resign
once the elected parliament had expressed a lack of confidence in
them. Continuing in this tradition, the Serbs made such significant liberal-democratic gains that within twenty years they were
to draft a new and model constitution, which reflected the progress they had achieved. Although suffering a temporary setback
in the '90's, the constitution of 1888 was firmly reinstated in
1904 under King Peter I, a true constitutional monarch. Under
him Serbia was governed in the best parliamentary democratic
tradition. Governments were responsible to the popularly elected
legislature. Freedom of speech and press, as well as other basic
freedoms, prevailed. Political parties organized without interference, free elections were held, balloting was secret, and the courts
were independent and impartial.

A remark of King Peter's as he rode through the countryside
in one of the earliest motor cars is indicative of the democratic
temper which prevailed in Serbia at that time. As they approached a peasant whose horses were frightened by the automobile, he said to his driver: "Take it easy, Joe, this isn't our
domain but that of the peasant!" And his onetime prime minister,
Nikola Pashich, expressed similar democratic sentiments when he
was being heckled in a Serbian village. "Go ahead, boys," he said.
"I fought for your right to heckle me."

World War I and Yugoslav Unification

The rulers in Vienna were very much aware that Serbia had
become the symbol of unity for the Yugoslavs within the Austro-
Hungarian Empire. They had been bitterly sensitive to Serbian
successes against Turkey in the First and Second Balkan Wars—
successes which, they were sure, would make the Serbs and
Croats in Bosnia and Herzegovina particularly restive. The assassination in July, 1914 of the Austrian Archduke Ferdinand in
Sarajevo, the principal city of Austria's newly annexed province
of Bosnia, afforded them the necessary pretext to humiliate Serbia. Although the archduke was killed within their own empire,
the Austro-Hungarian rulers held Serbia responsible on the
ground that the assassin, a Serb, had carried out his mission as a

member of an illegal anti-Austro-Hungarian organization which had been operating in Serbia without hindrance, and indeed with the encouragement, of Serbian authorities.

Irrespective of the truth of the Austrian allegations, no independent nation could have acceded to the demand made upon Serbia and still have retained her sovereignty. Although willing to negotiate an acceptable settlement, Serbia could not bow to the Austrian ultimatum. Thereupon Austro-Hungary, assured of Germany's backing, declared war, and World War I had begun.

Serbia, considerably outnumbered and outgunned, was not supposed to be much of a match for the great Habsburg Empire. But the Serbs held off the enemy for months at their frontier, and it was approximately a year and a half before Austro-Hungarian troops penetrated the interior of Serbia. By this time Bulgaria and Turkey, having entered the war on the side of the Central Powers, had made considerable inroads into Serbia. Consequently, King Peter I, his government, and the remnants of the Serbian army were forced to flee in winter through the almost impassable frozen wastes of the Albanian mountains, ultimately arriving on the Greek island of Corfu.

It was on Corfu in the summer of 1917 that an agreement was reached with respect to their future homeland between the Serbian government and the representatives of the Yugoslav Committee, composed for the most part of influential Serbs, Croats and Slovenes who had fled from Austro-Hungary at the outbreak of war. The future state was to be a constitutional, democratic and parliamentary monarchy under the Karageorgevich (Serbian) dynasty, and was to be called the Kingdom of the Serbs, Croats and Slovenes.

The Corfu agreement had not been reached without considerable difficulty, and many problems which would beset the new nation were left for future settlement. Yet the urge for unity was great and for the most part spontaneous. The armistice was just a week old when a delegation from the National Council in Zagreb, representing the people of Slovenia, Croatia and other Yugoslav areas outside prewar Serbia, presented an address to His Royal Highness Alexander Karageorgevich, acting as regent, expressing the desire of the people they represented to join in union with

Serbia and Montenegro to form the Kingdm of the Serbs, Croats and Slovenes. Many public pronouncements throughout the land indicated that the desire for unity was almost unanimous.

The Treaty of Versailles, merely ratifying what the Yugoslavs had already established, gave international recognition to the existence of the new state and helped in the fixing of most of its territorial boundaries.

Chapter 2:

Yugoslavia as an Independent Nation

ANY attempt to summarize the main lines of political development in Yugoslavia between the two world wars, although imperative to an understanding of Yugoslavia today, cannot expect to be fully adequate. Nor can Yugoslavia's successes and failures as a new nation be totally divorced either from her people's past experiences or from the interplay of European power politics. It is well, therefore, not to forget these two factors in making any survey of major Yugoslav political developments in the inter-war period or in seeking to appraise the meaning and significance of those developments.

New State Faces Internal Difficulties

The new state was destined to encounter internal difficulties at the outset. These obstacles were not simple, and no ready-made solutions were available. Attempts to simplify the problems which confronted the new nation and to place the blame for failure to find solutions on any one individual or groups of individuals simply will not stand the test of impartial inquiry.

Those who are inclined to view impatiently the difficulties confronting Yugoslavia after World War I should give thought to the divergent experiences of the Yugoslav people, living in some eight distinct areas, who were to make up the new state. If we begin north of Belgrade and move roughly counterclockwise, some aspects of these divergent experiences become more evident. The people of the fertile Vojvodina area, for example, were for years under Hungarian tutelage. They were educated under the Hungarian educational system; they operated within the framework of Hungarian legal and judicial doctrine; and they were a part of the Hungarian agrarian system. The people of Slavonia-Croatia, on the other hand, were more influenced by Austria. Yet they possessed a limited autonomy, and their educational and juridical systems were modified by the peculiar traditions of their own aristocracy. And in part because Vatican policy had viewed them as the first line of defense against the East, their basic organizational outlet was the church. To the north and west are the people of Slovenia who for generations lived between Germanic and Latin pressures. To survive, they developed discipline and organization. Closely knit and hard-working, they made good administrators. To the south of the Slovenes was Dalmatia. Considerably under the sway of Venice and Italy and enjoying some autonomy within Austro-Hungary, the people of Dalmatia engaged in world trade, felt the impact of Italian music, literature and education, and considered themselves far removed from the interior. On the contrary, the people of Montenegro, a continuity of the old Serbian state, were isolated in their mountain fastness, which even the Turks found unprofitable to attempt to conquer. To the north and east of Dalmatia and Montenegro are Bosnia and Herzegovnia. Feeling the impact of Turkish influence, this area—populated by Serbs, Croats and Moslems—afforded fertile ground for Austria's policy of divide and rule. To the east of Montenegro is Macedonia. Once the center of Serbia, it became partially populated by Turks and strongly affected by Ottoman barbarity and Ottoman culture. To the north of Macedonia is Serbia, with its own unique experiences: its successful struggle for independence, its autonomous church, and its indigenous democracy.

If in 1919 two Serbs had been introduced, one from Subotica (Vojvodina, near the Hungarian frontier) and one from Bitolj (Macedonia, near the Greek and Albanian frontiers), it would have been readily apparent that they had little in common. They would have had completely divergent cultural backgrounds; their concepts of law and justice would have varied; their educational experiences would have been totally different; their technical achievements and even their general outlook on life would have been dissimilar.

How much greater would be the contrast if the comparison were not limited to Serbs alone. Suppose a comparison were made between a Croat peasant from Bosnia and a Slovene city dweller from the Italian or Austrian frontiers—to say nothing of a number of equally striking contrasts which could be made! And one scarcely needs mention vocal and determined minorities.

Is it any wonder that the task of politically organizing people with such divergent historical experiences was so formidable, particularly in view of the economic consequences of the war and other postwar problems which faced the government.

It fell to Serbia, which had proportionately suffered more in World War I than any other allied power and yet had seen her armies return in successful offensives on the Salonika front, to assume the role of leadership. In the constituent assembly, elected to draft a constitution, there was much debate on the question of federal vs. unitary form of organization. Serbian leaders were not unanimous, but they finally took the position that the unitary form of government was to be preferred, and this view prevailed. Their own experiences had been limited to the unitary form. Moreover, they feared that federalism might bring disintegration, for the Slovenes and the Croats had had little or no experience in managing their own affairs. Serbian fears were sharply accentuated when the Croatian autonomists introduced a draft constitution which would have resulted in the loosest of confederations.

The rejection of the federal approach, however, resulted in immediate and serious dissatisfaction among the Croats. Represented overwhelmingly through the Croatian Peasant Party, they decided to withdraw from participation in parliament following the ratification of the unitary constitution. The Serbs constantly urged them to take their place in parliament, which they eventually did in 1924.

Decline of Parliamentary Democracy

For a time, and under the circumstances, parliamentary democracy worked tolerably well on the national level. Although local bureaucrats were occasionally heavy-handed and not infrequently insensitive to local wishes, sometimes out of caprice but more often out of ignorance and lack of training, a fair measure of democracy prevailed. Political parties functioned, freedom of speech and of the press were in large measure retained, elections were free, and the courts performed with little friction and with substantial impartiality.

There was one exception—the Communist Party. Having elected some fifty members to the first Yugoslav parliament, the party was outlawed in 1921 after one of its leaders had prepared a plot to assassinate the minister of the interior and was successful in his endeavor. The party, although continuing to function illegally and underground, remained formally outlawed throughout Yugoslavia's history prior to its military collapse in 1941.

The year 1928 saw the end of Yugoslavia's uneasy experiment in parliamentary democracy. In that year the leader of the Croatian Peasant Party, Stjepan Radich, died as a result of shots fired into him by a Montenegrin Serb during a session of parliament. His assassination symbolized the failure of parliamentary procedures to assuage the passions of extremist nationalism.

Sensing the acute dangers to the nation, King Alexander set aside the constitution and on January 6, 1929 proclaimed a government by royal dictatorship. The period of direct royal government lasted for approximately three years. During this time an attempt was made to sweep away much of the debris of historic particularism and to give the people a greater voice in local government. The emphasis was on Yugoslav unity: Serbs, Croats and Slovenes became Yugoslavs, both politically and before the law. Even the name of the realm was changed to Kingdom of Yugoslavia.

Apparently having no desire or intention to become an autocrat, Alexander modified the dictatorship in 1931 by introducing a new constitution. Under it parliament was shorn of many of its traditional privileges, and a regime created with vastly increased executive power and few limitations on its use. The result was a basically authoritarian regime, although admittedly less so than in the period of royal dictatorship.

Regency and Croatian Autonomy

In 1934 King Alexander, while on an official visit to France, was assassinated by the Croatian terrorists of Ante Pavelich, an extremist Croat nationalist, operating from Mussolini's Italy.

Since Alexander's eldest son was only eleven years old, royal powers were exercised by the regency council, headed and dominated by Prince Paul. Under him Yugoslavia continued as a semi-dictatorship. No one was in a position to challenge the government successfully. But opposition parties continued to function and elections produced sizable minorities for opposition lists. The opposition press continued in existence, but was subject to political censorship, although it was seldom rigid.

The most strong-willed of Prince Paul's prime ministers was Milan Stojadinovich, who was instrumental in orienting Yugoslav foreign policy toward a political and economic accommodation with the Axis Powers of Italy and Germany. He was constantly pressed by the Croats, who, taking advantage of the tense international situation confronting Europe, demanded that they be given autonomy within Yugoslavia. Stojadinovich negotiated with them, but no agreement was reached.

Shortly prior to Hitler's attack upon Poland in 1939, however, Stojadinovich's successor, Dragisha Cvetkovich, reached an agreement with Croatian leaders. Under this agreement, Croatia acquired a privileged position. She was to have a virtually independent governor and more local autonomy than any other area within Yugsolavia, including Serbia. But the war and revolution were soon to sweep all this away.

On the Eve of Catastrophe

Any impartial inquiry into the political, economic and social experiences of Yugoslavia between the two world wars can lead only to conditional and relative conclusions. How achievements, or the lack of them, are to be appraised will depend upon the standards of judgment employed. If one takes into account the magnitude of the problems which the Yugoslavs faced, the comparative experience of other new post-World War I states, and the conditions which have prevailed in Yugoslavia since World War II, then it can be said that Yugoslavia made considerable progress toward national unity, toward democracy and toward an improved standard of living in the years 1919–1941. And no one can know how much additional progress might have been

made had Yugoslavia been fortunate enough to enjoy another decade or two of peace.

Unfortunately for the new nation, there was rarely a meeting of minds between the Serbs and Croats. Instead of understanding, there was mutual recrimination. Wherever the Serbs, who had a decisive voice in public policy matters, failed to find solutions to their common problems, the Croats were inclined to attribute it to a lack of good will and a desire to dominate. The Serbs, on the other hand, believed that the Croats were deliberately impeding the finding of solutions by forever and always making new demands whenever it seemed that previous ones would be met. At one time, they point out, the Croats even demanded a separate postal system. Believing that they were purposely being hindered while working for the good of all, the Serbs did not sufficiently endeavor to explain either their aims or their methods. And on occasion they permitted what they believed to be unfounded Croat suspicions to lead them to shortsighted decisions which they later regretted.

The lack of understanding between Serbs and Croats was all the more regrettable because the overwhelming majority of all Yugoslavs—Serbs, Croats and Slovenes—aspired to the same high ideals of self-government, freedom, justice and dignity of the individual. But this cannot obscure the fact that the Croats were dissatisfied, or that these flames of discontent were fanned by Hungary, Mussolini's Italy and later Hitler's Germany. Their agents, principally extremist Croatian exiles, clustered around one Ante Pavelich, who in 1941 was to ride into Zagreb to set up an Axis satellite, the so-called Independent State of Croatia.

It must be added, also, that many achievements of Yugoslav governments fell into the category of too little and too late. The Croats were not alone in their dissatisfaction. Many Serbs and Slovenes, although sympathetically aware of the burdens which the government leaders had to bear, believed that progress was unjustifiably slow. Yugoslavia—Croatia as well as Serbia—simply did not, it seems fair to conclude, produce the imaginative and bold leadership which the times required.

The assassinations of the Croatian opposition leader and the Yugoslav king were incidents of no small magnitude in the turbulent and critical years of Yugoslav independence. The political instability which they dramatized was reflected also in the fact that there was no political party, having the support of an important segment of the population, which cut across national or regional lines. For Yugoslav unity, this was nothing short of tragic. The nearest approach to such a party was the Yugoslav Radical Union, formed in the '30's, but essentially constituting an artificial coalition of political groups, mainly Serbian and Slovenian. The parties commanding the greatest support were sectional (e.g., the Serbian Agrarian Party, Croatian Peasant Party, et al.).

Although the nationality problem and the question of political organization were to continue to plague the new state throughout its existence, there were also other difficulties. Religious differences (the Serbs being Orthodox and the Croats Catholic) contributed in no small degree to exaggerated suspicions and mutual distrust. Economically, too, the government seemed helpless in the face of difficult conditions, especially in the depression years.

Operating secretly and illegally, as they were forced to do, the Communists and their sympathizers cleverly exploited the prevailing dissatisfaction. Much of their effort was concentrated on university youth, many of whom were destined to become leaders in the Tito regime. Taking advantage of the students' poverty, the Communist leaders found fertile soil for their propaganda. Their analyses seemed to have a logical ring to these young people, and their promises were attractive. The apathy and indifference which was so prevalent among large numbers of intelligent non-Communists served only to aid the Communist cause.

It would be a mistake, however, to assume that the Communists enjoyed any significant popular following in Yugoslavia at this time or that they in any way constituted a threat to the established order. But war and enemy occupation, together with the enemy's attendant divide-and-rule policy, for the most part destroyed the established order, and brought about conditions which unscrupulous and determined Communists were to exploit successfully in their struggle for power.

Chapter 3:

World War II and Communist Seizure of Power

THE story of what happened in Yugoslavia during World War II is long and at times complicated. Rather than attempt to tell it fully, an impossibility in a book of this type, my main aim here is to survey its broad outlines in such a way as to show how and why the Communists were successful in seizing political power.

World War II and Yugoslav Collapse

- The Nazis, in order to facilitate the liquidation of Italy's war on Greece and thereby secure the southern flank of their planned onslaught against Russia, pressed the Yugoslav government in March of 1941 for adherence to the Three Power Pact, generally known as the Anti-Comintern Pact. Prince Paul, the regent, asked his government for advice. He was given a general staff memorandum which asserted that Yugoslavia could not possibly oppose Hitler, who had already overrun most of Europe, including France, which until then had been regarded as the strongest land power in Europe. The Soviet Union had not yet entered the war, nor had the United States, and England seemed to be tottering.

To Prince Paul this appeared to be sound advice, and on March 24, 1941, Yugoslavia signed the Three Power Pact. Expressions of hostility toward this decision were immediate, particularly in Serbia. Several ministers – all Serbs – resigned promptly. Confusion seemed to prevail in the armed forces. Neither Paul nor his government had taken sufficient pains to explain the basis of the decision which was to be made to important army and air force officers. Consequently, some officers fled to Greece, and others, seeing that the pact was to be signed, took their units to the hills. The latter, before many weeks went by, were to join the guerrilla forces of Drazha Mihailovich.

Elsewhere in the armed services a group of army officers (Serbs), unable to accept the humiliation of joining the Nazis in anything, effected a revolution on March 27, 1941. Prince Paul was deposed and King Peter II, then only seventeen, was placed on the throne. Members of the government which had signed the Three Power Pact were arrested. General Bora Mirkovich, who had led the revolt, stepped aside and General Dushan Simovich, commander of the Yugoslav air force, became prime minister. He formed a national government which included the principal Serbian, Coatian and Slovenian political leaders.

The Communists, who had gone completely underground after the signing of the Soviet-Nazi Pact in August of 1939, were caught off their guard by the events of March 27. They had not even known that a revolt was being prepared, and their response to it was to organize demonstrations against "imperialist England." [1]

Their reaction was in keeping with the resolution adopted by the fifth country-wide conference of the Yugoslav Communist Party held in October, 1940. This resolution emphasized the correctness of the 1939 Communist Party line which had proclaimed the Second World War "imperialistic." Moreover, it praised the "wise Stalinist policy of peace" and pointed out that "in the course of the past year the Soviet Union had liberated 23 million working masses from the nationalist and capitalist yoke." It asserted the need to unmask "the war aims of the imperialistic aggressors of both war camps," and called upon "all party organizations" to maintain "constant contact with their members in the army and to give them instructions in accordance with the instructions for work in the army which the leadership would work out." [2]

[1] *New York Times,* March 29, 1941.

[2] While the resolution was unavailable to me in published form, there would seem to be little reason to doubt its authenticity. In his report to the Fifth Party Congress, Alexander Rankovich quoted parts of it, including the

When Nazi and Italian armies, aided by Hungarian and Bulgarian forces, attacked Yugoslavia on April 6, 1941, the attitude of the Communists was best expressed by their oft-repeated query, "for whom and for what." Understandably, they had no interest in defending the old order, and only desired to see it crumble. Their instructions to party members serving in the Yugoslav army were, in accordance with the above-cited resolution: to disorganize resistance but to make it appear that an incompetent officer corps was responsible for defeat.

The Communists, who after 1945 claimed, ironically enough, that they were the initiators of the March 27 Revolution, can no doubt take take some credit for the fact that organized resistance in Yugoslavia collapsed within two weeks of the Axis attack. That the defeat was hastened by internal disorganization cannot be doubted, but not all sabotage was Communist directed. The Croatian *Ustashi* puppet regime, installed in Zagreb even before organized resistance came to an end, declared openly and publicly in one of its newspapers that the Serbs were "quite right" in their contention that "we betrayed them." The Croats "were actually the backbone of disobedience, sabotage and defeatism. . . . They took care that nothing was in order, that during battle nothing was in its place. . . . The Croats disobeyed orders, wrecked communications, spread panic." [3]

Some prewar Yugoslav army officers attribute the rapid collapse of the Yugoslav army to the "constant state of reorganization which it underwent between 1939 and 1941." This reorganization was most noticeable in the all-important antitank, border guard, air defense and assault units and in the air force. Since Croatians controlled the organization section of the general staff, these officers are of the opinion that the constant state of reorganization was deliberately perpetrated. It is important to remember, however, that irrespective of the contributions made by internal sabotage, the major reason for the Yugoslav defeat was to be found in the tremendous superiority of the Nazi war machine.

With the collapse of Yugoslavia imminent, King Peter II and his government went into exile, ultimately arriving in London.

---

section on party work in the army. Among the political tasks proclaimed by the resolution, he added, were "alliance with the USSR" and "struggle against the war." See his *Izveshtaj o organizacionom radu* (Belgrade, 1948), pp. 9–10.

[3] *Nova Hrvatska* (Zagreb), December 25, 1942.

Here they were to spend the bulk of the remaining war years, most of them, including the king, never to return again.

Yugoslavia was quickly dismembered. A large portion, designated the Independent State of Croatia, was set up as a puppet state. It was to be under the formal rule of an Italian duke, but actually under the Croatian quisling, Ante Pavelich, whom Mussolini's troops had brought to Zagreb. Slovenia was partitioned between Italy, Hungary and Germany, with Germany getting most of it. The greater part of Dalmatia was annexed by Italy. Bulgaria annexed southern and eastern Serbia and most of Macedonia. Hungary took over the rich district between the Danube and the Tisa. What remained of Serbia was placed under direct German occupation, although several months later the Germans succeeded in setting up a type of local Serbian administration under General Milan Nedich, which some writers have compared to the government of Marshal Petain in unoccupied France. Yet Nedich never disavowed his loyalty to King Peter, nor did the Nazis ever consider Nedich's Serbia independent, even in the puppet sense.

The consequences of war and occupation were catastrophic for the Yugoslavs. One needs to mention only a few facts. The Pavelich puppet regime, which could not do much to implement its declaration of war against the United States and Great Britain, sent at least a division to fight alongside the Nazis on the eastern front. More catastrophic for Yugoslavia, however, was the fact that the *Ustashi,* Pavelich's storm troopers, massacred by the most brutal methods well over a half million innocent Serbs who were living inside the boundaries of the so-called Independent State of Croatia. Soon to follow were the rise of guerrilla resistance, Nazi reprisals against the civilian population, and the determination of the Yugoslav Communist Party to seize power through the establishment of a separate guerrilla movement (only after the Nazi attack upon the Soviet Union), even at the expense of further destroying national unity and bringing on a bitter and bloody civil conflict.

Guerrilla Resistance and Civil War

The defeat of the Yugoslav army found many of its officers in out-of-the-way places with remnants of dispersed military units. Many of these rather than become prisoners of war decided to stay in the hills. One such officer was Colonel Drazha Mihailovich, who became the leader of the first guerrilla movement in World War II to begin armed resistance in an occupied country. His movement became popularly known outside Yugoslavia as *Chetnik* (literally member of a band or group), a name that had been used in previous wars to refer to irregulars. Officially it was designated the Yugoslav Homeland army, but in popular usage the name *Chetnik* prevailed. At a later date, the Communists were to emphasize the name *Chetnik* in an effort to discredit Mihailovich by making it appear that his movement was associated with a Serbian veterans' organization of the same name which was assisting the Germans.

Initially, the Mihailovich movement had no political aims save to assist the Allies in the defeat of the Axis Powers. The Yugoslav government-in-exile had recognized its existence, promoted Mihailovich to the rank of general and named him minister of war. Mihailovich considered himself a loyal servant of an allied government which enjoyed recognition among the Allied Powers. He had no political ambitions and did not consider it within his sphere to plan the future of Yugoslavia.

Only after it had long become evident that the Communists were determined to seize political power and to remake Yugoslavia in the Soviet image did Mihailovich's movement work out a liberal democratic and federalist program. This step was taken not so much out of fear that the Communists were winning over the population as out of a realization that the Communists were succeeding with the Allies in damning Mihailovich and representing their own movement, the so-called National Liberation movement, as being the popular and democratic one. The program enunciated by the Mihailovich-sponsored congress in January, 1944 was formulated with the co-operation of representatives of democratic political parties. Even the Republican and Socialist parties, although fundamentally antimonarchist, sensed the Communist danger and joined in the common effort.

Tito's regime has claimed exclusive credit for the Communist Party as the sole organizer of guerrilla uprisings against the Axis. But every Yugoslav knows that this is not true. Under the occupation the Communists did not lift a finger until the USSR was at war. Only then did they talk of needed action against the occupier. Milovan Djilas, one of Tito's closest collaborators, speaking in the name of the party's Central Committee, said on November 6, 1943: "We called the people to revolt only then when Hitler attacked the Soviet Union." [4] Moreover, it is evident from the following additional statement by Djilas that the Communists were interested in helping to liberate Yugoslavia *only* if they had a chance to rule it. "The participation of the Soviet Union in the war," Djilas declared, "gave a guarantee that the war would develop in the interests of true national liberation of the people, and not in the interests of reactionary circles abroad on whom the former hated rulers have leaned." [5] At that time, however, the party knew that it had little or no following in the country, and only by successfully concealing the primary aim of their movement, as well as the fact that it was Communist led, could they hope to attract members to it. Even the name of their leader, Josip Broz Tito, was not heard until many months after their guerrilla uprising was launched.

The core of their movement, popularly known as Partisan, was initially made up of Serbs who fled from Pavelich's Croatia to escape the *Ustashi* massacres. Some of these individuals were wandering over the country in marauding bands, others had been organized into guerrilla resistance groups by nationalist leaders. The Communists simply moved in on these unorganized, or at best loosely organized bands, liquidated the nationalist leaders and appointed men whom they could trust, with political commissars to re-enforce this trust.

Seeking to avoid giving their movement a political coloration, the Communists, contrary to their real convictions, made use of democratic and nationalist slogans. In order to attract people to their organization, they proclaimed their aims to be:

(1) Liberation of the country from the occupier and the attainment of independence and true democratic rights for all peoples of Yugoslavia.

(2) Inviolability of private property and full possibility for individual initiative in industry, trade and agriculture.

(3) No radical changes in respect to social life and activity except for replacement of reactionary local governments and gendarmes—

[4] Vladimir Dedijer, *Dnevnik* (Belgrade, 1946), Vol. II, p. 582.
[5] *Ibid.*, pp. 582–83.

who had placed themselves in the service of the occupier—with na-
tional-liberation committees which have a truly democratic national
character.

All the more important measures . . . will be decided after the
war by representatives of the people, who will for a fact be chosen
freely by the people themselves.[6]

In short, everything was to be done in the name of the people. An example of how much store they put in hiding their true
identity is seen in the fact that they strongly forbade talk about
"Communist actions" or about "Communist troops." Their two
principal military formations—the National Liberation army, and
the Partisan detachments—nowhere carried the name Communist, even though the latter was primarily a Communist elite
guard. One of Tito's top commanders, in a party magazine,
sharply rebuked comrades in Herzegovina for permitting a leaflet
to be signed not only by the command of the National Liberation
army, as it should have been, but also by the regional Communist
Party Committee.[7]

In reality, of course, the Communist leaders' primary aim was
to seize political power, a fact now readily admitted by them.[8]
In some areas of Yugoslavia, even at that time, the Communists
were unable to conceal their aims. One of these areas was Montenegro. There, under the command of Mosha Pijade, one of
Tito's top strategists today, Communist republics were set up, and
prominent nationalists, which meant nearly all intellectuals, were
quickly liquidated. At the Fifth Communist Party Congress in
1948, Tito spoke in general terms of the "errors" committed by
Communist leaders in Montenegro and Herzegovina.[9] He did not
reveal, however, that Pijade had barely escaped with his life
when a group of women, learning of the real Communist aims,
tried to kill him in a village on Durmitor Mountain where he was
hiding. Nor did he tell his comrades that the people of Montenegro were so incensed at Communist brutality that in 1942 they

[6] Leon Gershkovich, *Dokumenti o razvoju narodne vlasti* (Belgrade, 1948),
p. 141.
[7] According to a guerrilla soldier, whose name cannot be mentioned, this
statement appeared in a wartime issue of *Proleter* and was signed by Alexander Rankovich (Marko). This is partially confirmed by Rankovich, *op. cit.,*
p. 28.
[8] See Tito's Brioni speech, *Borba* (Belgrade), April 3, 1949.
[9] *Politichki izveshtaj* (Belgrade, 1948), p. 73. Also see Rankovich, *op. cit.,*
p. 23.

drove all the Partisans out and none was to be found there for a year and a half afterwards.

In Serbia, where the Mihailovich organization enjoyed the complete confidence of the population, the Partisans did not have any strength. In fact, after their withdrawal from Uzhice in November of 1941, the Partisans never came back to Serbia until Soviet troops arrived at the Danube in 1944. To be sure, there were a few scattered and isolated groups calling themselves Partisans. Although perhaps Communist led, they were for the most part composed of disgruntled men who had not found a position in the Mihailovich movement which was to their liking. But in Serbia they were like widely scattered islands in a vast Mihailovich sea.

Clearly, the essential difference between the two resistance groups is to be found in the fact that the Mihailovich movement pursued a national struggle of liberation from the occupier, while the Communist-led Partisans pursued a class war for the purpose of seizing political power. The former wanted democracy, the latter a dictatorship of the proletariat. This difference is the key to understanding all relations between the Communists and other wartime groups within Yugoslavia, as well as relations between the Partisans and the Allies.

Under these conditions, understandably, there could be no real or lasting agreement between the Partisan and Mihailovich movements. Indeed, conflict between them was inevitable. Tito has admitted that the Partisans struck the first blow in the civil war, but on alleged information that Mihailovich's forces intended to attack him the next day.[10] But it is not important to determine who was responsible for the initial outbreak. What is important is that given the avowed Communist aims, which they now admit and indeed proudly proclaim, the Tito forces would have done what they considered necessary to assure victory whether they had suitable pretexts or not.

The Communists first divulged their real aims by their complete insensitivity to Nazi reprisals against the civilian population which followed guerrilla actions. In October of 1941, for example, the Nazis massacred between 4,000 and 7,000 men be-

[10] Josip Broz Tito, "The Yugoslav Peoples Fight to Live," *Free World,* VII (June, 1944), pp. 496–97.

tween the ages of sixteen and sixty in Kragujevac alone, in retaliation for the killing of twelve German soldiers. The story was the same elsewhere. Mihailovich realized that he could not long justify bringing down upon the heads of the civilian population such merciless vengeance. But to the Communists, reprisals increased the disintegration of the existing order which they wanted to destroy. Then the multitude of the uprooted and desperate would grow, and the Partisans could hope to gain new recruits from their ranks. Eye witnesses report that Partisans went around in small groups, ambushing a German patrol here and there, thereby causing people to flee to the hills for fear of being taken as hostages by the Germans.

The Communists also revealed their real aims by a ruthless liquidation of political opponents. Members of guerrilla groups have told me how in the early days, prior to the existence of two distinct resistance movements, they had observed that able nationalistically inclined men disappeared one by one. It did not take the rank and file long to realize that the Communists, who reject no method as unscrupulous or unfair, were responsible. Similarly, the Partisans sought to mislead the enemy following attacks upon their convoys by leaving some of the captured booty as they withdrew through areas where the population was hostile to them. Frequently the result was a massacre of innocent people by enemy punitive expeditions. If such tactics had been used by Mihailovich's Chetniks, they would have been labeled by the Partisans as the most perfidious sort of collaboration with the enemy.

Moreover, the Communists unmistakably demonstrated their true intentions when they began setting up a "new people's authority" in the guise of People's Liberation Committees wherever the Partisans went. Mihailovich saw in these actions, and rightly so, an armed rebellion against the Yugoslav state, the throne and the constitutional order. That it was clearly incumbent upon him, as the chief legal representative of his government, to resist these actions there can be no doubt.

The final proof of Communist intentions was to be found in their diligent and ceaseless efforts to destroy Mihailovich and his movement politically, particularly in the eyes of the Western Allies. The quickest way to destroy him, they reasoned, was to proclaim him a traitor. And they did so as early as late 1941, although the Germans continued to offer the identical reward for his and Tito's head at least as late as the middle of 1943! [11] Even the Kremlin did not believe Tito's rantings about Mihailovich's alleged treachery, and said so.[12] And gestapo Colonel Fuchs, when questioned during his trial in Belgrade in December, 1946 about alleged collaboration between Mihailovich and the gestapo, declared that not only did the gestapo have no connection with General Mihailovich, but always considered him the number one enemy of the German people. The Germans, he said, always believed that his national movement in Serbia represented the greatest danger to the security of German troops in the Balkans. Similarly, when the Nazi economic representative for Serbia, Franz Neuhausen, was tried after the war in Belgrade as a war criminal, he asserted that the Germans had not taken out of Serbia any of the 1944, and only part of the 1943, wheat crop. When the surprised Communist judge asked him ironically: "I presume you lacked railway cars and manpower?" Neuhausen answered: "No, we could not take out anything because of Drazha Mihailovich's Chetniks."

But this testimony was not, of course, available at the time the Communist charges were having a telling effect. Nor were leaders in the West yet aware that Tito defined treason as any act which disputed what the Communist Party wanted to do or challenged its right to a monopoly of political power. And it was not then evident that the Communists were employing every conceivable trick "to prove" the existence of treason. Composite photographs were produced to show enemy and Chetnik "friend-ship." Sometimes uniforms taken from captured Mihailovich men were put on Communist stooges who were then photographed in friendly poses with captured enemy soldiers. Communists were even sent to join the Mihailovich movement under the guise of true patriots, later to return with valuable information and to testify to "Mihailovich's treachery." Through such unscrupulous techniques the Communists were diabolically successful in creating the impression that patriotic men were deserting Mihailovich's home army and joining the Partisans.

[11] *Novo vreme* (Belgrade), July 21, 1943.
[12] See articles by Mosha Pijade, *Borba,* March 22 and 23, 1950.

The Titoists have often made the assertion that collaboration between Mihailovich and the Germans was clearly shown by the fact that a Nazi attack upon their movement was frequently accompanied by a simultaneous attack launched by Mihailovich troops against the Partisans. A British officer who was in Yugoslavia when these things happened explained them in terms of Nazi strategy. Their favorite tactic, it seems, was so to attack the Partisans that they would be forced to move into territory held by Mihailovich's men. The latter, thinking this an attack upon them, would resist fiercely.[13]

The Partisans accused Mihailovich of trafficking with the enemy, but they have readily admitted making similar deals themselves (i.e. exchange of prisoners, obtaining ammunition from the enemy through various channels, etc.) [14] Moreover, they never hesitated to inform the enemy about the location and disposition of their rival's forces. One Mihailovich officer who was captured by the Nazis told me how a German officer advised him in detail about having received information from a Partisan source that revealed their whereabouts. Whatever the truth or falsity of this German's report, it should be recorded that the enemy sought to exploit domestic discord to his advantage. It was in the Nazi interest to have each group believe the worst about the other, and they made full use of their resources to this end.

It is no doubt true that some of the self-styled Chetnik organizations outside of Serbia, which recognized Mihailovich as supreme commander but over whom he never had full command, collaborated with the enemy in fighting Partisans. They undoubtedly did so not because they were pro-German, but because they believed they were the best judges of how the Communist menace should be handled in their localities. For that reason some Chetnik commanders chose to disregard Mihailovich's orders against collaboration. He in turn was hesitant to condemn their actions, since he was powerless by other means to protect the people concerned from Communist brutality.

At Mihailovich's trial in 1946, his accusers produced "orders"

---

[13] Jasper Rootham, *Miss Fire: A Chronicle of a British Mission to Mihailovich, 1943–1944* (London, 1946), p. 28.
[14] See, for example, Tito, *Politichki izveshtaj*, p. 58.

from him approving collaboration with the enemy. He denied that these were his orders. But Mihailovich had unwisely given to some of his commanders blank pieces of paper with his signature so that they could issue orders in his name. Since the Titoists have admitted that some of these had fallen into their hands,[15] it cannot be determined whether the orders were those of Mihailovich, his subordinate commanders, or the work of Tito's agents who could thus manufacture any kind of evidence desired.

Before shooting him, the Communists also alleged at the trial that Mihailovich collaborated with General Nedich. It is no doubt true that Mihailovich had his men in the Nedich administration, but not for the purpose of helping the Nazis. On the contrary, they were able to furnish Mihailovich with valuable information about German plans and even surreptitiously to extend some material assistance to him.

The Germans did not trust Nedich. They knew that, unlike Pavelich in Croatia, Nedich was an unwilling and untrustworthy collaborator, who hoped to utilize his position to minimize the terror of the occupation. That they distrusted Nedich can be seen from what happened to his secretary. The gestapo called him in and asked what were the connections between Nedich and Mihailovich. When he said he did not know, the gestapo immediately put him in prison. A fellow prisoner asked him about his crimes, and the young man recounted what the gestapo had asked him, and added that he would no doubt be free within a few days. Actually, the Nazis shot him the next day for the simple reason, it seems, that they did not want him to be able to tell Nedich what they were trying to find out.

Partisan Ascendancy

To what extent Communist charges of Mihailovich's "treachery" were accepted in the West, and thereby became a factor in the Allied desertion of Mihailovich in favor of Tito, may never be fully ascertained. More important, it seems, was Churchillian pragmatism of aiding those who were "killing the most Germans." This policy, bearing the official stamp of Big Three decisions at Teheran, was to result first in extending more aid to the

[15] Dedijer, *op. cit.*, p. 408.

Communist-led Partisans, secondly in withdrawing all assistance
to Mihailovich, and finally in compelling King Peter II to re-
nounce Mihailovich and to ask the Yugoslav people to support
Tito.

The Allies rationalized their abandonment of Mihailovich on
the ground that he was doing no fighting against the enemy,
whereas the Partisans were. Little or no weight was given the
fact that Mihailovich had engaged in actions against the Germans
but was forced temporarily to abandon them because of the
fearful reprisals. Nor were Mihailovich's successful efforts to
save and return American airmen who had been shot down over
Yugoslav territory duly appreciated. And seemingly no account
was taken of the contradiction in Allied policy of instructing the
underground movements in France, the Low Countries, Poland
and Norway to lie low until the decisive moment came, while
criticizing Mihailovich for doing that very thing. Moreover,
instructions which he received from the Mediterranean and Middle East Allied Command had contained the same type of orders: to prepare and train men but not to dissipate their strength
needlessly. At this time, interestingly enough, the Bulgarian
Communists also believed that the time for rebellion was not at
hand.[16]

All of a sudden Mihailovich was supposed to fight. Although
he had a sizable organization, he was desperately short of arms
and other equipment. The "few droppings from aeroplanes" to
which Churchill referred in the House of Commons on February 22, 1944 was about all the aid Mihailovich had received. A
British officer who was with the Mihailovich forces in eastern
Serbia has reported that for five months (October, 1943 to
March, 1944) not a single British or Allied aircraft brought
them anything.[17] On the other hand, upon his arrival in Italy,
after the mission had been withdrawn, a fellow officer told him
that "on one occasion sixty sorties had been dropped to the
Partisans in one night. In eastern Serbia," he observed ruefully,
"we had received twenty-seven sorties in twelve months." [18]

[16] See Tito's Skoplje speech, *Borba,* August 3, 1949.
[17] Rootham, *op. cit.,* p. 130.
[18] *Ibid.,* p. 214.

But the Partisans were successful in convincing the West, especially Great Britain, that they were inflicting considerable damage upon the enemy. Yet a careful examination of the principal chronicle of the Partisan movement, Dedijer's three-volume diary, reveals that their fighting against the Germans consisted for the most part of one rearguard action after another. They never undertook a single major action against the Axis. In their official history books, the Titoists place great emphasis on the "Seven Offensives," but these were enemy offensives against them. They even admit that they were badly beaten each time, but attempt to portray each as a victory by virtue of the fact that they were not completely annihilated.

To be sure, the Partisans did engage in some sabotage, but much of it was of questionable value. Most of their actions took place in the mountainous regions of Bosnia and Herzegovina. Factories were destroyed, although they were not in operation; bridges were blown up, although they were of no consequence to Hitler's army. Moreover, these actions took place on the territory of the puppet state of Croatia, where it was in Hitler's interest to curry favor with the population rather than evoke their hostility by shooting countless hostages as a result of these Partisan activities. The Partisans would have been insensitive to reprisals against the civilian population in any case, as was demonstrated in other areas. The absence of reprisals in the puppet state of Croatia, however, benefited them indirectly, for the wrath of the local population would have been turned against them, too, as was indeed the case in those areas where reprisals were carried out.

In Serbia, on the other hand, where Mihailovich's forces were to be found and where communications were exceedingly important to the Nazi army, several surrounding villages were burned for one destroyed bridge, and hundreds of young men were shot, imprisoned or carted away to Germany as forced laborers.

Not only were Partisan military contributions to the Allied cause magnified out of all proportion to their true worth, but in addition, the extent of Partisan-held territory within Yugoslavia was falsified. Areas through which they passed were quickly put down as "liberated territory" even though it was obvious that these areas could not be held, and usually no effort was made to hold them. But it was clever propaganda.

When the Allies were increasing their aid to Tito, the Partisans were principally entrenched in the mountains of Bosnia and Herzegovina. They had some groups in Slovenia, but they were competing with a pro-Mihailovich movement. In Croatia proper there were virtually no Partisans. They had been driven out of Montenegro, but were able to return in some areas after the capitulation of Italy. And in Serbia they were nonexistent, not appearing until *after* Soviet troops had crossed into Yugoslavia. The fact that they did not arrive to greet the Red army for over a month after it had reached the Yugoslav frontier is rarely admitted by the Yugoslav Communists. A wall calendar for 1949, issued by *Gospodarski list,* organ of the ministry of agriculture of Croatia, however, has the following entries: "September 6, 1944 —Arrival of Red Army at Yugoslav border. . . . October 10, 1944—First meeting of National Liberation Army with Red Army."

Russian troops, as a matter of fact, were met at the Danube by Mihailovich's forces under the command of Colonel Velimir Piletich. Another Mihailovich commander, Colonel Keserovich, liberated Krushevac and turned over some 800 German prisoners to the Russians when they arrived. The Russians accepted this co-operation. But when Tito's General Peko Dapchevich, whose troops had been on a forced march from Montenegro, arrived, the Chetniks were pushed aside and the Partisans took over.

Everything seemed to move with perfect synchronization in Tito's favor. Soon after the Allies had decided to help his Partisans, Italy collapsed. For the most part Tito's troops were in a better geographical position than Mihailovich's forces to seize Italian equipment. But Mihailovich commanders who were on the spot have told me that the Italian troops had received Allied-dictated orders to surrender only to the Partisans.

The Italian capitulation not only signified more suitable bases from which aid to Tito could be dispatched, but also indicated to the forces of Pavelich's puppet Croatia that the Germans would certainly lose the war. Consequently, they began to abandon the sinking ship, but where could they go? Mihailovich was not near by, and besides, they feared that he might seek to avenge the more than half million Serbs who had been massacred by Pavelich's storm troopers. Therefore, they began joining the Partisans in ever-growing numbers, confident that their sins would be atoned by assisting the Partisans in gaining their ends.

While everything seemed to move in Tito's favor, the opposite was true in the case of Mihailovich. Although receiving no more aid from the Allies, he nevertheless continued to have confidence in their ultimate decisions. Members of the American Mission who were still with him assured him that he would not lose at the "Green Table," after having erroneously assured him that Russian troops would not cross the Danube.

Such optimism on the part of American representatives was not warranted by developments which had been taking place. King Peter II had yielded in May, 1944 to strong British pressure and dismissed his government, appointing the former governor of Croatia, Ivan Shubashich, as his new premier. The purpose of this change was to negotiate an agreement with Tito, which was consummated promptly, and to which further reference will be made below. Tito and Shubashich agreed that Mihailovich should be dismissed as commander-in-chief, but King Peter was reluctant. Finally, he again yielded to resolute British pressure, and thereby dealt a death blow to the Mihailovich organization. Hardened soldiers wept, and people committed suicide. One commander sent word to King Peter, saying that his proclamation "was more difficult to bear than the twenty-seven wounds" he had received fighting the Nazis, but added significantly, "we know you are not a free agent."

The dismissal of Mihailovich, by uncanny coincidence, came just as Soviet troops were approaching Yugoslav soil. Their arrival, occurring so soon after the abandonment of Mihailovich by the Allies and by his own government and king, broke the back of the Mihailovich movement and sealed the fate of its supporters.

While convincing the West, especially Great Britain, of his military prowess, Tito had at the same time volunteered assurances that he had no intention of imposing or introducing Communism in Yugoslavia. As late as 1944, in a conference with Prime Minister Winston Churchill in Italy, Tito gave that assurance orally.[19] Moreover, in response to Churchill's question as to whether he would allow individual freedom after the war, Tito replied in the affirmative, and added that "democracy and the freedom of the individual" were basic to their principles.

It is worth noting at this point that while the Titoists were busy assuring the West of their respect for democracy, private property and individual freedom, there was substantial evidence that they were playing a deceptive game. As early as November of 1942, for example, they created a revolutionary government in the Anti-Fascist Council of National Liberation (AVNOJ). This was the national counterpart of the revolutionary People's Liberation Committees which were being set up locally at least a full year earlier, and which were declared to be the successors of the prewar institutions of local government.[20] The day it was created, AVNOJ condemned the Yugoslav government-in-exile, and publicly and officially proclaimed Mihailovich a traitor.[21]

It is true that they sought to conceal their plans to establish a dictatorship of the proletariat. But once in power, Tito and his collaborators did not feel at all abashed at proclaiming to the whole world that this had been their aim all along. But even if Churchill had doubted Tito's allegiance to democracy at an earlier date, the outcome still might not have been different, for he does not appear to have been greatly disturbed by the prospect of a Communist government in Yugoslavia. Shortly after the Teheran Conference, Fitzroy Maclean, who was the ranking member of the British Mission to Tito, warned Mr. Churchill that Tito and his cohorts were avowed Communists and that as such they would no doubt set up a system along Soviet lines and would no doubt orient Yugoslavia towards the Soviet Union. Churchill's answer was to ask Maclean if he intended to make Yugoslavia his home after the war. And when Maclean replied in the negative, Churchill said that neither did he, adding, "And, that being so, the less you and I worry about the form of Government they set up, the better." [22]

[19] Stephen Clissold, *Whirlwind: An Account of Marshal Tito's Rise to Power* (London, 1949), p. 196. Since these pages were written Churchill has confirmed this fact in his *Triumph and Tragedy* (Boston, 1953), p. 89.

[20] Gershkovich, *op. cit.*, pp. 15–21.

[21] *Ibid.*, p. 103 ff.

[22] See Fitzroy Maclean, *Eastern Approaches* (London, 1949), pp. 402–03.

Partisan ascendancy, and the material and moral aid from the West which so much contributed to it, left the Mihailovich movement in a state of utter confusion. Bewildered and at a loss to explain Allied support of Tito, many of Mihailovich's commanders engaged in mutual recrimination and more and more went their separate ways. Morale progressively deteriorated, and the organization, never strong in discipline, became further weakened. Had it not been for an almost blind faith among Mihailovich's leaders and followers in the ultimate actions of the West, the movement would no doubt have collapsed much earlier than it did.

Communists Consolidate Power

For the Communists, the Tito-Shubashich Agreement was but another tactical move toward their ultimate goal. They took advantage of the "legal continuity" and the façade of a coalition government, which the agreement provided, and behind which their acts could be sheltered.

In spite of all favorable developments, however, the Communists were desperately worried for a time in the autumn of 1944. Despite the mortal blows dealt to the Mihailovich movement, the Partisans had no support in Serbia. Only by a forced march from the mountains of Montenegro by one of the Partisan units was it possible to link up with the Soviet troops which had crossed into Serbia. For a time the Soviet troops were having hard going against the Germans in eastern Serbia. Belgrade, the Yugoslav capital, was still in German hands, and known to be strongly pro-Mihailovich and anti-Partisan. The situation seemed critical and yet neither Partisan nor Soviet troops were nearby.

Fearing that Mihailovich forces would capture Belgrade, Tito made a desperate move to forestall that eventuality. A reprensentative from the staff of Tito's General Kocha Popovich, a Mr. Tomovich, made contact with the members of one part of the Mihailovich Central Committee, which had been dispersed geographically into two groups. He asserted that events had decided the Tito-Mihailovich struggle in favor of Tito, and asked the Mihailovich representatives to assist in implementing King Peter's request that all armed groups join Tito's army and accept its discipline. After analyzing events, the committee declared that it had always been for a united struggle against the occupier and that it was at this moment willing to ask its supporters to join Tito's ranks for the final battle against the enemy. At the same time, the committee believed Tito's staff, in calling upon all people to join the struggle, should announce (*1*) that after liberation the people, with appropriate guarantees, would have complete freedom to decide concerning the political regime under which they would live, and (*2*) that all acts committed in the civil war would be forgotten.

The Mihailovich representatives even selected two delegates who would go to General Popovich's Staff, as soon as they were called, to work out the details. But this being only a delaying action, the Communists turned their backs as soon as the withdrawal of German troops from the front in eastern Serbia removed the danger of Mihailovich's capture of Belgrade. And, of course, nothing came of the talks.

Once in Belgrade, however, Tito moved rapidly to consolidate his position. The firm hand of dictatorship was immediately felt. No time was lost in liquidating actual and potential opponents rapidly and efficiently. Tito's secret police, then known by the initials OZN, were quick on the trigger, and expeditious in filling the torture chambers. People disappeared at night, in Soviet style, never to be heard from again. With the aid of UNRRA-furnished American jeeps its agents rapidly covered the countryside, ferreting out opponents even in the most remote areas. OZN, with its new-found mobility, seemed everywhere. Now, *after* "liberation," the Yugoslav people for the first time began to appreciate the full meaning of one of the Atlantic Charter's honorable war aims—freedom from fear.

It should be noted in passing that relief supplies of all types, sent to Yugoslavia by UNRRA, served to stabilize Tito's regime economically. Food, trucks, clothing, medicines and a whole host of other articles, at that time exceedingly scarce or nonexistent in Yugoslavia, were poured in. The Yugoslav Communist Party determined who should get the major share, with the army and the secret police at the top of its priority list.

Before a majority of the people were aware of what had happened a police state was established. The dictatorship of the proletariat controlled everything. A few newspapers and other enterprises which had begun to function independently soon learned that they could not exist and still remain independent and free. Those who attempted the impossible not only ceased to exist but also found themselves at the mercy of Communist justice.

Simultaneously, Tito moved to liquidate the coalition government which he and Shubashich had devised. Non-Communists, like Shubashich, Milan Grol and others who had believed that co-operation with Communists was possible, found themselves bitterly disillusioned. They were pushed aside and, although holding ministerial posts, not permitted to know what was going on in their own departments, much less to make decisions of any consequence. One by one they were driven by frustration to resign their posts. Those like the independent socialist, Dragoljub Jovanovich, who attempted to stay on and do verbal battle with the Communists, soon found themselves not only out of the government but also in prison.

In place of the liquidated coalition, Tito substituted the typically docile Communist front organization which he called the People's Front. Into the front were brought individual representatives of prewar political parties who, with one or two singular exceptions, were third- or fourth-rate men who had no support among the members of their respective parties. But even these weaklings were not permitted to make speeches or to have party meetings, although their parties had to register with the authorities. And the only really active party—the Communist Party—chose to ignore the formality of registration!

Initially the Communists rewarded these collaborators with insignificant places on their electoral lists. As time went on, they were moved slowly and quietly to even less significant positions. Others were eased out entirely by being pensioned. Until finally all posts of any importance were filled by Communist Party men.

The Tito-Shubashich Agreement, which had received Big Three sanction at Yalta, was now understandably forgotten. The right of the people to choose the form of government under which they were to live became an empty hope. The promised plebiscite on the future of the monarchy was never held.

Anxious to launch a regime on the Soviet model, Tito rode

roughshod over all who would stand in his way. In a speech on
March 27, 1945, he openly warned everyone who would stand in
the way that he "will be run over like a worm." [23] A few months
later, in November of 1945, Soviet-type elections for a constituent assembly were held. Understandably, the constituent
assembly did not engage in any lengthy or detailed deliberations.
It declared the monarchy at an end and proclaimed the creation
of a republic. A constitution, almost a verbatim copy of the
Soviet basic law, was promulgated. And with that last formal
act in the Communist seizure of power, Yugoslavia was catapulted down the road to Communism.

[23] Josip Broz Tito, *Borba za oslobodjenje Jugoslavije, 1941–1945* (Belgrade,
1947), p. 275.

Chapter 4:

Sources of Communist Success

THE principal reasons behind the Communists' successful seizure of power in Yugoslavia have become in large part apparent from what has already been said. Yet it would seem worthwhile to catalog them, even though there may be some argument as to which were the really decisive ones. The following classification may seem arbitrary, but I believe it embodies the main sources of Communist success. The first four are primarily internal and the last two basically external.

Clear-Cut Ideology and Firm Purpose

From the beginning the Communists knew what they were fighting for. They had a goal beyond immediate victory over the Axis. That goal—a Communist state—was their guiding light. Everything was subordinated to one central purpose; no sacrifice was considered too great in the process of seeking its attainment. All their actions became but means to an end, and no means were rejected, no matter how repugnant, if they served to advance the desired goal.

The Mihailovich resistance movement, faced with the Communist clarity of purpose and a determined ruthlessness in achieving it, was at a distinct disadvantage. Mihailovich's principal purpose was to assist the Allies in the war against the Axis Powers, while the Communists were utilizing that war to carry out a revolution. Mihailovich's adherence to at least a semblance of a code of honor and his respect for democratic methods left him the victim of a ruthless foe. Men who spent years with the Mihailovich forces told me how they had refrained, upon captur-

ing young Communists or their sympathizers, from taking drastic
action against them. They were often forgiven, and attempts
made to rehabilitate them, simply because there were among
their captors men who pleaded that they came from good families
or insisted that they were misled. Such leniency, more often than
not, was rewarded with escape and treachery.

Corresponding prisoners in Communist hands experienced
no such leniency but were shot without further ado. Such disregard for life, an attitude which characterized the Communist
view toward Nazi reprisals against the civilian population, por-
trays the fury of their zealous determination. Without doubt they
would not have altered their fanatical course even if the cost
would have been the annihilation of one half or more of the
entire population.

Disciplined Organization

The nucleus of the Partisan movement was the small but
well-organized and disciplined Communist Party. Working
through its established chain of command, it never left any doubts
as to how the movement was to be organized or who the responsible leaders were. The general staff of the movement, the Central
Committee of the Party, relayed its decisions and its orders
through trusted party men in key positions in a welter of Com-
munist-created organizations.

Aware that its own popularity was not great, the party used
its hierarchical and disciplined organization to create the impression that the Partisan movement had a wide and popular
base. By always keeping the party in the background, its leaders
were able to mobilize unsuspecting patriots in such seemingly
nationalistic groups as the People's Committees, the People's
Youth Organizations, and the National Liberation Front. Moreover, even the activities of various political parties and religious
groups were tolerated so long as they did not openly work against
the Communists.

To Western representatives, Tito's men always sought to
portray the Liberation Front (later People's Front) as something
much bigger than the Communist Party. In 1948, however, the
Titoists, stung by Cominform charges that they had dissolved

the party in the People's Front, proudly proclaimed that the Communist Party was always the real ruler of the People's Front. And, in effect, admitted that they had used the front, as well as other ruses, as techniques for capturing innocent liberals and mobilizing them for Communist ends.

Unlike the Communists, Mihailovich had no previously developed organization. By sheer force of circumstances he was catapulted to lead a heterogeneous and loosely organized movement. The autonomy which individual commanders enjoyed frequently resulted in the rise of rival commanders who often refused to obey the supreme commander. It was not difficult for the Communists to infiltrate such a loosely organized undertaking. One Chetnik commander, for example, was able to hold his post for two years, although he was a Communist!

In their conversations with me, men who served in different capacities in the Chetnik movement attributed nothing but the highest motives to Mihailovich. But they were of the opinion that he had not been a sufficiently strong personality to hold tight rein over the movement. Some of them questioned his political wisdom, and all agreed that many of his commanders were politically immature. This was particularly significant, they said, in a movement that tried to hold itself to certain standards of conduct although facing a foe who had no scruples.

Clever Propaganda

As the resistance leader of a recognized Allied government, Mihailovich believed that all loyal citizens should concentrate their efforts in assisting in the winning of the war. He did not consider it his place either to defend the past or to paint a glowing picture of the future society. To him the common cause was clear and unmistakable, and he was sure that it was equally so to his compatriots.

To the Communists, on the other hand, the common cause was but a convenient vehicle to be employed in reaching their ultimate objective. Consequently, a well-organized and cleverly devised propaganda was imperative, both for internal as well as for external consumption. From the outset, and during their most difficult days, Tito's general staff was always accompanied by the Agitation and Propaganda Section (*Agitprop*) of the party's Central Committee. To the extent that wartime conditions permitted, *Agitprop* published newspapers and leaflets, organized political meetings, and otherwise developed a full-scale indoctrination program among the people. The foreign audience was told of Partisan exploits over Radio Free Yugoslavia, purportedly broadcasting from Partisan-held territory, but in actuality from Tiflis in the U.S.S.R.

The tactics of Partisan propaganda, as previously indicated, were devised for the purpose of convincing the Yugoslavs, as well as the Western Allies, that the Partisan movement had a broad popular base and that its goals were democracy, freedom, justice and a better future for all. The Mihailovich movement, by contrast, was painted as reactionary and in the actual service of the enemy. No technique was rejected, no matter how unfair or unscrupulous, if there was hope that it would advance the party's propaganda objectives.

A telling illustration of the value which the Communists placed on propaganda is the case of Vladimir Nazor and others of similar stature. Perhaps not a great poet, but well known in parts of Yugoslavia, Nazor, although weak and decrepit, played a useful propaganda role for the Communists. By getting him to join them in the hills—although often several Partisan soldiers were immobilized carrying him on a stretcher—the Communists added respectability to their camp and thereby induced others to follow suit. The fact that Nazor had written a panegyrical ode to the Nazi puppet Pavelich and that it had been published in an *Ustashi* journal apparently did not bother the Communists.

It must be added, however, that many Yugoslavs were receptive to Partisan propaganda. Promises of democracy and a better life were attractive, especially in areas where people had been dissatisfied with prewar Yugoslav governments. To many whose material well-being had left much to be desired, the Communists offered a philosophy of life—an explanation, a meaning and a promise. This was particularly true of underprivileged young intellectuals, who saw an opportunity to improve their status and to gain psychological satisfaction from championing the cause of the underdog. And many who did not join the

Partisan movement were nevertheless sympathetic with its pledge of a "broad people's democracy."

In many areas, on the other hand, Partisan propaganda had a hollow ring. In Serbia, where the people knew the Mihailovich movement to be truly patriotic, charges of collaboration with the enemy found few or no believers. Similarly, in Montenegro and Herzegovina, where Communists had engaged in ruthless extermination of political opponents and in an unadorned confiscation of property, Partisan propaganda was nothing short of detestable mockery.

Strategic Location

The main centers of Partisan activity, it will be remembered, were the mountain ranges of Bosnia, Herzegovina and surrounding territories. These areas were in the puppet state of Croatia, and it was here that Pavelich's *Ustashi* massacred some half million Serbs. It was in these areas, too, that many escaped the massacres by fleeing to the mountains only to be mobilized by adroit Communist leaders. Their passions inflamed by what had happened to relatives and friends, these men were eager to fight.

Aside from providing recruits for Partisan ranks, this area, with its forests, its high mountains and deep gorges, afforded the best protection against Nazi punitive expeditions, always referred to by Partisan leaders as "enemy offensives." Moreover, the proximity of these areas to Italian garrisons proved useful when Italy collapsed in the summer of 1943. Yet, on reflection, it can be seen how weak the Partisan movement really was by the fact that the Nazis were able to regain control, within a few days, of most of the towns and cities which the Italians had held.

The strategic location of this territory was even more evident when it was becoming clear to all, especially to those who were in the military ranks of puppet Croatia, that the Nazi empire was crumbling. Pavelich's soldiers were induced to come to the Partisans in large numbers by being promised that not only would they not be treated as enemy prisoners of war, but that in addition they could become members of the new Yugoslav army, and in most instances could retain a rank corresponding to that which they already held.

Western Aid

By far the most important source of Communist success, it seems to me, is to be found in the Big Three decision at Teheran which, in effect, made Tito's Partisans the chosen instrument of Allied policy in Yugoslavia. The actual arrival of Soviet troops on Yugoslav soil, while closely related to this and other Allied decisions (such as the one not to invade Europe through the Balkans), is treated separately in the section to follow. There can be little doubt that Teheran opened the floodgates of aid from the West, which, in an ever-growing torrent, was to engulf Mihailovich and sweep Tito to victory.

It is interesting to note that Tito received no aid from the Russians until late in 1944, when the die had already been irrevocably cast. And Western aid continued to flow even after it had become evident that here was an attempt to set up a regime which one day would become an enemy of the West. Many Yugoslavs were completely at a loss to explain Allied aid to Tito. Some tended to be charitable and attributed Western actions to ignorance. But, more recently, after having learned from Fitzroy Maclean's *Eastern Approaches* that Churchill had told him not to worry too much about Yugoslavia's future government, since neither one of them would be making their home there, they have become exceedingly bitter, particularly toward the British. I found many Yugoslavs who had always viewed the Germans as enemies now saying that the Germans had been more honorable. "We did not expect freedom from the Germans, but we did from England," was an expression I heard frequently. But we Americans do not escape our share of the blame either.

The Red Army

Many Yugoslavs insist that in spite of all the weaknesses of the Mihailovich movement and in spite of Allied aid to Tito, the Partisans could not have been victorious if the Soviet army had not come to Yugoslavia. While this assertion may not be subjected to tangible proof, a careful study of the situation would reveal that such a conclusion is far from unsound. And it can be said with considerable certainty that if the Red army had not crossed into Yugoslavia, making it possible for Partisan units to link up with it, Tito could not have won without a prolonged civil war, and there are certainly doubts as to whether he could have won at all. In any case, the fact remains that while Tito had some units fighting with the Russians, it was really the Red army which drove the Germans out of Belgrade (and out of Serbia) and turned the capital over to him.

PART TWO

DICTATORSHIP OF THE PROLETARIAT: PARTY AND GOVERNMENT

ONCE in power, Tito and his eager comrades proceeded to set up a dictatorship of the proletariat. Guided more by Soviet experience than by Marxian writings, they religiously copied Soviet institutional and organizational forms in both party and government. Since their historic break with Moscow in 1948, however, and more concretely within the past year or two, they have made widely advertised changes in the operation of the government and the economy, which they contend are at sharp variance with Soviet practice. But they insist that these reforms are in harmony with classical Marxian teachings and, consequently, that they did not stem from any misgivings on the part of Yugoslav Communists about the wisdom of Marxian dogma, but presumably from doubts as to the efficacy of Soviet methods in pursuit of Marxian objectives. As we look at current Yugoslav practice, therefore, it would be interesting to keep two questions in mind: Do the Yugoslav reforms constitute radical departures from Soviet practice? And, are the similarities or the differences in the two systems more striking?

To pose these questions is not to say that the Yugoslav approach to the implementation of Marxism is not in itself interesting or instructive. On the contrary, contemporary Yugoslav Communist concepts of Marxism, the role which the party and the government are supposed to play, as well as the nature of their concrete organizational hierarchies, constitute an expressive and meaningful commentary on

45

the type of society which the Yugoslav Communists lose no opportunity in proclaiming as superior to Western democracy. To understand how this society functions is to appreciate in no small measure
the nature and the far-reaching implications of the ideological challenge with which the world is today confronted.

Chapter 5:

Marxism and the Role of Party and Government

No PENETRATING GRASP of the Yugoslav Communist dictatorship is possible without a knowledge of basic Marxian theory, or at least that part of it which concerns itself with the role of the Communist Party and the government once the Communists succeed in capturing political power. In the following brief summary, however, it is impossible to undertake more than a consideration of the most elemental features of these theoretical concepts.

Ideological Basis for Monopoly of Power

Unlike other philosophical systems, Marxism provides a plan and an instrument for its own realization. According to Marxian theorists, the proletarian revolution against capitalism will result in the destruction of the bourgeois state and its replacement by a workers' state. The workers' state in turn will give way, after classes are abolished, to a stateless society. During the transition period—the period of the workers' state—political power is to be exercised by a dictatorship of the proletariat. More specifically, political power will be in the hands of the most conscious segment of the working class, the Communist Party.

Yugoslav Communists are fully in accord with this view, although they have made some changes in terminology. They now seem to prefer the term "socialist democracy" instead of dictatorship of the proletariat, and at their Sixth Congress in

November, 1952, they changed the party's name to "League of
Yugoslav Communists." At the same congress, however, Tito
reaffirmed what he and other Yugoslav Communists have been
saying since (as well as before) their rise to power: "In order
that the realization of socialism would develop normally. . . .
Communists must be on top." [1] Other leaders have even asserted
that the role of Communists was being strengthened.[2]

And there is nothing in current Yugoslav practice or in the
utterances of any Yugoslav leaders to indicate that they intend
to abdicate or share any of their monopoly of power. On the
contrary, everything, including firsthand observations and in-
formal conversations with Yugoslav Communists, points to an
unvarnished determination on the part of the party (or league)
to remain the sole repository of power. The façade of an elaborate governmental organization, paralleling the party hierarchy,
but presumably elected by and responsible to the people, is a
familiar Communist device to convey the impression of popular
support. Similarly, the employment of a vast network of mass
organizations, such as the People's Front (recently renamed the
Socialist Alliance), does not signify any diminution in the
power of the party. And, in the final analysis, the Communists
do not seem to make much of an effort to hide the fact that all
important decisions are made by the party and that no decisions
can prevail if they are not in accord with the party line.

It was the party's Central Committee, for example, that decided in 1952 how the Yugoslav constitution was to be amended,
although the power of amendment is vested in the national legislature. One of the Communist leaders, Mosha Pijade, defended
this as natural, for "in the building of our socialist democracy"
the party "possesses political initiative and leadership." [3] Six
months before the amendments were adopted, Tito indicated
what the new system would be like,[4] and at the party's Sixth Congress the changes to be made were described in greater detail.[5] It
was also at the Sixth Congress that the party decided upon far-
reaching changes in the People's Front and its activities.

---

[1] *Borba* (Belgrade), November 4, 1952.
[2] Milovan Djilas in *Partiski radnik* (Belgrade), August 27, 1952.
[3] *Politika* (Belgrade), June 12, 1952.
[4] *Borba,* August 21, 1952.
[5] *Borba,* November 4, 1952.

Party's Tasks in the Transition Period

According to classical Marxian doctrine, the party, acting through the institution of the dictatorship of the proletariat (army, police, bureaucracy, etc.), has two fundamental tasks to perform before the goal of the stateless society can be reached. The first is to do away with the old order: "lay low the exploiters" and liquidate the bourgeoisie as a class. The second is to build socialism: transform the nature of the economy from private to collective enterprise. When these tasks are accomplished, the result will be a classless society, and the state, which exists only because there are classes (as an instrument of the dominant class), will no longer be needed and will "wither away."

Just how these tasks were to be accomplished, no Marxian theorist had explained. Marx had prescribed the dictatorship of the proletariat as the appropriate political instrument, but he had devised no detailed blueprint. Lenin, the leader of the Russian Communists, had declared in 1917 that force and utter ruthlessness must be employed. And the Yugoslavs, as had the Russians earlier, adopted Lenin's formula of a ruthless dictatorship. But the dictatorship of the proletariat was to be only a transition period, yet no Marxist thinker had indicated how to proceed beyond it or how long it might be expected to continue. But the lack of theoretical precision has not hindered the Yugoslavs, any more than the Russians, from talking earnestly and incessantly about their current tasks and about their ultimate goals.

Much of their discussion is in the abstract. The party is referred to as "a conscious instrument . . . of the class struggle of the proletariat," [6] and as the "political and ideological leader of the people's masses in their struggle for the building of socialism." [7] It is said to be struggling "for the building of socialism, preservation of national independence, brotherhood, unity and equality of the peoples of Yugoslavia." To achieve these aims it utilizes "all political and organizational means; it moves and

---

[6] Djilas, *op. cit.*

[7] Alexander Rankovich's report to the Sixth Party Congress, *Politika*, November 7, 1952.

mobilizes the broadest people's masses." This involves "education of the masses in the spirit of socialism," as well as the development of initiative and actions looking toward the broader participation of the masses in the "economic, social and political life of the country." [8]

In short, Yugoslav Communists are steadfastly adhering to the Marxian creed as they interpret it. Wherever one looks, in political utterance or official deed, there is no indication that the party has any intention of abandoning its basic program, or that it has any less confidence than before in the wisdom of that program, or in its ability to carry it out. Methods and techniques, as well as the tempo of development, are being re-examined and revalued, but the goal remains undisturbed.

Recent party decisions reveal, however, that while the party will continue to make the basic decisions and maintain an appropriate supervision to see that they are properly carried out, it will in the future devote far more time to the task of political education than it has done in the past. At the Sixth Party Congress, for example, Tito stated that the "role of Communists consists of re-education and education of the citizens of our country in the socialist spirit," and that "socialist education is one of the most important and most responsible fields of work for Communists." [9]

From Tito's report, as well as from the utterances of other important Yugoslav Communists, the increased stress on political-educational work seems to stem primarily from external sources. There is the need of conducting a "struggle against Cominform-Soviet revisionism of Marxist theory and practice," which will be no inconsequential task in view of the admission that there is a "low ideological level among a fairly large part of the party membership." [10] Secondly, it is imperative to combat the "concepts foreign to socialism," which have increasingly penetrated Yugoslavia as a result of closer association with the West. The Yugoslavs do not reveal which of these two problems they consider more formidable, but if we are to judge by their utterances both have become increasingly acute. And the greatest amount

[8] *Ibid.*
[9] *Borba,* November 4, 1952.
[10] Rankovich, *op. cit.*

of damage is apparently being done inside the party itself. Soviet-Cominform propaganda finds little fertile soil among the general population, whose friendly inclinations toward the West and whose utter hostility toward Communism in all its forms are well known. In the party, on the other hand, Tito has admitted that some "harmful Western concepts" have taken root. And it can safely be assumed that pro-Soviet sympathies are far from being eradicated.

It may also be that there is a primarily internal reason for the new stress being given to the party's political-educational tasks. One of Tito's close collaborators alluded to this when he said that the "process of class struggle is not nearly finished. It merely takes on new forms." [11] He suggested that in seeking to establish Socialism, ideational and political arguments would take the place of administrative measures. "If we Communists want to insure a really democratic and a really socialistic development," he said, "we have to struggle politically and ideologically; we must write and write . . . and discuss and discuss." These words, no doubt principally conceived for export, can at best be but expressions of wishful thoughts, for there is nothing in Yugoslavia to signify that political arguments, although they may increase, will at any time in the foreseeable future replace administrative measures. Moreover, in view of the vast proportions of existing politico-ideological work, discussed in considerable detail in Part III, it is difficult not to conclude that it has already passed the point of diminishing returns.

Government as Agent of the Party

Since political power is an exclusive prerogative of the party, and since it consequently formulates policy, all governmental forms, as well as the whole fabric of organizational and institutional life in a Communist society, are at the beck and call of the party. They constitute the administrative apparatus for implementing party policy and party aims. This is the central point to remember about all organizational activities under Communism. All else is subordinate. The much advertised reforms in the Yugoslav governmental structure, which were inaugurated early in

[11] Djilas at Sixth Party Congress, *Politika*, November 6, 1952.

1953, have not in any way altered the basic Marxian concepts concerning the primary functions which institutions of government under Communism are supposed to perform.

But the party does more than decide policy. Keeping one eye on the performances of bureaucratic agencies and the other on the Marxian text, it acts as a driving force, pushing its will through a variety of channels. It is not only the judge of ultimate results but also the instrument which guides, encourages, and, in the final analysis, demands acceptable performance. The techniques which it employs to this end, that is the means and methods of harnessing the masses to the dictatorship, are discussed in Part III.

Yugoslav Communists are anxious, however, to preserve the fiction that governmental policies stem from local and popular initiative. In doing this, they seem to be motivated by at least two considerations. First of all, they are seeking to make it less obvious to their own people that the Communists "run everything," hoping thereby to minimize popular hostility against them, and believing that indirect control may actually afford them more time for other vital jobs. Secondly, American congressmen and other influential persons from the West have told them that they should pay more attention to public opinion. As long as they continue to need assistance from the West, therefore, they will want to create an impression that they are responsive to popular demands.

In fact, the Yugoslavs are going one step further. They are earnestly talking about the "withering away of the state." Unlike the Russians, who long ago stopped discussing this vital Marxian concept as something imminent, the Yugoslavs, although not setting any target date either, are talking about it as coming "by degrees" and through the elimination of "its individual functions." [12] Evidence now available, however, does not point to any rapid or significant withering away of the Yugoslav state.

[12] Tito's report to Sixth Party Congress, *Borba,* November 4, 1952.

Chapter 6:

Party Organization

THE Yugoslav Communist Party (or League, as it is now called) has an intricate organization. The size and nature of its membership, its organizational forms and its leadership all contribute to an understanding of the sum total of its activities. These features serve in large measure to explain the manner in which the party wields its vast powers, a process described in the latter part of this and in subsequent chapters.

Party Membership

Outlawed in 1921, the Yugoslav Communist Party continued to function underground. Although growing from a mere 3,500 members in 1929 to approximately 12,000 in 1941, it was still but a drop in the bucket compared to an estimated total population of nearly sixteen millions.[1] In an overwhelmingly peasant country such a small membership was perhaps understandable. But even among industrial workers the party had attracted only a relatively small number of members.

Of the 1941 membership only 3,000 survived World War II, but the party emerged from the war with a total membership of 140,000. Countless thousands of new members had been recruited during the war, chiefly from peasants who had fled to the hills to escape the *Ustashi* massacres, and were there mobilized into the Communist-led Partisans. An increased number of the extremely poor workers also joined the party in this period. Fol-

[1] See Rankovich's report to the Fifth Party Congress for membership figures at various times in the party's history, *Borba,* July 23, 1948.

lowing the Communist consolidation of power, the party membership continued to grow until it had reached a total of 468,000
in 1948, and at the time of the party's Sixth Congress in November, 1952, the total membership was reported to be 780,000.[2]
This figure represents less than 5 per cent of the total population
and slightly more than 8 per cent of the total adult population.
In maintaining a comparatively small, well-disciplined party, the
Yugoslavs are merely adhering to Leninist precepts and Soviet
practice.

Although Communist parties are generally regarded as having a working-class base, the Yugoslav Communist Party had
less than 30 per cent workers in 1948 and nearly 50 per cent
peasants. Intellectuals made up approximately 15 per cent of the
total, with about 5 per cent unclassified. Twenty per cent of the
1948 total were women. By 1952 the social composition of the
party had not been greatly altered. The number of workers had
increased by only 2.5 per cent, a distinctly insufficient increase,
according to official statements at the Sixth Party Congress.[3]
From time to time the party press points to specific places where
party membership is "unjustifiably" small (in one mine, for example, out of 122 miners only nine were party members). By
1952, however, the number of peasants had decreased by 7 per
cent, which was regarded as desirable. Yet the small increase in
the percentage of workers and a slightly larger decrease in the
percentage of peasants was not regarded as much of an improvement over 1948, particularly in the light of the fact that more
and more individuals had become workers, providing an increased source of recruits in this group. Likewise, it was considered clearly undesirable that there had been a decrease in the
student membership by 3 per cent and that women now made up
only 13 per cent of the total membership.[4]

The social composition of the party is not, however, reflected
in the leadership. At and near the top, for example, intellectuals
predominate. On the local level, on the other hand, workers are
predominant, and intellectuals occupy approximately as many
positions as peasants, although the latter are considerably more

[2] See Rankovich's report to the Sixth Party Congress, *Politika,* November 7,
1952.
[3] *Ibid.*
[4] *Ibid.*

numerous than either of the other two groups.[5] This can no doubt
be explained in part by the lack of education among many Communists, particularly those recruited from the peasant areas. It
was officially admitted in 1948 that the majority of party members had had only four years of elementary school, and 32,000
no formal education at all.[6] It is not surprising, therefore, that
intellectuals should predominate among the leaders. Nor is it
difficult to perceive why the extent of Marxist learning among so
many Yugoslav Communists is limited to the simplified handbooks prepared by the party leaders. For only a precious few
among the rank and file have really dug down into the writings
of Marx, Engels, Lenin and other Marxian theoreticians.

It should be noted in passing that scores of opportunists
joined the party at different times, but especially toward the end
of World War II, when it was becoming increasingly evident that
the Communists would capture political power. Even men with
a conservative or a reactionary past were accepted, particularly
if they had attained any position of honor or respect in the community, for their actions could be utilized to attract others and,
in general, to create the impression that the new order was ir-
resistible. The life histories of some of these opportunists—men
who were willing to sell their souls—make interesting reading.
Unfortunately, in a work of this kind it is possible only to mention a few cases in passing. One of the most striking is that of Ivo
Andrich, an able writer and president of the Association of Yugoslavia Writers. He is a member of parliament and a big wheel
in Tito's regime. Yet before the war he was Yugoslav ambassador
to Nazi Germany (he considered Hitler a great man), and was a
firm admirer of his fellow Rotarian, Milan Stojadinovich, a onetime Yugoslav prime minister who to the Communists was the
epitome of reaction. Another case is that of the legal advisor of
the Yugoslav foreign office, Milan Bartosh, an eminently able
professor of international law before World War II, and bitterly
hated by the Communists. But during his sojourn as prisoner of
war he seems to have found accommodation with the Communists, although some of his friends doubt that he is at heart a
Communist even today. In a similar category is the head of one of

[5] Rankovich's report to Fifth Party Congress, *Borba,* July 23, 1948.
[6] *Ibid.*

Yugoslavia's law schools. An early convert to Marxism, he left the fold in the '30's after attaining a position on the faculty. At that time he was severely criticized for betraying Marxism by some of Tito's present close collaborators. Another man, appointed by the Nazis to reorganize the medical school during the occupation, was able to become head of that school under the Communists. It is a well-established fact, too, that many faithful servants of the Fascist *Ustashi* regime in Croatia were able to obtain positions of trust under the Communists. And there are some opportunists like Nenad Jovanovich, who, now holding a good job, even deny that they were once strong supporters of Drazha Mihailovich.

Party Governing Bodies

In theory the Communist Party is a democratic organization. Ostensibly its governing bodies and individual officers, from top to bottom, are in one fashion or another elected. And they are presumably accountable to those who choose them. At the same time, however, the party is an hierarchical and highly disciplined association. Its top governing bodies literally possess powers of life and death over its subsidiary organizations, and indeed over the entire membership. In reality, therefore, such an organization is not democratic but authoritarian.

According to official party rules, the supreme governing agency of the party is the congress, which should be convened at least once every four years. Composed of delegates chosen by basic party organizations (formerly called party cells), the congress is supposed to determine the party's line of policy and to elect the Central Committee, which is the party's supreme agency between congresses. Moreover, the congress hears, and presumably passes upon, the reports of the Central Committee. And it elects a Central Review Commission whose professed job is overseeing the "material-financial dealings" of the Central Committee. As a matter of record, however, the congress merely applauds the reports of the Central Committee and rubber-stamps its proposals. It exercises no visible initiative on its own accord.

While the Central Committee, now exceeding one hundred members, has a greater voice in formulating party policies than does the congress, it is nevertheless in large measure a creature of its Executive Committee, formerly called the Politbureau or Political Bureau. The Central Committee is charged with electing the Executive Committee and the General Secretary of the party, as well as the Central Control Commission, the latter being given jurisdiction in deciding cases involving violations of the party program and party rules, as well as passing on complaints. Moreover, the Central Committee elects a Secretariat from among the members of the Executive Committee.

The General Secretary, a position held by Tito, and the Executive Committee, of which he is a member, constitute the essence of political power within the party and therefore within Yugoslavia. Historically, the composition of this body (then known as the Politbureau), like the makeup of similar Communist leaderships in other countries, was approved by the Comintern in Moscow. During the war, however, some members were killed and the Yugoslavs apparently added new ones without reference to Moscow. Since the war three members have been purged, all allegedly because of pro-Cominform-Soviet sympathies. Although in theory elected by the Central Committee, the Executive Committee is in fact a self-perpetuating body. It is extremely doubtful that any new additions would be proposed by the Central Committee unless they were first recommended by the Executive Committee. Any such effort would no doubt be looked upon as a power challenge, euphemistically described as "fractionalist activity" designed to undermine the "monolithic unity of the Party," and, of course, not tolerated.

This all-powerful body of thirteen men (previously the official membership was nine) has now been reduced to twelve through the death of Boris Kidrich. The group functions as a unit and as individuals, in conformity with the division of labor which makes each member responsible for a separate sphere of governmental activity. Working under the respective members are such little publicized units of the Central Committee as *Agitprop* (the Agitation and Propaganda administration), and the full time party organization-instructional staff. Moreover, the army and the secret police (UDB), more than other governmental agencies, are direct party agencies in that they have the novel and weighty task of preserving and protecting the party dictatorship.

The party governing bodies described above, except for the

General Secretary, are duplicated in each one of the six republics which now make up the Yugoslav state. Understandably, party organizations in the republics must function within the general framework of policy laid down by the national organization. In each republic there are regional, district and local party units, all set up on the hierarchical principle of organization.

Party Leaders

The top party leaders are the twelve members of what was the Politbureau, now called the Executive Committee. Five of these (Josip Broz Tito, Edward Kardelj, Alexander Rankovich, Milo- van Djilas, and France Leskoshek) were in their positions prior to the party's Fifth Congress in 1948. At that time four were added (Boris Kidrich, Mosha Pijade, Ivan Goshnjak, and Bla- goje Neshkovich), the first one is now dead and the fourth one was dropped in 1952 for alleged Cominform sympathies. At the party's Sixth Congress, held in November, 1952, five new mem- bers were inducted (Svetozar Vukmanovich-Tempo, Djuro Salaj, Djuro Pucar-Stari, Lazar Kolishevski, and Vladimir Bakarich).

All of the main nationality groups are represented in this body, but it is well to remember that these men are Communists first and only secondarily representatives of their respective na- tionalities. Yet nationality feeling has persisted to a degree even among Communists. Where this happened among Serbian Com- munists, interestingly enough, it was regarded as anti-Marxian, bourgeois-nationalist, and by implication indicative of sympathy for prewar Serbian-dominated governments. Consequently, such Communists were immediately purged. On the other hand, where nationality feeling cropped up among the other nationalities, notably among Croats or Macedonians, it was for the most part regarded as a continuation of the prewar protest against alleged Serbian nationalism and Serb-dominated regimes, a protest in which they had been joined by the Communists. And, therefore, it has in large measure been tolerated.

By far the most important men in the Executive Committee are Tito, Kardelj, Djilas and Rankovich. These four were at- tacked by name in the now famous Cominform Resolution of 1948, which expelled the Yugoslavs from the Cominform family.

Tito is a Croat, Kardelj a Slovene, Djilas a Montenegrin, and Rankovich a Serb. Tito is the over-all chief, paying close attention to all aspects of party activities. Kardelj and Djilas are Marxian theoreticians, which means that hardly any phase of the Communist program escapes their scrutiny. In the past the former has focused his attention on political organization and foreign affairs, while the latter has concentrated on agitation and propaganda. Rankovich, a former tailor, is the ruthless head of UDB, the Yugoslav secret police.

Democratic Centralism

The democratically sugar-coated authoritarian process which operates within the party has been given the name "democratic centralism" by Communist theoreticians. Simply stated, democratic centralism signifies that party governing bodies are directly or indirectly elected by rank and file members. They in turn are supposed to submit to the centralist (authoritarian) decisions of these bodies. At appropriate intervals, however, they are supposed to have an opportunity to choose a new leadership. And they theoretically retain the right to criticize the work of party officials and party governing bodies.

In practice, all Communist parties have discovered that, once established, party leaderships are altered only in a manner prescribed by the leaderships themselves. Secondly, they have found out that the direction of criticism is from the top down and not the reverse. The Yugoslav Communist Party, far from being an exception, runs true to form.

In discussing democratic centralism before the Sixth Party Congress, Minister of Interior Alexander Rankovich noted at least two erroneous tendencies.[7] In some instances, he said, criticism was carried to the point of ignoring instructions from higher party authorities, while in other cases there was no criticism at all. He reported that some party organizations, notably in universities and in administrative establishments, had assumed too much democracy. They had developed the notion that while party organizations may carry out decisions of the higher leadership they were not obliged to do so. Similarly, in other party cir-

[7] *Politika,* November 7, 1952.

cles the idea that it was not necessary to attend party meetings or pay dues took root. And in the peasant areas, party members, "supposedly in the name of democracy," had not reacted to the "slandering of the people's authority." In some party circles, he observed, criticism had been forestalled by the fact that lower civil servants hesitated to criticize those above them. In other cases there was no criticism, because "familiarity in party relations" had served to cover up weaknesses.

Rankovich admitted that criticism had been made difficult by the practice, now allegedly abolished, of having the secretary of the local party organization also serve as head of the local unit of government. Consequently, any criticism of him would constitute criticism of the party, an unpardonable offense. He admitted, moreover, that some valid criticisms had actually resulted in the critics being proclaimed enemies. In other instances, criticism had not been forthcoming because of the harmful petit-bourgeois notions to which some party members had succumbed.

Interlocking of Party and Other Organizations

The party organizational setup described above was partially camouflaged in the postwar period. Although operating through a welter of party-sponsored mass organizations, Yugoslav Communists did not identify themselves as party members until some time after their rift with Moscow. They were numerically insignificant and apparently believed that they should seek to perpetuate the fiction, at least until they were well entrenched, that the Tito regime represented a broad popular movement. When Moscow accused them of having dissolved the party in the People's Front, however, Yugoslav Communists began to come out into the open, and to proclaim that they had always been the real leaders of the People's Front and the other mass organizations.

Within the past few years it has become plainly evident that party members are in fact the leading officers in the so-called mass organizations, one of the methods employed to harness the masses to do the bidding of the dictatorship. Of the twenty-six-member top governing body of the Socialist Alliance (formerly the People's Front), for example, twenty-one are members of the party's Central Committee. While party men may not hold all important offices in these organizations at all levels, the Communists do not hesitate to say that they should. Recently, their principal organ, *Borba,*[8] declared that every Communist should "be an active member in other social organizations," for it is through their participation that "the Party exerts its influence and indirectly runs those organizations." And Rankovich, at the Sixth Party Congress, stated openly that party organizational units at different levels receive instructions as to their work in the mass organizations.[9]

In addition to a considerable overlapping of officers, there is a comparable overlapping of membership between the different organizations. Yet some Communists do not always take themselves seriously enough. Many of them, for example, do not join mass organizations, and others are members in name only. It is this lack of vigilance, according to Yugoslav Communist leaders, which accounts for the infiltration of "unfriendly influences" into Yugoslav organizational life.

[8] July 31, 1952.
[9] *Politika,* November 7, 1952.

Chapter 7:

Organization of the Government

THE structure of the postwar Yugoslav government was fashioned after Soviet experience and in conformity with the Marxian concept of the role of government during the period of the dictatorship of the proletariat, discussed in an earlier chapter. The Yugoslavs now contend that they have rejected much of Soviet experience, principally its centralist and bureaucratic tendencies. But they continue to assure all interested parties that they are not deviating from Marxism or from the Marxian concept of the primary role of government during the so-called transition period. In order to appreciate fully the nature of their present governmental structure it is necessary to keep this fundamental concept in mind. Its essence is oneness of purpose. Governmental organization, unlike that existing in democratic states, is concerned primarily with ends instead of means. There is a common aim—to build a Communist society. No one must challenge the validity of this aim or the wisdom of those who are seeking to accomplish it. And it is understood that the Communist Party is the sole repository of all wisdom as well as of all political power. Literally everything, therefore, is dedicated to this oneness of purpose.

Federalism and the Nationality Question

Borrowing from Stalin's thesis that the way to solve the nationality question is to let each nationality preserve its individual identity, the Yugoslav Communists decided even before they came to power that Yugoslavia should be organized on a federal basis. Each unit in the federation was to be based primarily on

nationality, not geography, economics or some other consideration. But mixtures of population and particularistic pride among
some of the top Communists made for compromises, and resulted
in six republics instead of three, which would have corresponded
to the three traditional nationality areas (Serbia, Croatia and
Slovenia). Bosnia-Herzegovina was made a separate republic
partly to prevent Serbia from becoming "too large" and partly because it would have been difficult to draw a line between the
Serbs and Croats in this area, to say nothing of the sizable Moslem element. Macedonia was made a separate republic principally to deny Bulgaria a propaganda weapon which she had
utilized so effectively in the pre-1941 period: the claim that the
residents of Macedonia were really Bulgars. But the need to satisfy local Communist pride and the hope of eventually annexing
at least parts of both Bulgarian Macedonia and Greek Macedonia also entered in its creation as a separate republic. Montenegro, economically poor and having only about a third of a million
inhabitants, was made a separate republic almost solely because
many top Communists came from there and wanted it as an individual republic.

Yugoslavia is a federation in name only, however. It cannot
meet the traditional tests of federalism, for the individual republics do not possess substantial powers which cannot be taken
away without their consent. It is amply clear that power radiates
from the center, and it is the center which decides when and in
what manner the powers of local initiative are to be extended or
withdrawn. This situation should surprise no one, for a one-party
dictatorship is scarcely the place where one would expect to find
federalism in operation.

The regime insists, however, that at least the nationality problem has been solved. And some casual observers have concluded
that the Communists have brought national unity. Anyone who
talks to Serbs and Croats will easily discover that this is not so.
What the Communists have done, they will tell you, is to draw
some geographic boundaries, proclaim the problem solved, and
impose stiff penalties on anyone who would betray disagreement
by an attempted discussion of any issues or complaints involving
the different nationality groups.

In actuality, the government has aggravated the problem by

making it impossible to discuss unresolved issues. In such an atmosphere suspicion and rumor have produced anything but mutual confidence. Both Serbs and Croats have told me that the nationality problem has never been more acute than it is today.
Among Macedonians, it is only fair to state, there is some feeling
that having gained recognition as a separate nationality group,
they have made least partial progress.

In addition to making it a crime to discuss issues involving
differences between nationality groups, the government has taken
at least two other steps to inflame nationality suspicions. First, it
officially adopted the policy of seeking to build up economic
equality among the republics. The poorest ones (Macedonia,
Montenegro, and Bosnia-Herzegovina) would get the most, and
the richest (Serbia, Croatia, and Solvenia) would contribute the
most.[1] This, in essence, was the policy of prewar governments, a
policy then severely criticized by Croat politicians, who contended
that the rich areas of Croatia were being sapped to keep the backward regions alive. At that time the Communists joined in the
criticism, but now concrete problems have forced Tito, a Croat
ironically enough, to adopt the policy of his political predeces-
sors.

Secondly, prewar governments were criticized for sending
Serbian civil servants into non-Serb areas. If this was a mistake,
Tito has compounded that error several-fold. He has not only
sent many non-Croats to Croatia, but non-Serbs to Serbia, etc.
When on one occasion I was making an official tour of a number
of offices in Belgrade, I noticed that most of the people introduced to me were Croats and Slovenes, but I did not give it a second thought. On my way back to the office, however, the person
who had accompanied me said: "That was typical. You can go
from office to office in Belgrade and you hardly run into a Serb.
They are either Macedonians, Croats, Slovenes or Montenegrins."

The nature of the Communist solution of the nationality
problem was brought to me rather forcefully when at a later date
a Croat in Zagreb told me that Tito's government was "a Serbian
regime." When I reported this conversation to a Serb who had
been in the Mihailovich movement, he could hardly believe what

[1] See Tito's speech, *Borba,* July 11, 1949.

he had heard. "How incredible," he said, "when you recall that we were the only ones who fought against the Communists' getting to power!"

Elective Principle

Yugoslav Communists have not been entirely consistent in their statements about elections. In utterances designed for foreign consumption they have made much ado about the "fact" that all of their governmental officials, from top to bottom, are in one way or another elected by the people. In some of their domestic propaganda, too, they have emphasized popular election of officials as a cardinal tenet in the political philosophy of the new regime. At other times, however, they have publicly revealed that the purpose of elections is not to choose those who will govern. During the election campaign of 1950, for example, one of the Politbureau members, Milovan Djilas, stated that the purpose of elections was *"to strengthen the dictatorship of the proletariat."* Moreover, "elections are to confirm the line of development which the election campaign has to expose and to explain, for it is evident that *the question of whether the candidates will be elected is of secondary importance, because under such conditions and under such a system they certainly will be.* The important question is the conscious activity and participation of the masses in the election campaign." [2] In other words, elections are principally a propaganda vehicle, affording the party one more opportunity to put forth its message in a different context.

These were Soviet-type elections, with one carefully selected list of candidates and one candidate for each office to be filled. And there were no opposition lists or alternative political programs from which the voter could choose. He could either vote for the official list of candidates or vote against it.

During 1952, however, the Yugoslavs began introducing certain alterations in their electoral processes. The most important of these is the possibility for the presentation of more candidates than there are offices to be filled. Since this will not mean two lists

[2] Speech to students of Belgrade university, *Narodni student* (Belgrade), March 20, 1950. Italics mine. For similar and more recent statements see the electoral proclamation in *Borba,* September 20, 1953.

of candidates, the voter will choose among individuals for each office. Such a possibility would seem to afford the voter a greater element of choice, but it may be hazardous to forecast at this time how meaningful this choice is apt to be, if indeed a choice is to be made available. Yet it is possible, on the basis of a general understanding of Yugoslav Communist leaders and their aims, to set forth certain conclusions which are not likely to be proved wrong.

First of all, Yugoslav Communists will not permit the utilization of whatever electoral reforms they have made, or in the future might make, by any person or groups of persons to present to the electorate a program at variance with their own. Tito's statement, made in the electoral campaign of 1950, that "two programs cannot exist" in Yugoslavia, will no doubt continue in force. If someone wants to achieve another program, he said, it is "a program hostile to socialism and naturally we cannot allow such at the elections." [3] In the electoral campaign of 1953, Tito referred to his would-be opponents as "boils on a healthy organism . . . which must be removed." [4] He cautioned his listeners that a second operation was always more painful, but left no doubt that he would "operate again" if certain elements did not make peace with the inevitable.

Secondly, the Communists will, as in the past, make every effort to be in full and complete control of the nominating process. According to the electoral law of 1953, nominations are to be made at scheduled and planned meetings of voters.[5] As heretofore, the chief participants in this process are the Communists and their sympathizers. In November of 1952, the Yugoslav press reported that in some local elections "enemy elements, former politicians, and in some instances church committees" attempted to put forth "politically compromised men as candidates." [6] While these efforts, according to the same report, in the main failed, the Communists issued a public warning that the persons elected "should be men known by their personal efforts, ability and worth in the field of social affairs, men highly regarded because of their

---

[3] *Borba,* February 19, 1950.
[4] *Politika,* October 5, 1953. For similar statements by other Yugoslav leaders see *Borba,* September 19 and 20, 1953; also *Politika,* October 5, 1953.
[5] *Borba,* September 8, 1953.
[6] *Politika,* November 12, 1952.

honesty and loyalty toward their socialist fatherland." [7] Prior to the national elections of November, 1953, Communist leaders told their associates openly that they "must be active in the preparations for and the conduct of the meetings of voters," and that they "must not allow reactionary elements . . . to be nominated." [8] For the time being, therefore, it is highly doubtful that the party's monopoly of power may be undermined by means of the nominating process.

Thirdly, the Communists will still continue to count the ballots and to proclaim the results. And this is all-important. Assumptions that Communists, although they may be dishonest in other respects, tabulate and report electoral results honestly are inaccurate and misleading. I shall cite two instances of their dishonesty which I was able to verify, but it is not possible to reveal the sources. During the first Tito-controlled election in the city of Pozharevac several thousand ballots were cast, of which Tito received only 380, yet the newspapers reported that 87 per cent had voted for the government list. In the 1950 national elections the city-county vote of Bachka Topola was nearly 12,000, of which the regime list received 13 per cent although the official report put the figure considerably higher.

These two cases are of additional interest in that the regime was apparently not supported by those from whom it might reasonably have expected support. In the first case, Partisan soldiers guarding the Pozharevac prison (there were less than 200) were voted several times, so that the total soldier vote cast was nearly 600, indicating that Tito did not get nearly all of their votes. In the second instance, Bachka Topola, populated mainly by poor peasants settled there by the Tito regime, could have been expected to vote for their alleged benefactors, but did not do so.

Consequently, the question arises as to why Communists hold elections at all. It has already been suggested that they offer a useful context within which to couch propaganda messages. Secondly, elections provide a convenient façade by means of which the regime can claim popular support, especially in its contacts abroad. Finally, elections serve to destroy an individual's sense of

[7] *Ibid.*
[8] *Borba,* September 19, 1953.

personal integrity. No hater of Communism can go through the symbolic approval of what he hates without a certain sense of degradation. Communist elections cannot but help to create a climate of moral despair, of futility and hopelessness.

During the Yugoslav elections of March, 1950, for example, many persons told me that they were sure they would suffer at the hands of the government if they did not vote, that they were afraid a vote against the government list would be detected and that it really did not matter how the votes were cast, because "the government had already decided by how much it will win."

In their zeal to emulate the Russians, Yugoslav Communists at one time even introduced such moronic things as "socialist competition" in elections. Adding insult to injury, various voting places would challenge others to see which ones could complete their balloting in the shortest time. In one ward persons were urged to be at the polling place by seven o'clock on a bitterly cold Sunday morning. In at least one instance progress was being tabulated every two hours. In another ward an army major came about noon to ask a woman why she had not voted, despite the fact that the polls were not due to close until six in the evening.

The National Government

Early in 1952 Yugoslav Communist leaders decided that major revisions were needed in their constitutional structure. Allegedly, they wanted to extricate themselves from a hopeless web of centralism which their Stalinist constitution had cast over them. Their new theme, "decentralization," was persistently employed to describe their avowed aim of reducing the size and jurisdiction of the central government and of transfering more and more functions to the lower units of government. By the end of the year their proposals to revise the constitution were put in concrete form for ratification by the parliament, in which is lodged the formal power of constitutional amendment. In January, 1953, as was to be expected, the parliament adopted the party's proposals.

While subsequent sections of this chapter will portray the nature of these changes, particularly as they affect policy making and administration, one or two preliminary observations may be in order at this juncture. First of all, one must never lose sight of the fact that no matter how elaborate the façade of governmental organization, the Communist Party will continue to be the key to its functioning. Secondly, any assumption that the intricately designed governmental forms can in practice function as such forms operate in the West is totally erroneous, at least as long as the Communists hold the monopoly of power.

But even when one looks at the "new" governmental structure, things are not what they are supposed to be. Far from reducing the powers of the central government, the new constitutional changes seem in the main to revamp its structure and to amplify and redefine its prerogatives. As one reads the sections dealing with the rights of the central government and the powers of the Federal People's Assembly (parliament),[9] the conclusion is inescapable that it would be difficult to conceive of a constitution which lodged more authority in the national government and left less real power to be exercised by its component parts. Among the many exclusive powers of the Federal People's Assembly, for example, are the power to amend the constitution and the power to decide whether the constitutions and the laws of the constituent republics are in conformity with the federal constitution and federal laws.[10] Additional evidence of the centralist nature of the present Yugoslav constitution will be found in the pages to follow.

Federal People's Assembly

As heretofore, the Yugoslav constitution declares that the Federal People's Assembly is the supreme governing body of the national government. The assembly's composition, however, has been altered. The two previous houses, the Federal Council and the Council of Nationalities, have been combined into one house, the Federal Council, but for certain purposes they continue to maintain their separate identities. The Federal Council is composed of two groups of people's deputies chosen every four years. The first group is elected directly, one deputy for every 60,000 inhabitants. The second group, ten deputies from each of the six republics (including six from an autonomous region and four

[9] See constituent law promulgated January 13, 1953, Articles 9–23.
[10] *Ibid.,* Article 15, Sections 1 and 10.

from an autonomous area), is elected by the respective republican, regional or area assemblies from among their own members. Within the Federal Council, under certain circumstances (such as amendment of the constitution and the enactment of the national social plan), this group of deputies acts as a Council of Nationalities, thereby preserving the fiction of equality of the republics.

The second house of the Federal People's Assembly, the Council of Producers, is a new creation. It is designed to accord representation to various sectors of the economy. For this purpose the economy is divided into three groups. In the first are industry, mining, forestry, transport, construction, commerce, hotel industry and communal activities—all nationalized pursuits. The second group is supposed to represent agriculture, but only insofar as peasants are associated in some form of co-operative or collectivized organization. The third group includes artisans and craftsmen engaged in their trades.

The size of the Council of Producers will be determined on the basis of one deputy for every 70,000 producing inhabitants. But the number of deputies allocated to each of the three groups will be in proportion to each group's contribution to the country's total production. This means that the first group will receive by far the largest bloc of deputies. Yugoslav Communist leaders have not attempted to hide the fact that the Council of Producers was designed as an instrument of class policy. Under this plan of economic representation, the numerically fewer industrial workers will have many more representatives than the great peasant majority.

Unconcerned with violating constitutional provisions, the Titoists in September, 1953 promulgated an electoral law which denied the third group a separate representation.[11] Instead, the artisans were amalgamated with the first group (industry). This group was accorded 135 representatives, or approximately one deputy for every 30,000 producers, while agriculture is represented by sixty-three deputies, or one deputy for every 150,000 producers.

In the main the two houses possess relatively equal powers,

---

[11] See *Borba*, September 8, 1953. A future parliament will no doubt be asked to amend the constitution so as to conform with the electoral law.

especially in all matters pertaining to the economy, labor and social insurance. It is envisioned, however, that the Federal Council will have exclusive functions in the more strictly politico-governmental sphere. In the event of a jurisdictional dispute between them, the matter is to be settled by the two houses meeting in joint session. The membership of the Council of Producers, it should be noted, is approximately two-thirds that of the Federal Council.

While the Federal People's Assembly is declared to be in permanent session, this apparently applies to the Federal Council only. Its members receive regular monthly salaries, while the members of the Council of Producers are only entitled to expenses incurred in performing their functions as deputies and compensation for lost earnings during the same period. Members of both bodies are ex-officio members of the corresponding councils of the people's committees in the districts or towns from which they were elected.

Two other innovations are interesting enough to merit at least a passing note. The Federal People's Assembly is authorized to submit legislative proposals, before or after passage by the assembly, to the people. Their decision shall be binding, and at least two years must elapse before the matter can again be raised. Previously unknown to Yugoslavia, the referendum has been transplanted from abroad, and it is difficult to conceive of its serving any other function than to mislead foreigners. The second innovation is a nine-member legislative commission, authorized to issue binding interpretations of federal laws. Such interpretations, however, must be submitted to the competent house for subsequent confirmation.

President of the Republic

The executive power is vested in a President of the Republic and a Federal Executive Council. Both are elected by the Federal People's Assembly from among its own members. The President of the Republic is at the same time President of the Federal Executive Council. It was evident from the first discussions concerning constitutional revision that this office was being created for Tito.

Aside from being the formal head of state, the president is endowed with substantial powers. He is commander-in-chief of the armed forces. He presides over the national defense council, a body seemingly independent of parliament. Its organization and authority stem from the Federal Executive Council, which also chooses its members, but only upon recommendation of the president. Moreover, the president is given power to hold up acts of the FEC with which he does not agree, but is obligated to submit the disputed question or questions to the first session of the Federal Assembly for decision.

Federal Executive Council

The Federal Executive Council, consisting of from thirty to forty-five members elected by the Federal Assembly from the ranks of the Federal Council, takes the place of a similar collegial executive, the Presidium. All republics are supposed to be represented in the FEC, and the presidents of the executive councils of the republics are ex-officio members of the FEC. At the first election, held in January, 1953, thirty-seven members of the Federal Council were chosen to constitute the FEC. Thirty-four of them were members of the Party's Central Committee!

Unlike the former Presidium, the FEC has vastly enlarged powers.[12] While retaining most of the functions of the Presidium (although presumably not the power to issue decree laws except in an emergency), it has in reality also inherited the powers of the Council of Ministers, which has been abolished. The FEC not only has broad powers in carrying out legislative enactments of the Federal Assembly, but is also expected to study legislative proposals and to submit recommendations concerning them to the assembly. In case of war or other extraordinary occurrence it possesses wide emergency powers.

In order to perform the actual tasks of governing, the FEC appoints and dismisses the secretaries and undersecretaries of state who head the five secretariats of state (foreign affairs, national defense, internal affairs, national economy, and budget) which the revised constitution has established. While additional secretariats can be created only by law, the FEC has the power

[12] See Articles 79–89 of the constituent law, passed January 13, 1953.

to establish enterprises and to set up independent agencies and other forms of federal administration. It also appoints and dismisses such high functionaries as the public prosecutor and the governor of the national bank. It has the power to suspend acts of the executive councils of the republics if they conflict with federal laws and regulations. And in similar circumstances, it has the power to request the councils to cancel or annul the acts of republican administrative agencies.[13]

The Federal Executive Council is responsible to the Federal Assembly, to which it is obligated to report on its work. None of the members of the FEC can be an officer of the Federal Assembly or a member of its committees, although all of them are members of the lower house of that body. FEC members may, however, attend and participate in committee sessions, but without the right to vote. And they are obliged to answer questions and to furnish information about their work to the appropriate committees. The secretariats of state and other federal administrative agencies are responsible to the FEC.

Local Government

An additional commentary upon the centralist nature of Yugoslav politics is the new constitutional provision that the republics "will independently enact their own constitutional laws" so as to amend their present constitutions to conform with the changes made in the national constitution.[14] It was a foregone conclusion that the republics would do as they were told. Actually, there was little for them to do, for the amendments to the national constitution specified the main legislative and executive bodies, as well as their powers, which each republic was to have.[15]

In general, the governmental structure in each republic was patterned after that existing on the national level, except that there is no office comparable to that of the President of the Republic. Unlike the previous system, the People's Assembly in each republic is bicameral, a Council of Producers having been added. As on the national level, the Council of Producers is designed to

---

[13] *Ibid.*
[14] *Ibid.*, Article 112.
[15] *Ibid.*, Articles 100–114.

provide economic representation. Both houses are said to have equal powers when it comes to amending the constitution, enacting the social plan for the republic, passing on the budget and other laws concerning the economy, labor and social security. The remaining powers, although not specified, presumably reside in the Council of the Republic.

The executive authority in each republic is vested in an executive council of fifteen to thirty members chosen by the assembly, but exclusively from the ranks of the Council of the Republic. The respective executive councils select secretariats of state, councils and other agencies through which the actual tasks of governing are carried out. These agencies of republican governments are obligated to execute federal laws as well as the laws of their respective republics. These agencies, moreover, are responsible to the executive council, which in turn is responsible to the People's Assembly in each republic.

At the base of the Yugoslav governmental hierarchy are the so-called people's committees, some of which were organized by the Communists as early as September, 1941, and perhaps earlier. It is through these agencies of local administration that the people have felt the full impact of the policies of the Communist dictatorship. In the past, the members of these committees were "elected" without any opposition candidates allowed. Recent laws, however, as noted previously, supposedly provide that more than one candidate may be presented for each position to be filled.[16] It is understood, of course, that all candidates will support the program of the Communist Party.

In the past, these committees merely "rubber-stamped" the proposals and acts of their executive committees, whose membership was frequently identical with that of the local Communist Party cell. Their decisions were reached in secret, and even the meetings of the full committee were not open to the public. Now, however, the executive committees have allegedly been abolished. Major decisions are now supposed to be reached after discussions in full committee, whose sessions are said to be open to the public.

All people's committees have been organized pursuant to national laws and the most minute instructions emanating from

[16] *Borba,* August 2, 1952.

the center of power in Belgrade.[17] The instructions set out in detail how these institutions of local "government" are to be organized and what functions they are to perform. Following the national and republican pattern, each committee is a bicameral body, having a county or city council and a council of producers. In each people's committee there are five councils, which are designed to be the initiators and bearers of "the entire activity of the people's committee." [18] These councils concern themselves with internal affairs, education and culture, social and health services, economy, and communal affairs. Under each council there is a secretariat to carry out the council's instructions, with a separate administrative secretariat operating under the committee as a whole.

It seems obvious that the purpose of such uniform and detailed organization of local people's committees, as well as the prior determination of their functions by central authorities, was to establish a spiritless administrative apparatus to carry out centrally determined Communist policies. To the extent that the work of these local committees is not directly guided by agents of the central government, it is supervised by appropriate republican authorities, who "have the right to inspect the administration of, and the right to initiate disciplinary procedures against the officials of people's committees in republican disciplinary courts." [19] Moreover, the executive council of each republic has the power directly to oversee the work of people's committees, to annul their "illegal" acts and to dissolve them or their councils if their work is clearly against the Constitution and the laws.[20]

Paradoxically enough, the discussions which preceded the constitutional reforms of 1953 placed a great deal of stress on decentralization and on the need of stimulating local initiative, and such sentiments continue to be expressed. In practice, however, institutions of local government have tended, it seems, to move towards one of two extremes. They have either retained the "old system" of promulgating orders in an authoritarian fashion, or they have moved toward "too much" local autonomy. The

[17] See *Sluzhbeni list* (official gazette) VIII (July 23, 1952), pp. 706–718.

[18] Petar Aligrudich, "Rad i organizacija administracije narodnih odbora," *Narodna drzhava* VI (Belgrade, 1952), p. 151.

[19] *Ibid.*, p. 153.

[20] *Republika* (Belgrade), January 27, 1953.

Communist leaders want local initiative, but they want it to be exercised in a manner which will best advance the party program at any given time.

The Courts

As early as 1941 Yugoslav Communists began destroying the legal and judicial machinery of Yugoslavia and systematically replacing it with a system of Soviet-type "people's courts." [21] These courts form the basis of the present Yugoslav judicial structure. It consists of the Supreme Court of Yugoslavia, a supreme court of each republic, approximately sixty regional or district courts and about 360 county courts. The whole judicial system has been set up through national legislation, and the Federal People's Assembly is declared to possess the exclusive prerogative in passing legislation concerning the judiciary.

Yugoslav courts are collegial, consisting of a judge and two judge-assessors, a practice borrowed from the Soviet Union. In courts of first instance, the judge is supposed to possess legal training. The two judge-assessors, although usually not possessing a legal education, have as much power in deciding cases as the judge. Where county courts sit as courts of appeal, however, all three members must be jurists. Members of the supreme courts are always jurists. In cases of extraordinary seriousness (e.g. cases involving the death penalty), the Supreme Court of Yugoslavia is made up five justices instead of three.

In practice, especially in the early years of Tito's regime, these requirements were not always adhered to. The number of politically acceptable men who possessed legal training was far too small to meet the needs. Even the two judge-assessors, although Communists and hence constituting a majority, could not always be relied upon not to be misled by a clever jurist, as experience demonstrated in a number of cases. Consequently, there are even today a number of judges who have no legal training.

County and district courts are chosen by the respective people's committees for an indefinite time, but they can be removed at any time by the body which elects them. Supreme court justices

[21] Vladimir Kalember, "The Organization of Justice in the FPR of Yugoslavia," *New Yugoslav Law* I (Oct.–Dec., 1950), p. 10.

are chosen by the People's Assemblies in the republics, and by the Federal People's Assembly in the case of the nation's highest tribunal. They serve for indefinite terms, and may likewise be removed by the body which elects them.

Interlocking Personnel: Party and Government

When after World War II the Yugoslav Communists erected their governmental structure, they faithfully copied the Soviet Union, including the practice of having party men occupy the key governmental positions. From top to bottom of the party and governmental hierarchies there was an interlocking of personnel. Key positions in the party and in the government at various levels were frequently held by one and the same man. At the local level, for example, the secretary of the party organization was also head of the local unit of government.

At the party's Sixth Congress, however, one of Tito's close collaborators revealed that the party, having concluded that this practice was erroneous, had set out in June, 1952 to have it abolished.[22] It was quite evident, he said, that criticism of those who hold office was difficult, if not impossible, under such conditions. This does not mean that Communists cannot hold key governmental positions, which they will no doubt continue to occupy, but only that the authority and the prestige of the top party man in any particular area will not be at stake when things go wrong.

In making this change, Yugoslav Communists contend that they are reversing a practice which in the Soviet Union has made for an entrenched bureaucratic caste, and has consequently stifled progress toward socialism. As a result, they insist, the economy of the Soviet Union has evolved into "state capitalism." And as long as the bureaucratic caste continues to exist there, they argue, there can be no talk of a workers' society, much less a withering away of the state.

[22] See Rankovich's report, *Politika,* November 7, 1952.

Chapter 8:

Party and Government: Policy Making

THE structure of Yugoslav politics, as portrayed above, reveals two inseparable and closely integrated hierarchical organizations—the party and the government. In this dualistic association, so characteristic of contemporary one-party dictatorships, it is necessary to distinguish between form and substance, between shadow and reality.

Party as Policy Maker

A great deal has already been said to indicate that the Communist Party has a monopoly on over-all policy making. The party as a whole, of course, does not make policy. Its Central Committee is charged with that function, and all party policy decisions are issued in its name. But it is the Central Committee's inner circle, formerly the Politbureau and now the Executive Committee, which decides fundamental issues. On occasion, however, it might submit questions for a rather full discussion within the Central Committee, but as a general rule it has specific recommendations to present, and these are promptly ratified.

Prior to 1948, policy making by the party, although sensed at every turn, was largely invisible. The party was still operating in secretive ways, reminiscent of its prewar illegal activities. Stung by Cominform accusations that it had sunk into deep illegality, the party began to admit and to proclaim that basic governmental decisions were first of all party decisions. Discarding its secretive past rapidly, the party in 1952 went the Cominform one better by declaring that in the future, meetings of party organizations would be public, and hence open to all citizens. But no Yugoslav citizen is under any illusion that these will be anything but more or less formal gatherings, with fundamental decisions having been reached at higher levels and within the confines of the party family.

High party policy makers, in arriving at their decisions, are guided first of all by an ideology to which they are all devoted. Facts and figures are furnished almost without exception by party organizations and party staff experts. Sometimes information is submitted in the form of reports of party units, and at other times in the form of reports of governmental agencies. In conformity with the division of labor which exists within the Executive Committee, all pertinent information coming through the secretariat is funneled to the appropriate member or members, who from time to time submit reports and recommendations to the committee.

For the most part, high Communist policy makers concern themselves with questions of major importance. But problems of minor import are not infrequently referred to them. On one occasion, for example, the Politbureau discussed and decided what charges were to be brought against a certain man and what sentence should be meted out to him. On another occasion, it decided that a certain individual should not be brought to trial for fear that he might be too clever in court. In the case of party members, even their private lives have been the subject of Politbureau or Central Committee discussions. More than once, high party policy makers have made binding decisions concerning marriage or divorce without respect for the wishes of the party members concerned.

One or two examples of major policy making might be cited by way of illustration. Reference has already been made to the fact that, although the Federal People's Assembly (parliament) was designated in the Yugoslav constitution as the competent body for deciding on constitutional amendments, the party for at least six months prior to the convening of the assembly discussed and proposed comparatively far-reaching changes. At the Sixth Party Congress the delegates were even told what these changes would be. Consequently, no one was surprised that the People's

Assembly, when it met in January, 1953, ratified the party decisions. At the same congress the party's guiding role was illustrated by its avowed decision to change the name of the People's
Front, and to set up for it vast new, and, what will no doubt turn
out to be costly, tasks—all without consulting the People's Front
organization itself. Earlier, at the Fifth Party Congress, the party
decided to merge the Communist Youth and the People's Youth
organizations without waiting for an expression of opinion, let
alone a decision, on the part of the members of these groups.[1]

Moreover, proclamations of domestic changes and reforms
are usually accompanied by references to party initiative or by
citation from, or reference to, letters or resolutions of the Central
Committee. The Yugoslav press is replete with examples such as
the following: "Letter of CCCPY, sent to the Communists in the
University.[2] . . . The letter concerning cooperatives sent by the
CCCPY.[3] . . . The letter of CCCPY to the Student Federation.[4]
. . . "Resolution of the third plenum of the CCCPY concerning
schools.[5] . . . The CCCPY took the point of view that the legal
profession should.[6] . . . The second plenum of the CCCPY also
decided to accept in principle the division of the people's republics into regions.[7] . . . The second plenum of the CCCPY en-
dorses the policy of the Politbureau of the CCCPY concerning
the economic plan for 1949. . . ."[8]

In a more general sense, every important utterance in the
party press constitutes a policy directive. The party's official program is widely proclaimed and publicized, and the party-controlled press and radio are utilized to explain, expound and amplify it. Party-determined aims and goals are constantly reiterated,
and "deviations" from them openly and severely criticized.

Parliament a Rubber Stamp

Dramatic proof that the party is the real policy maker is to
be found in the fact that the theoretical policy making body, the

[1] *Borba,* July 29, 1948.
[2] *Univerzitetski vesnik* (Belgrade), November 1, 1952.
[3] *Borba* (Zagreb edition), August 27, 1952.
[4] *Narodni student* (Belgrade), March 5, 1952.
[5] *Politika,* October 4, 1952.
[6] *Borba,* July 15, 1952.
[7] *Ibid.,* March 22, 1949.
[8] *Ibid.,* February 3, 1948.

Federal People's Assembly, is no more than a rubber-stamp legislature. While some of its sessions were of longer duration prior to
the liquidation of recalcitrant non-Communist members, they
have averaged no more than one week since the summer of 1947.
During these brief sessions, the parliament merely went through
the motions of enacting what was put before it by party leaders.

I was fortunate enough to be in the diplomatic gallery
throughout every sitting of the entire regular session of the assembly which convened on May 25 and adjourned on May 28,
1949. It was in actual session less than nine hours, half of which
time was consumed in two speeches, one by Kardelj and the other
by Kidrich. Although there were several other speeches of considerably shorter duration, there was still time to pass eight laws.
But this is perhaps understandable in view of the fact that at no
time was an amendment offered from the floor; at no time did a
single person speak against any measure; at no time did anyone
propose a new law or discuss any subject except those placed on
the agenda by the government.

Moreover, it was of interest to me that there were no quorum
or roll calls, and all laws were passed by a unanimous vote. Some
laws, to which the major speakers had not even referred, were
enacted in record time. The law nationalizing the drugstores, for
example, required five minutes to pass. Similarly, a law on the
People's Courts took three minutes; a law on authentication of
signatures required two minutes; a law on navy flags consumed
five minutes; and a law transferring a certain settlement from one
republic to another consumed another five minutes of the parliament's time.

It was also of interest to note that many of the deputies were
seemingly little interested in the proceedings. Several of them
walked out of the chamber during speeches, but in view of the
dullness of some of the speakers this was perhaps justifiable even
among Communists. At times there was much whispering, and at
one time at least two of the people's deputies were making paper
boats out of newspapers.

Since that particular session the Titoists have talked much
about reforms, about socialist democracy, about decentralization.
But when I sat through a session of the assembly of the People's
Republic of Serbia in September, 1952 I could observe little

change in the basic pattern. The session convened one evening and adjourned the next afternoon. Several laws concerning people's committees were enacted without fanfare, opposition or dissenting votes. It would be difficult to conceive of a duller session, and perhaps the best proof of this was to be found in the fact that aside from two Yugoslav newsmen, I was the only person in the galleries. Whatever else Tito's recent reforms may signify, therefore, they are not likely to lead to decentralization in fundamental policy making, which, as heretofore, will remain a jealously guarded prerogative of the party's high command.

Chapter 9:

Party and Government: Administration

SINCE policy making is exclusively a Communist Party function, all government under Communism is, in essence, little else but administration. Consequently, the much-advertised "decentralization reforms" in the Yugoslav government, which do not alter basic policies nor the means by which they are arrived at, must be viewed as reforms in administration only.

But it is also well to bear in mind that administration in a country where the state controls everything is a vast and complicated affair. Its vastness is augmented by the creation of separate bureaucracies in the six republics, to say nothing of bureaucracy on the local level throughout the country-wide network of people's committees. The far-reaching scope of the bureaucracy may be illustrated by the fact that the Yugoslav government at one time went so far as to forbid the private exchange of postal stamps with the outside world, and created a philately bureau through which all such exchanges had to clear. And yet, ironically enough, the bureaucracy, the favorite whipping boy of all Communists, is nearly always blamed for failures, which can never be acknowledged as consequences of Communism itself.

The nature and scope of Communist Party goals, it seems to me, must almost inevitably require a highly centralized or a centrally supervised bureaucracy. The very essence of Communist regimes has been centralism. It remains to be seen, therefore, to what extent the Yugoslav Communists can decentralize an essentially centralist system.

Party Directs Administration

Reforms in the Yugoslav administration do not mean that the party will not continue to furnish the general over-all administrative directives. On the contrary, streams of instructions and directives from the party continue in a fairly constant flow. But, contrary to past practice, these directives do not attempt to set forth in detail the means and methods to be utilized in carrying them out. Recipients of administrative directives are more and more being shouldered with the responsibility of adapting local resources to achieve the tasks set out for them.

Party decisions are, as heretofore, being transmitted through appropriate channels. Since most of the national ministries have been abolished, however, party organizations and the institutions of local government are being increasingly employed for this purpose. Mass organizations also continue to be harnessed to the party dictatorship and to play their assigned roles. Moreover, the quantity and quality of party men in key spots in local administration was increased somewhat with the transfer to the respective republics of many Communists who had heretofore staffed the now abolished national ministries.

These men have been told to exercise their influence. At the Sixth Party Congress, for example, local party functionaries were criticized for having taken too literally higher party orders not to interfere too much in the actual operation of plants.[1] At least some local party bosses had interpreted such orders to mean that in the future they should concern themselves with "some type of general and higher policy questions." Consequently, they became passive and did not "participate in a proper way" in the election of workers' councils. This attitude, they were warned, was completely erroneous.

Hence, the guiding role of the party cannot be considered any less important than in the past. Some techniques are being replaced, others modified, and new ones subjected to trial tests. And for the recalcitrant and unco-operative there is still the secret police, with its prisons and labor camps, affording "opportunities" for repentance and dedication to the glory of the "socialist fatherland."

[1] See Rankovich's report, *Politika*, November 7, 1952.

The Character of Communist Administrators

The vast majority of Yugoslav administrators are uneducated, untrained and inexperienced men, who have sought to compensate for their deficiencies by adopting the techniques of rigidity, force and ruthlessness. In many cases their sole qualification for administrative office consisted of the fact that during the war they had joined the Partisans. Frequently they were men of little ability or achievement—opportunists who came in at the last moment—men who knew little or nothing about Marxism, but who were taken into the Communist Party because they were the only persons locally available as officials of the new regime. Since they had been so little respected in the past as members of their respective communities, it was not surprising that now, as officials of the local people's committees, they should become detested symbols of a hated regime. These facts are set forth not to excuse Communist excesses, but rather to explain them, and what is even more important, to indicate the kind of wretched and miserable person which the Communist-dominated Partisan movement so often succeeded in attracting.

The primary qualification for positions of administrative responsibility was political reliability. Communists were to make the decisions in spite of their ignorance. But the lack of education and training among Communists impaired more than the functioning of individual offices. The whole administrative apparatus suffered because the Communists controlled the personnel divisions, which they staffed exclusively with party members. These divisions, and the persons who manned them, had little appreciation of how governmental offices should function. They were principally interested in ferreting out individuals who were suspect for one reason or another. They did not tolerate familiarity. If in one office two people seemed friendly, for example, one of them was certain to be transferred. To be sure, there were capable people in various offices, but they were not trusted and they either possessed no initiative or were afraid to exercise it.

Of the Yugoslav bureaucrats no more than 10 per cent are university graduates, and as noted earlier, a large percentage of them possess only four years of elementary school education. In the central government the picture is slightly better, but at the local level it is considerably worse. Although special schools and individual courses were devised to "lift" their educational level through easily obtainable degrees and diplomas, these bureaucrats continued to have difficulties. The educational process could be accelerated on paper, but transforming the individual was another matter. A budgetary specialist, for example, told me that his chief had only four years of elementary school, and "did not know the first thing about budgets." And while specially devised courses might assure him of an academic degree, they would not necessarily produce a man who really knew something about budgetary matters.

Most of these bureaucrats are keenly sensitive of their educational and cultural inferiority, and seek to compensate for it by resorting to authority, bluster, and an exaggerated notion of self-importance. Many office or bureau chiefs, for example, became annoyingly unapproachable. They set aside certain hours when they could be consulted, and did not permit interruptions at other times even though urgent matters might arise. They refused to see minor officials, because they "communicated only with equals." Some directors even refused to read letters which were addressed to them but which had ommitted their full titles. Yet, at times, Communist bureaucrats found themselves confronted by insurmountable psychological hurdles. A local ward secretary, for example, faced the difficult task of asking the university professor in his street to attend the local ward conference where he, a former cobbler, would deliver a lecture on the "importance of the people's loan." In this particular instance he could not surmount the psychological barrier and consequently did not go to ask the professor to attend.

The feeling of inferiority, which characterizes so many Yugoslav Communist bureaucrats, does not stem, however, from educational and cultural shortcomings alone. It arises also from an awareness that they were not chosen by the popular vote of a free electorate. Appointed by their party superiors, and having no sense of responsibility to the people, they developed a set routine of carrying out party directives with dispatch and rigidity.

Yet they could not escape a feeling of weakness and mediocrity. Even as an American diplomat I experienced a number of discomforts as a result of their bureaucratic rigidity. On one occasion, for example, I was turned back at the Yugoslav frontier about five o'clock in the afternoon, although my family and I had diplomatic passports and all of our papers were in order. The border authorities had received an order, about which none of us had been told, that no border crossings were to be permitted between sundown and sunrise. No argument could prevail. I was not even allowed to telephone Belgrade! Had it not been for the courtesy of the Hungarian border authorities, who permitted us to return to a Hungarian city to spend the night, even though we had checked out of Hungary and had no visa to return, we would have been forced to spend a cold November night in our car, parked on that short strip of no man's land between the two road barriers.

On another occasion, I had stopped to buy some fruit in a peasant area which I later learned was particularly hostile to the regime. Someone had reported our presence there, and an armed militiaman was sent out on a bicycle to bring us to local police headquarters, about two miles away. Despite the fact that my papers were in order and that he replied in the negative when I asked if I had done anything wrong, he could not deviate from his orders. He even used physical force to prevent me from shutting the car door to keep him from riding in our car. Since he had a gun, I did not believe in further contesting his "right" to ride with us on our way to see his chief. At headquarters, his chief, after looking at my diplomatic identity card, simply said, "Excuse it," and waved us on.

Top Yugoslav Communists know that their bureaucracy, still replete with men who joined the party as dissatisfied, disgruntled, half-literate opportunists, has been badly run. With little education or experience, these men hold most of the all-important middle, as well as most of the lower, layer of administrative positions. Yet party leaders have been virtually powerless to do anything about it. On the one hand, they did not seem to want to believe that the regime had been irreparably discredited, and therefore assumed that the situation could be saved by improvements in administrative personnel and administrative practices. On the other hand, such a step would require the removal of many old party comrades who would thereby become ready recruits for Cominform propaganda.

The party's approach to this problem would seem to be two-fold. Officially, even men who have failed miserably are defended as individuals who can learn from experience and from appropriate "criticism and self-criticism." Unofficially, ways are being found to replace incompetent officeholders as soon as better trained men are available. The much heralded decentralization was supposed to accelerate this process by the dispersal of the more talented administrators who were found concentrated in the main centers. The replacement of some officials who hold key local posts was made possible in part by the party's decision in mid-1952 that the secretary of the local party organization should not also be head of the local government unit. Ostensibly, this separation was decided upon in order to create conditions which would enable the party "to take a critical stand toward the work of governmental organs." [2] But it does not seem unreasonable to conclude that the need of finding a satisfactory way out of the administrative chaos was the more important reason.

Easing Communist Party members out of their administrative positions of power and reducing their influence is proving to be a troublesome matter, for even though no longer occupying key positions, they cannot easily accept the notion that their ideas should be any less important. Moreover, having become accustomed to seeing local matters settled authoritatively by the executive committee of the local people's committee, they are finding it difficult to accept the notion, put forth by the party high command, that now decisions should be made by the people's committee as a whole. Habit and fear of local repercussions, for the time being at least, combine to frustrate in large measure the adoption of new and less dictatorial administrative procedures.

The Meaning of Administrative Decentralization

A number of reasons no doubt motivated the Yugoslav Communists to attempt a decentralization of their governmental apparatus. Certainly among the most important was the need to devise an administrative structure which would prove workable in implementing party decisions, particularly those involving the operation of the economy. After the break with Moscow in 1948,

[2] See Rankovich's report to Sixth Party Congress, *Politika*, November 7, 1952.

Yugoslav Communists began, hesitatingly and gradually, to wonder if the abominable state of their economy was perhaps not
traceable to the top-heavy centralized bureaucratic structure
which they had copied from the Russians. Finally, after nearly
three additional years had elapsed, they decided to reduce and to
eliminate centralized operation of the economy. Industry was
ostensibly turned over to the workers to operate, and workers'
councils were created for that purpose.

But party leaders soon discovered that if party economic objectives were not to be lost sight of and if consistency in economic
policy was to prevail, political organization with appropriate
authority had to be created at corresponding levels of economic
activity. Hence, the alterations in the governmental structure
described earlier in Part Two. One common purpose dictated
the uniformity of governmental and administrative organization
from top to bottom, and one common desire called for a
streamlining of the bureaucracy. That one common purpose or
desire was to convert the republics and the local people's committees into effective executors of party decisions. One important
party member even described the future people's committee as "a
picture of the social plan in fulfillment." [3]

A second reason motivating the "decentralization" effort was
to somehow find ways and means of engaging the Yugoslav people in the work of local authorities, and thereby giving them the
impression that they were participating in governmental decisions. Party leaders knew that there was something wrong with
the existing way of doing things. But since they were unwilling to
consider that the weaknesses might be inherent in Communism
itself, they were frequently confused. According to their theory,
people should show an interest in the work of local authorities,
but they discovered that these "offices were nearly always
empty." [4] People complained and criticized, but not at the established places. Even members of local people's committees often
failed to attend meetings, let alone perform needed tasks.[5] But
since dialectical materialism admitted of no impossibilities, the
Communists were convinced that an answer could be found if

[3] See statement by Nikola Shulentich, *Borda*, July 15, 1952.
[4] *20 Oktobar* (Belgrade), December 3, 1948.
[5] *Borba*, July 15, 1952.

they tried hard enough. If one effort resulted in failure, it should be followed with a new or revised attack.

Yet to non-Communist observers it was evident that people were afraid to criticize, and well they might be when they learned what had happened to those who had taken the Communists at their word that criticism was desired. Likewise, the non-Communist observer could also perceive what had happened in the smaller provincial towns. Instead of the towns and cities helping to raise the villages to a higher level, they had themselves been brought down to the level of the villages. Unlike the prewar political leaders, who were men of some education, travel, achievement and experience, the new Communist rulers of the towns and cities were former village dwellers, whose standard was the standard of the backward village. But Communist leaders seemingly never understood nor did they seem even to be aware of this particular impact of their rule.

Yet they were cognizant of the need that something be done and, more specifically, that the political structure should be adjusted to mesh with their economic decentralization. They also realized that policital decentralization, even though our definitions of the concept might be at considerable variance from theirs, offered them opportunities to stress for foreign as well as domestic consumption the "democratic" nature of these developments.

It cannot be denied that Yugoslav Communists succeeded in selling these developments as democratic and progressive to some foreign circles, and thereby achieved a certain modicum of respectability. The Yugoslav people, however, were less easily deceived. When I asked some of them why they did not seem much excited about the new laws and the proposed reforms, one wise Serb put it vividly when he said: "People have come to know that laws in themselves mean nothing. What really counts are the instructions from the Central Committee [of the party] as to how any particular law is to be applied in practice."

The Future of Administrative Decentralization

The future of Yugoslav administrative decentralization will no doubt depend upon the extent to which it accomplishes the basic purpose for which it was established. It was not devised to bring about local autonomy nor to permit units of local government and local economic enterprises to operate freely and independently. On the contrary, it was designed in the expectation that it would constitute an effective instrument by means of which the party could facilitate the successful functioning of a "decentralized" collectivist economy. Hence, the future of administrative decentralization hinges not only upon its own efficiency as an administrative technique, but also upon the workability in Yugoslavia of the concept of economic decentralization itself. While a consideration of the latter must await a future chapter, it may be useful to record at this point some of my own reactions to administrative decentralization as it was being put into practice at the time I was in Yugoslavia.

Basically two questions were and will no doubt continue to be involved: personnel and procedure. In the case of the latter, it still remains to be seen how quickly and how effectively local officials, accustomed to carrying out detailed instructions from above, can accommodate themselves to the new governmental machinery. During the interval between the decentralization of the central economic apparatus and the establishment of the new decentralized governmental forms, local bureaucrats found things extremely confusing. They were often left confounded by directives which did not indicate *how* to proceed at each step of the way. Their tasks were made even more difficult by the disruption of the familiar administrative hierarchy, leaving them completely at a loss about where to refer their questions. But getting accustomed to new administrative forms and procedures may be only a matter of time.

In the matter of administrative personnel, however, some stubborn obstacles have arisen. The party high command might have been sincere in desiring to lift the bureaucratic level of local units by sending to them some able men from the center. But in practice the process has not worked out smoothly. First of all, there has been a strong reluctance on the part of Communists and non-Communists to go to the smaller provincial towns, frequently resulting in outright refusals to go even though they have been penalized by the loss of their jobs. Party leaders discovered that in the struggle of who would be sent to the provinces, the Communists, having come to enjoy the benefits of urban living and possessing the advantages of a closely knit group, were winning out. Consequently, it was the non-Communist for the most part who was being "decentralized." Party leaders insist that this situation will be "corrected."

Moreover, local authorities have been far from co-operative. Frequently, a man sent to a small provincial town has discovered that there was no job for him. Take the case of a legal counsel. The local enterprise already has one, and has no need for a second. Even if the new man should be more able, why should the present job holder who has been capable enough to hold the position for the past several years now no longer be considered adequate? Even the official Communist press has admitted that knowledge gained on the job may entitle a person, even though he has little schooling, to retain his position.[6] Such obstacles have not been easy to surmount. On the other hand, in many instances where the newcomer has had a job when he arrived, he has found no housing and local authorities have not helped him. Yet, if he should attempt to return to Belgrade or some other larger center from which he had departed, he may discover that he has no right to residence there unless he is employed in that city.

Many unfortunate circumstances may ensue. Knowing this, the person receiving transfer orders has often sought to evade carrying them out. One Belgrade doctor, for example, argued that he could not go to the designated place because his wife, also a doctor, was employed in Belgrade, because they owned their own home, etc. The authorities promptly knocked out his principle reason by also transferring his wife; whereupon he resigned. The authorities then issued an order that he could not be employed anywhere in Belgrade for a period of two years. Nevertheless he decided to stay, and to become a porter or perform any other menial tasks in order to eke out a living. But the Belgrade housing authorities came to him and told him that he no longer had a right to his apartment, although he is the *owner* of the apartment building in which he lives!

While it may be difficult to forecast the future of Yugoslav administrative decentralization, one thing seems certain. Regardless of the regime's efforts, new problems will doubtless continue

[6] *Borba,* June 16, 1952.

to arise, and the likelihood of the discovery of simple and effective solutions is extremely remote. Further improvising, within the Marxian concept of the role of government, can be expected in the future.

Chapter 10:

Party and Government: Law and Justice

THE judiciary, no less than the Communist-controlled political and administrative setup, has its assigned role to play. Here as elsewhere in their governmental system, however, the Yugoslavs insist that they are making significant changes. The key to these changes is to be found in the alleged aim of eliminating certain admitted evils without changing the basic principles of Marxian justice. As we look at Yugoslav judicial practice, therefore, it is important to bear in mind the nature of these principles and the function which the judiciary is expected to perform within the framework of their political system.

Concept of Law and Justice under Communism

As a general rule, laws and the means employed to enforce them are but a reflection of the ideas and principles which characterize any given political system. In this respect Communist law and Communist justice in Yugoslavia hold true to form. The primary objective of their laws and their courts is to preserve the regime and to aid and protect those who faithfully seek to carry out its program. And conversely, to strike down those who attempt to get in the way, as well as those who are suspected of such an attempt. In other words, all of those who are not for the party program should be punished in one way or another. Punishment may vary from the death penalty to being denied a housing permit or being expelled from school.

In view of the Communists' clear-cut and all-embracing politico-economic program, the need for a uniform and centralized system of law and courts becomes evident. Although the principle of indirect election of judges is preserved, the fact remains that they must support the objectives of the regime. And no Yugoslav citizen is under any illusion about the basic aims of Communist laws or about the primary functions of their courts.

The public prosecutor and his many local assistants are the guardians of the Communist order. Immediately after the establishment of the Tito regime their biggest job was that of purging antiregime elements. Their next most onerous task involved the prosecution of countless peasants who had not delivered the requisite amount of grain and other products demanded by the government. In the summer of 1952, the public prosecutor of Yugoslavia told me that the principal problem facing them involved the numerous malpractices (forgeries, fraud, theft, embezzlement, etc.) occuring in various economic enterprises. He also told me that the prosecutor's office could no longer exercise certain judicial functions, such as suspending acts of administrative agencies, and determining how long a prisoner might be held without formal charges and without trial, functions which it had heretofore performed.

Historical Note on Yugoslav Communist Justice

Following their rise to power, the Yugoslav Communists faithfully copied the Soviet judicial system, and proceeded to impose upon their people the now familiar Soviet pattern of justice. One of the most telling commentaries I heard about their judiciary was the story of two Yugoslavs who were talking about incongruities. "Look at Hungary, for example," said the one, "they have a navy department, yet no navy." "Brother, that's not so strange," replied the other. "Look at us, we have a ministry of justice!"

But in those days (1947–1950), Yugoslav Communists stoutly defended their system of justice, and denied the existence of miscarriages of justice with which we were all too familiar. More recently, however, they have admitted such gross miscarriages of justice so far as to make the darkest picture we possessed in those days pale into insignificance by comparison. The admissions come from none other than Alexander Rankovich, head of the secret police.[1]

Bearing in mind the probability that much still remains concealed, it seems nonetheless astounding that Rankovich should reveal that 47 per cent of secret-police arrests during 1949 were unjustified.[2] Among his other almost unbelievable revelations were the following: ". . . our courts (as well as UDB and public prosecutors) are sometimes inclined to convert ordinary crime into political criminal offenses [3]. . . the court accepts the matter of fact as stated in the indictment regardless of evidence to the contrary.[4] . . . Individual courts apply punishments which do not exist under the law [5]. . . the People's Committee in Trebinje . . . sent its officials on the terrain and gave them blank signed decisions which provided for a sentence of three months forced labor [6]. . . an individual has been punished for collaboration with the enemy who during the occupation was imprisoned in the invader's concentration camps.[7] . . . There are examples where directives are given on how a sentence will be passed in a concrete case, and also that even concrete instructions are given in advance with respect to the amount of punishment to be meted out to a person. . . ." [8]

Many other equally damaging admissions could be cited from Rankovich's report to the party's Central Committee. Moreover, case by case documentation from other sources could be furnished were it not for the fact that these admissions make that unnecessary. Even the president of the Yugoslav supreme court, in a conversation with me in the summer of 1952, said that at one time judges of local people's courts simply asked their respective local party secretaries what verdict they should hand down.

Rankovich's report was apparently designed to demonstrate the party's desire to eliminate injustices and to rectify faulty

[1] See his report to the party's Central Committee (June 3, 1951), *New Yugoslav Law*, II (October–December, 1951), pp. 3–34.
[2] *Ibid.*, p. 16.
[3] *Ibid.*, p. 8.
[4] *Ibid.*, p. 11.
[5] *Ibid.*
[6] *Ibid.*, p. 31.
[7] *Ibid.*, p. 11.
[8] *Ibid.*, p. 19.

judicial procedures. These shortcomings he attributed to over-zealousness of local party leaders, to the lack of legal training among many judges, to ignorance of the law by prosecutors and judges alike, and to a deliberate determination on the part of some officials not to let anything stand in their way when carrying out orders from above. But while describing the changes that would have to be made, Rankovich was careful to point out that this did "not involve the changing of the basic principles of our justice." [9]

The Central Committee of the Communist Party, in endorsing Rankovich's report, formulated several decisions concerning law and the judiciary. The reforms which followed certainly improved upon the existing situation. Arbitrary arrest and detention are at least in theory eliminated. Moreover, the right of the police and the party to arrest and sentence individuals for certain categories of offenses without due process of law, a procedure known as "administrative punishment," was allegedly abolished in 1951. Yet, detailed instructions on the reorganization of local people's committees in the summer of 1952 refer to "administrative-punishment" functions in the "secretariat for internal affairs." [10]

To the extent that some of the avowed reforms are put in operation, they will no doubt facilitate a greater measure of justice, at least in some cases. But one cannot be sure to what extent these new guarantees will be observed, for it should not be forgotten that legal requirements are never a substantial hindrance to the pursuit of basic Communist objectives. It was not surprising, therefore, that nine months after the above cited Rankovich report, which, among other things, called for raising the professional qualifications of judges, the party launched a campaign to purge politically unreliable judges. [11] It was not explained how politically hostile judges were able to survive nearly a decade of Communist rule, but it was made plain that they would be replaced with younger men who would work with the party to clean up the courts. [12] Assuming, however, that the much-advertised reforms are carried out, Yugoslav justice, as the following paragraphs will demonstrate, leaves much to be desired

[9] *Ibid.,* p. 4.
[10] *Sluzhbeni list,* VIII (July 23, 1952), p. 709.
[11] *Borba,* March 3, 1952.
[12] *Ibid.*

among those who have become accustomed to the guarantees of Anglo-American jurisprudence.

Some Procedural Practices

In conformity with general continental practice, the Yugoslavs operate on the Roman Law principle that the burden of proof rests on the accused. Unlike the Common Law doctrine which presumes a man innocent until proved guilty, the Roman Law requires that the accused disprove the charges brought against him. It is significant, too, that in court he is never referred to as the defendant, but always as "the accused." In democratic nations, such as France, with the attendant guarantees of a free press and a legislature whose laws cannot be declared invalid by the courts, Roman Law justice has been eminently satisfactory. But in countries whose judges are agents of a police state dictatorship the results have been particularly odious. The accused are rarely given a real opportunity to defend themselves. They cannot be in consultation with their attorneys. They dare not comment upon the methods utilized by the police to obtain confessions. And in court they are browbeaten by the judges, who do all of the questioning.

Before a prisoner is ever brought to trial, however, he may have been held in prison for months or even years. I personally knew of a number of cases where more than two years elapsed before formal charges were made and the man brought into court. Since there is no such thing as *habeas corpus* in Yugoslavia, persons can be, and are, held in jail for long periods of time without their families, friends or defense lawyers being allowed to see them or even learning what the charges against them may be.

Some trials are secret and some public. There may be several reasons for secret trials, one of them being to protect informers. An illustration of this was provided when in 1951 a person was tried in secret on a blackmarketing charge. The defense attorney, noting that twenty-odd people were listed in the accusation as being involved in the alleged blackmarketing ring, asked the court to summon all of them as witnesses. Of twenty-six who were summoned, only four appeared, and three sent excuses. The trial was delayed, and upon the insistence of the defense, a new summons went out to the same twenty-six people. Only seven appeared, the four who had appeared before and the three who had sent excuses. Thus, while the Yugoslav Communists talk about preserving legality, their courts could not compel the appearance of nineteen witnesses in this one case. In view of the fact that these nineteen persons in no way responded to either summons, there could be little doubt about their being secret police informers, and hence above the law. The case was also a vivid portrayal of the fact that the Communist Party and its decisions are more important than legal forms or constitutional guarantees.

It seems to be an unwritten principle of Communist jurisprudence that no one should be brought to public trial until he confesses. Consequently, during these periods of incarceration the secret police seeks to obtain a full and complete confession, preferably one which implicates others. One confession may follow another, as additional persons are apprehended and as further questioning reveals omissions in the previous confession. Where necessary, various forms of barbaric torture are utilized to extract confessions. I witnessed one court scene where a young man denied his guilt. The judge sought to browbeat him by fanning the air with his "confession" and asking why he had signed it if he was not guilty. The young man started to say something, but as soon as he had uttered the words "secret police," the judge cut him off. A few moments later, however, he was able to blurt out a brief sentence, saying that he had signed the confession "after a ten-day treatment on the cement slab." This did not, of course, affect the verdict.

When in the summer of 1952 I asked the president of the Yugoslav supreme court about these long periods of pretrial imprisonment, he readily admitted that they had occurred, but tried to assure me that they were a thing of the past. There were instances, he asserted, where a person was arrested and held, pending efforts to apprehend others involved, and "sometimes the authorities simply forgot about them." It should be recorded that some of these were never heard of again. When I asked him a few moments later about Yugoslav Communists with Cominformist sympathies, he made an interesting admission by saying: "We did not even want to bring them to trial; we sent them to correctional work camps." At least insofar as Cominformists are concerned, therefore, they are in a separate category, for the much-advertised judicial reforms apparently do not apply to them.

It is also interesting to note that under Yugoslav justice there is no protection against double jeopardy. A person may be tried for the same alleged offense any number of times. Shortly after World War II, for example, the Communists arrested a man for having been a German spy. Actually, the man had been anti-German to such an extent that he had refused to carry German products in his store, although he handled products from other foreign countries. At his trial it became obvious that the case was ludicrous, and he was acquitted. He was brought to trial a second time, and again acquitted. After a time he was again brought to trial on the same charge. This time he "admitted," among other things, that he had traveled to Berlin ten times, although he actually had not been there once. This time he was convicted. It was not insignificant that the judge in the first trial went to jail, while the judge in the second lost his job because he "had not been objective."

Moreover, under Yugoslav judicial practice, it is possible for the prosecution to appeal from what it considers light sentences, and to obtain stiffer penalties from higher courts. In 1949, for example, the directors of the prewar Foreign Investment Bank were brought to trial for alleged wartime collaboration with the enemy. They were found guilty, but their sentences were not severe enough to permit confiscation of their property. An appeal to a higher court, however, resulted in longer sentences and, of course, confiscation of property.

The practice of allowing the prosecution to appeal for increased penalties serves as a useful technique for deceiving foreigners. A man may be brought to trial and given a relatively moderate sentence in the light of his crime. When these facts are published in the local press, the foreign observer may not get an unfavorable picture of Yugoslav justice, for the appeals and the heavier sentences are not, as a rule, given any publicity.

A little known and curious aspect of Yugoslav jurisprudence requires that a guilty person serve out his sentence, alive or dead. Two cases are personally known to me where men died in prison before the expiration of their sentences. In both instances the respective families claimed the bodies, but were told that they could get the remains only after the expiration of the time for which the men were sentenced. One family had about two years to wait, the other approximately nine years.

Some Examples of Communist Justice

Communist propagandists have had some success in convincing many persons outside their orbit that while their laws may not reflect political and economic ideas with which the non-Communist world agrees, they are nevertheless enforced impartially and scrupulously adhered to by those who enforce them. Such a view is, of course, erroneous. Many examples might be cited to illustrate the lack, or the nonobservance, of legality in a Communist state. In addition to such cases as I may have noted elsewhere in this book, it seems appropriate at this point to record several other examples of a lack of respect for legality, by way of illustrating the nature of Yugoslav Communist justice.

When the Communists came to power in Yugoslavia, the people still believed that the courts would dispense justice, for although prewar Yugoslavia had had its good and bad administrations, the courts had been good. The people had confidence in them. One lawyer with thirty years' practice told me that in all of his experience he would not have suspected more than two or three judges who might have been subject to corruption. But the people discovered the hard way that unjust accusations could not be disproved so easily in courts controlled by a Communist dictatorship, for the Communists had little respect for law or justice.

In 1945, for example, a peasant who had been a courier in the Mihailovich movement landed in jail. His cellmate, an urban dweller and also a Mihailovich supporter, asked him how it was that the Communists caught him, since it was so easy to hide in the rural areas. The peasant replied that they would never have caught him if he had not read the amnesty proclamation. After reading it, and knowing that he had not killed anyone or committed any other crime, he put the newspaper in his pocket and went to the authorities to receive the required identity papers. But the authorities threw him into prison. When he pulled out his

newspaper and called their attention to the amnesty proclamation, the police said to him: "That is only for fools! How do you
think we would have caught you otherwise!"

The Communists' disrespect for law was also illustrated when
valuable property was taken over without compensation or with
the owner's being compensated for only a fraction of the property's worth. In one instance with which I am personally familiar
the authorities did not even bother to inquire as to the ownership
of a plot of land. When a friend met the owner one day, he asked
him what he was building on that plot of land down by ————.
"Nothing," replied the confused owner, whereupon he hurried to
investigate. He discovered that his friend was not joking; a half-
finished building stood on his property. Some government ministry had not been much concerned about the clause in the Yugoslav constitution which stated that "private property and private
initiative in economy are guaranteed." [13]

A case involving a similar disregard for private property
came to my attention in early 1949. In one village a man's milk
cow was taken and slaughtered to feed some 200 soldiers who
had been assigned to pest control work in that particular village.
The owner did not mind the fact that he was paid a ridiculously
low price for the cow quite so much as the fact that he was de-
prived of an exceedingly scarce item—a rich milk supply.

It has happened that men have been arrested on fabricated
charges for no other reason than to confiscate their property. One
day, for example, the owner of a printing shop was notified that
his shop was being confiscated. In response to his demand for an
explanation he was told that he had worked for the Nazis. When
he protested and proved that his shop had been closed during the
occupation, he was thrown in jail. After a time he was released
and, understandably, he protested no more.

Similarly, several years after the execution of General Drazha
Mihailovich, the attorney who had defended him, Dragich
Joksimovich, was arrested, tried, convicted and sentenced to
three or four years imprisonment. The alleged crime was a desire
to overthrow the Tito government. The principal piece of evidence consisted of the fact that at a private dinner one of the
group proposed a toast in which he is reported to have addressed

[13] Article 18.

Joksimovich and said: "I hope you will be our next president."
His arrest was in reality motivated by the government's desire to
get its hands on materials concerning the defense of Mihailovich,
which were in his possession and which might prove embarrass-
ing to the government at some future date. It may be of historical
interest to note that Joksimovich died in prison, and that despite
a thorough search by secret police agents, the sought-after materials were not found.

A different commentary on Yugoslav justice occurred more
recently. The chief financial officer of the parliament was arrested, and while no reason was ever given, informed sources
believe that he was suspected of having revealed financial information which would embarrass the government. His wife, by
virtue of the job her husband held, was in a position to know and
to reach important political leaders. In response to her request
for an explanation, she was told not to worry, that her husband
would be released soon. After a few days she made a further
inquiry and was given the same answer. Yet on that same day
she accidentally learned that her husband was dead and was
being buried that afternoon. Afterward the local papers reported
his death and attributed it to a heart attack, but it is significant
that his widow was not even allowed to open his coffin, much less
to have an autopsy performed by the family doctor.

It is also interesting to note that Communists are not bothered
by such things as consistency. Immediately after World War II,
for example, individuals were shot for having signed an anti-
Communist proclamation during the Nazi occupation. Yet it was
considered proper for Communists to have signed the same
proclamation in order to save their heads. A Communist who
signed one of these proclamations even became president of the
Serbian Academy of Science.

A Word of Caution

Those who may be interested in pursuing the study of Communist law and justice must always be on guard against dangerous pitfalls. As in the case of other institutions (political, economic, or social), law and justice must be studied within the
context of the total political situation. To condemn a system of

law and justice, for example, and thereby leave the impression that it could come near our own standards of justice while remaining an integral part of the dictatorship, is not only fruitless but also in the highest degree unscientific.

Moreover, the difficulties of getting at the facts cannot be exaggerated. Long, patient and painstaking effort is required. Much of what transpires in a Communist-controlled country is never reported, and what is reported needs careful and critical evaluation, for Communists are not at all above falsifying the facts in the most ordinary type of reporting. In 1950, for example, about a dozen young men were brought to trial for allegedly conspiring to overthrow the Tito regime. There was no advance public notice of the trial, but I learned of its existence and attended. No report of the trial appeared in the local press until after the second day of the trial, after it had already been reported to the Yugoslavs by the Voice of America. At that time the press carried a brief story which reported that all of the accused had admitted their guilt. Yet I had sat in the court room and heard all but two or three deny being guilty!

PART THREE

HARNESSING
THE MASSES
TO THE DICTATORSHIP

COMMUNIST dictatorships have perfected a variety of elaborate techniques for regimenting the masses. It is no exaggeration to say that these are both more intensive and more extensive than those devised by any other despotism known to man. Like other Communist totalitarian governments, Tito's Yugoslav regime brooks no opposition and tolerates no passivity. In its determination to obliterate opposition and to harness the people to do its bidding, the regime has left no stone unturned.

Chapter 11:

Refining the Techniques of
Force and Fear

NO REVOLUTION is without its brutality and its innocent victims. And, sooner or later, no revolutionary regime fails
to modify or refine its terroristic methods. Unlike revolutions of
past centuries, however, modern-day Communist uprisings are
characterized by a more systematic, determined and cold-blooded
ruthlessness, and by an all-encompassing surveillance of the people within the domain of their power.

Purges and Imprisonment

The Yugoslav Communists did not wait until they had formally assumed power to liquidate anti-Communist elements.
While still presumably fighting the Nazis, the Titoists were busy
systematically compiling lists of their intended victims. As some
of these fell into their hands they were first tortured in an effort
to implicate others and then killed, usually without trial or at
most a perfunctory and meaningless hearing.

Once in power, the Titoists shot thousands of actual or potential opponents. Many of these fell even prior to the formal
organization of the state, i.e. prior to the drafting of the constitution and the holding of elections. Scarcely is there a city or
town in Yugoslavia where a number of leading citizens (usually
doctors, lawyers, judges, teachers, merchants, journalists and
writers) were not summarily liquidated, many of them without
benefit of judicial process. Some were given a summary and

often farcical trial. One seventeen-year-old boy, for example, was brought before a "judge" who asked him if he had a girl friend. Blushing, the young man replied that there was a girl whom he liked. He was asked if he had been intimate with her. Blushing all the more, the youth said no. To this the "judge" retorted: "Well, it is too late now, for you will not have another opportunity. You are sentenced to death." This was the extent of his "trial." Fortunately for him, the sentence was commuted to twenty years' imprisonment, hence he was able to tell his story to a fellow prisoner, since released, who told it to me.

During the purge period some of Tito's judges made no effort to conceal their depraved partiality even in open court. Impatient with the efforts of the defense at a Belgrade trial in 1946, the presiding judge turned upon one of the attorneys for the defense, and with utter contempt blurted out: "You Belgrade lawyers may delay the trial but the accused will grease the stake!"

Heads rolled easily in the immediate postwar period. At a big dinner celebrating the liberation in the city of Novi Sad, for example, several reserve officers who had been invited to the dinner took exception to the exclusive praise showered upon the Red army and upon Tito's Partisans, and asked what about the contributions of England, the United States and other allies. Several of these officers were shot that same night.

In another instance a young man, who was fortunate enough to get out alive, told me that while in prison he had witnessed secret police agents taking out hundreds of prisoners to be shot the night before the first amnesty was proclaimed. That they must have known about the amnesty was attested to by the fact that long printed lists of those shot were posted by early morning, an indication that there had been a need to meet a deadline, for the lists must have been in the printer's hands *before* the men were shot.

In the summer of 1952, Tito told an American visitor [1] that Rankovich (head of the Yugoslav secret police) "had not shot anybody with or without a court sentence since 1947." In view of the fact that Yugoslav newspapers have carried announce-

---

[1] Louis Fischer, "How Much Freedom in Yugoslavia," *The Saturday Review,* August 16, 1952, p. 36.

ments of executions every year since 1947, Tito's statement constitutes an admission that Rankovich was a law unto himself prior to 1947, a fact confirmed by hundreds of Yugoslavs. One Yugoslav woman, for example, told me of an agent who barged into her house right after the war to take an inventory of her property. After she was able to show him that he was in error, he said, without an apology: "This is a mistake. We are taking an inventory of the property of those who fled with the Germans, were shot without trial, or were sent to the Black Sea" (a reference to deportations to Russia).

There were hundreds of thousands whose immediate liquidation was not considered necessary, but who were looked upon as sufficiently dangerous, in the sense of being potential anti-Communist leaders, to warrant their arrest. Some were later liquidated, some sentenced to varying terms of imprisonment and some were released after being held in jail for months without even any charges being filed against them.

Sometimes whole families were arrested, each member being put in a different cell or even in a different prison. The full impact of such arrests can be more adequately appreciated by citing a fragmentary case history of a Slovenian family. Late one night an eleven-year-old boy was pushed into an overcrowded prison cell. Awakened by the new arrival, his cellmates were interested in his story. He reported that the entire family had been arrested —father, mother, an older sister and he. When they were led away the police locked their house. In the midst of this family tragedy, the boy's main thoughts were with his pet rabbit who had been left in the kitchen. "What will become of him?" he asked his cellmates.

After two weeks of incarceration, the boy was led out for a hearing one night about eleven o'clock. When he came back some time later, he told his cellmates that his interrogators had informed him that he could go home if he told the truth. If not, and at this point his inquisitor pulled a gun out of his pocket and laid it on the table, this is what was in store for him! The boy readily admitted that he had painted signs on buildings and fences reading, "Long Live the King." But the interrogators wanted to know who told him to do it? Who bought the paint and brush for him? Did his father and mother know about it?

Did his sister know? Who else was painting such signs? The boy took full responsibility, implicating no one.

By sheer chance, my informant met the boy's father at a later date in another prison to which he had been moved. The father did not know anything about his son, but he related how secret police agents had brought his daughter in front of him and his wife, and told them that "she will not be good for man or God" when they got through with her if she did not tell the full story. The parents told their daughter to tell the truth. She replied that she had already done so, but to this the secret police agents retorted with voluble abuse. Then the parents told her to tell "what was necessary." At this point the girl threw her arms around her parents and said there was nothing to tell, except what she had already told, i.e. that she had painted signs reading, "Long Live the King." Thereupon the agents took her away and put her in a dark cell in the U-shaped cell block across from where her parents were. They could see nothing, but that she was brutally tortured was evident from the cries of pain which echoed throughout the cell block.

What eventually happened to this family or its individual members, my informant did not know. And no one can ever know the tragedy and pathos in the history of many another unfortunate Yugoslav family. Nor can anyone ever have more than the most limited appreciation of the magnitude of the brutality of the Tito regime. Certainly, its victims were far more numerous than ever came to the attention of the outside world. Some clue as to the number of people hailed before the "people's courts," however, was provided by the minister of justice when on March 28, 1947 he reported to parliament that "during 1946 a relatively small number of judges decided over 1,100,000 various judicial cases." [2] The next day a non-Communist deputy declared: "The Minister of Justice said that in the past year there were over 1,100,000 criminal decisions. That means that every eleventh citizen in this country was convicted!" [3] None of the other deputies made any effort to deny this assertion or to offer any explanation.

[2] *Stenografske beleshke* (Treche redovno zasedanje, March 26–April 28, 1947), p. 98.
[3] *Ibid.*, p. 169.

UDB—the Secret Police

The liquidation and imprisonment of actual and potential opponents was only the first step in Tito's determination that the people should respect the mailed fist. For those who were not executed or imprisoned there was UDB, with its ubiquitous secret agents, ready to put them through the torture chambers in the interests of Marxian unanimity.

Serbia was probably hardest hit by UDB brutality, for the Serbs had not only supported Tito's opponent, Mihailovich, but in addition their history recorded only too well the unhappy fate which their past tyrannical rulers had met. Montenegro, Slovenia and Bosnia-Herzegovina, where Tito's Partisans had operated during the war, had already experienced considerable terror, and more was to come later. While Croatia and Macedonia were far from free of brutality, the Tito regime did make a deliberate attempt to minimize it in these regions, in the hope of gaining and holding popular support, for it was in Croatia and Macedonia that antiregime sentiment had been strongest before the war. While these efforts were largely unsuccessful and while popular opposition toward Tito's government is not confined to any one region, many Croats and Macedonians believe that hostility toward the regime in their regions is not so deep-seated as it would have been had they suffered the degree of brutality endured by Serbia, Montenegro, or Bosnia-Herzegovina.

Communist terror was also visited upon young people. It occurred in its rawest form in Belgrade, where the Communist leaders did not like the opposition to the regime which they found among the youth. It was necessary, they thought, to frighten young people and to teach them to be quiet and obedient. In order to do this, physical beatings were systematically organized by Communist youth leaders in the winter of 1946–1947. This was the pattern: Evening conferences of students were called, but the teachers were not notified. As the students assembled the doors to the building were locked and three-member Communist goon squads were stationed in the assembly hall, just outside the door, at the head of the stairs and at the door leading to the outside of the building. One by one certain students were called and accusations of the most general nature

read to them. There was no opportunity for defense. Before the
accused could begin to speak, the president of the youth group
would push him into the hands of the first goon squad, whose
members kicked and otherwise beat the victim, pushing him to
the squad waiting outside the door. Again he was beaten and
delivered to the squad at the head of the stairs, which, taking
charge of an already dazed and partially conscious youngster,
saw to it that he was kicked or pushed with sufficient force so as
to end up at the foot of the stairs. From there the last goon squad
would take over, throwing the victim outside as if he were a
corpse. Students who dared voice any protest, and even some
who did not applaud the bestial actions of the Communists, were
put through the same routine.

From one school alone nine students were taken to the hospital on stretchers. Bloodstains remained on the school's stairway
wall until the following summer when the whole building was
calcimined. In another school sixty-five students were beaten.
When a militiaman approached one of the schools, after hearing
shouting and screaming, he cried out: "What are you doing?
Can't you see that there are dead ones below?" But the superintendent of the school approached him, whispered something in
his ear, and the militiaman walked away. This same superintendent later referred to the three-member squads as "conscious
youth which is squaring accounts with reaction."

For a time after the war savagery knew no bounds. In an
effort to extract confessions from persons whom they regarded as
political enemies, Tito's secret police subjected men and women
to various forms of torture. Hot needles were driven under finger-
nails; hot irons were applied to legs; persons were forced to
spend as long as three days and nights in water up to their necks;
men were put on tables with heads hanging down over the edge
and water poured into mouths and nostrils; in summer victims
were wrapped in winter overcoats and placed near hot stoves,
later to be thrown on cement floors while cold water was poured
over them. At times several days of torture were followed by a
day or two in a large and comfortable room, with good food and
with servants coming in at frequent intervals to inquire if there
was anything that the victim wanted. Then back he would go to
the torture chambers. This is but a sample of UDB techniques,

and many Yugoslavs could tell about others from firsthand experience.

Today the UDB is not so obviously crude, arrogant and direct. In June of 1952 it was even "transformed" from a military to a civilian agency. But its chief, Rankovich, declared that this did not constitute any change in the "principles on which it is based," and warned one and all not to come to the conclusion "that they may organize and fight against the existing internal order." [4] UDB techniques of force and fear, however, have been refined. Individuals are no longer arrested on the spot as political prisoners. Rather, they are taken in by the militia (police) on charges of speculation, blackmarketing, or some similar count, and then turned over to UDB.

After the Tito-Stalin break the UDB realized that no longer was "Big Brother" nearby, in whose company it could feel safe. Moreover, since Tito was in need of assistance from the West, with its abhorrence of police-state methods, it was imperative to refine police-state techniques and even to hide their existence. Finally, the UDB terror had already achieved its major aim—to cow and to terrify any would-be rebels into submissiveness.

But all direct and brutal actions have not been put aside. Where it is deemed necessary, UDB organizes goon squads to deal with recalcitrants. One such incident occurred in Belgrade University during the 1951–52 school year, when several students were severely beaten for questioning the wisdom of a governmental decree which they said had so adversely affected their material well-being that it was difficult for them to stay in school.

For the most part, however, UDB has the situation well in hand. Most of the really dangerous persons have been liquidated, imprisoned, or completely cowed. In order to make doubly sure, persons known to be anti-Communist or prodemocratic are periodically summoned to appear at an UDB office. Here they may be questioned or even imprisoned for a time. Each new summons carries with it the frightening thought that this time the "visit" to UDB may be of a more permanent nature.

UDB tactics are many and varied. Agents are frequently provocateurs, posing as opponents of the regime. They seek to set up antiregime organizations among unsuspecting victims, and

[4] *Borba,* June 26, 1952.

later in court become star witnesses, admitting all. Some of them
spend days in prison, readily admitting their "crimes" in order
to learn as much as possible from fellow prisoners. Others, posing as personal friends of the imprisoned, visit relatives and
friends in an effort to collect evidence and to implicate others.

On one occasion in Belgrade after the war, during a church
celebration in honor of visiting English churchmen, secret police
agents, in the guise of press photographers, snapped pictures of
enthusiastic student participants. A day or two later they visited
schools in the vicinity with pictures in hand. The students whom
they identified were questioned as to what they had been saying
at the time the pictures were taken, what orders or encouragement they had received from parents, teachers, or others.

UDB, although paid from taxpayers' funds, is in no way
responsible to the people, who know neither the size nor the
budget of the secret police establishment. And the fact that a
large proportion of UDB activities is waste motion, resulting only
in voluminous files, does not seem to bother the Yugoslav regime.

Supplementing the work of UDB is the counterintelligence
service, KOS (*kontra obaveshtajna sluzhba*), whose members
were in large measure recruited from the polite technical and
industrial intelligentsia. These agents are well dressed; they go
to concerts, the opera, movies and the best hotels. They pretend
to be anti-Communists. They have the right to arrest anyone on
the spot, and they are directly responsible to Tito.

Secret Police Auxiliary: Informers

Obviously UDB agents cannot be everywhere at all times.
Consequently, they have set up a whole network of informers, an
auxiliary arm without which they might have difficulty in functioning. These informants are strategically placed—in government
enterprises, apartment buildings, schools, restaurants and hotels,
and even in the army. The colleagues of a young woman teacher
in a Belgrade school, for example, insist that she is not competent
to teach. Her real function is that of a secret agent who informs
on other teachers, including the superintendent, even though he
is a Communist. Servile underlings of various party-sponsored

organizations do their best to report what people say, buy or do. On the pretext of telling people about forthcoming political conferences or other gatherings, they call at homes during lunch or dinner time so that they can observe what is on the table. Their reports note those houses where cakes are made and what kind of cakes (with eggs or without, how much sugar, butter, etc.). Once cherished privacy is no more.

Some persons are willing informers, expecting thereby to demonstrate their loyalty and consequently hoping for better treatment in the future. Many more are unwilling victims, detesting themselves and the regime which has forced them to stoop so low. Yet it is not difficult to perceive how individuals are forced into becoming informers. There is a limit to human endurance. A number of Yugoslavs told me more than once that they could not stand another imprisonment. They are at the breaking point. As their resistance is broken down by threats, imprisonment and economic discrimination, as they are forced by circumstances (such as U. S. aid to Tito) to become more and more resigned to the regime, they are enlisted as informers. Often a man's close friend informs on him. One Yugoslav told me that UDB agents had even showed him a letter sent to them by a man he regarded as a close friend, informing on him.

Another Yugoslav, employed in one of the ministries, told me about a girl in his office whom UDB sought to enlist as an informer. One day she came into the office looking as white as a sheet. Her fellow employees asked her what was the matter, but received no answer. They gave her a stimulant, but still no answer. The next day she told her whole story to one of her coworkers. She had been asked by UDB to become an informer, but refused. Subsequently she was reached by telephone and told of her appointment with a UDB agent, an appointment which she failed to keep. Later an agent came to the office, threatening her with arrest. When she still refused, the agent handed her a statement to sign, which read, in part, that she "refused to inform on the people's enemies." Of course, she could not sign such a statement, and that evening told her parents about the whole affair. Because they knew a relative of someone high up in the government, they sought his help. He told them not to worry.

Yet, in spite of his intervention, she was arrested and held for several days before he could get her released. Others have not been so fortunate.

Why did this girl so object to becoming an informer? What did they want her to do? Quite simply, they wanted her to report office conversations. The agent pointed out to her that when people came to the office in the morning they usually talked about what they had read in the papers or about what they had heard on the radio, and UDB was interested in what they said. She knew, first of all, that other and more difficult tasks would be assigned her in the future, and if she refused to perform those more onerous assignments later, she could be accused of being disloyal and insincere even in her first undertaking. Secondly, she was sure that there would be other informers in the same office, and any discrepancies in their reports would be used to prove disloyalty and dereliction of duty. She knew that once she became enmeshed in the wheels of the secret police there would be no turning back and only grief ahead.

Chapter 12:

The Public Opinion Monopoly

No COMMUNIST regime can afford to limit its control over the masses to techniques of force and fear. But in discussing public opinion in a Communist dictatorship, it is necessary to make one point clear at the outset. Unlike democratic governments, Communist regimes are not interested in public opinion in the sense of seeking to satisfy popular demands. They are interested in it only to the extent that they may thereby obtain knowledge to help them promote their program and to get the people to believe what they think the people should believe. They are aware that if left alone, people will continue to do some thinking even if they cannot express themselves publicly. Hence, it is imperative to channel this thinking along desired lines. It is not unexpected, therefore, to find that in attempting to get their views accepted, Communists not only strive for ownership and control of the instrumentalities of public opinion, but in addition seek to exclude competing influences to the utmost of their ability.

Ownership and Control of Instrumentalities of Public Opinion

Although a few independent newspapers were able to begin publishing in Yugoslavia immediately after liberation, they were snuffed out or taken over by the government soon after the Communists were firmly in power. Today every means for conveying public opinion is either owned by the government or at its mercy.

It is impossible to appreciate the extent of the government's monopoly in the field of public opinion unless one keeps in mind the fact that there are no privately owned newspapers, printing presses or stocks of newsprint. There are no privately owned movie houses; no private producing or importing film enterprises. There are no privately owned theaters and no privately produced plays. There are no privately owned radio stations or privately produced programs.

It is well to remember also that there has been a great increase in the publishing field. Where one newspaper or magazine existed before the war, today there are several. Some of these are the result of planned expansion by Communist propaganda strategists. Some have resulted from half-baked ideas of enthusiastic regime partisans who desired to make a place in the sun for themselves. The number of these ventures which were dropped after a few issues approaches, if it does not exceed, the total number of newspapers and periodicals in existence in Yugoslavia when World War II began.

But successes and failures are lumped together by Yugoslav Communist propagandists to produce a statistically impressive appearance of cultural growth. They are convinced that foreigners can be impressed with statistics, and the fact that publications are not continued is of minor importance to them. Some of their ventures are costly, too. Recently, the Communist Party organ, *Borba,* announced that since the war nearly 300 books had been translated and published in the Albanian language.[1] But *Borba* did not indicate the cost of this enterprise, which certainly was not economically profitable, nor the extent to which the partially literate Albanian minority had made use of these books. In another instance, the Yugoslavs claimed that in one year they had translated more works from foreign languages than had any other country in the world.

The ambitious nature of the regime's strategy can be seen from the efforts of Yugoslav Communists to curry favor with minority groups in Yugoslavia by producing a variety of publications for them. In the summer of 1948 they described some of this publishing activity in the press and periodical field.[2] Most of the publications were weeklies, although there were some dailies and a few fortnightlies and monthlies. These publications were edited by party-sponsored People's Front or other mass

[1] August 28, 1952.
[2] *Rad* (Belgrade), August 13, 1948.

organizations. Some were designed for adults, others for youth and children (Pioneers). The number of publications for each minority was reported as follows: Hungarian, nine; Italian, nine; Albanian, four; Czech, three; Rumanian, three; Slovak, two; Russian, two; Turkish, one.

But even this recitation of government ownership and control of the instrumentalities of public opinion does not fully convey the extent to which the government is engaged in the battle for men's minds.

No One Can Stand Aside

Yugoslav propaganda strategists do not stop with ownership and control of existing facilities or the rapid expansion of such facilities to meet their needs. They stress "quality," too, by which they mean that no one should be permitted to stand aside or remain aloof from political polemics. "Freedom of the press" is extended even to those who may not desire it, by the creation of special newspapers for all groups in the population.

No longer can poets, musicians, writers, or artists argue that theirs is a nonpolitical life. During the brief electoral campaign of 1950, for example, over twenty of their leading writers contributed from twenty to sixty lines each in two issues of *Knjiz-hevne novine* [3] (Literary News), all expressing their happiness and thankfulness to Tito and the Communist Party. Adding to this chorus of unanimity, a group of musicians, in another newspaper, proclaimed that a vote for the regime was "a vote for the greater blossoming of art." [4]

Communist propagandists are always on the lookout for appropriate occasions to mobilize writers, local political chieftains and cultural and educational leaders. In 1949, for example, they proclaimed "Presheren Week," in honor of France Presheren, a Slovenian poet who died in 1849. Special newspaper articles, theater performances, and pilgrimages to his birthplace and grave were featured, in an effort to demonstrate his influence in the leftward process which finally culminated in the Tito-led revolu-

[3] Published in Belgrade and, like the Soviet *Literary Gazette,* designed especially for writers, March 14 and 21, 1950.
[4] *Narodni list* (Zagreb), March 9, 1950.

tion. Such celebrations are manifestations not so much of a high cultural appreciation under a Communist regime as of the lengths to which Communists will go to find pegs on which to hang their propaganda.

University professors are also the objects of special attention, for they are also provided with a newspaper of their own, the *Univerzitetski vesnik* (University Herald), in which they are expected, and indeed asked, to go on record along established lines laid down by the Communist Party.

Methods sometimes vary. If a factory employs some competent and respected engineers, the political commissar, desirous of exploiting their prestige among the workers, will get them to participate in political meetings or conferences. An engineer may beg off, perhaps once, by pleading preoccupation with overtime work or some other valid excuse. But the persistent party secretary will suggest that he "come and speak for just five minutes." The engineer may protest that he is a poor speaker or that he does not have time to prepare a speech. If the party secretary sees no other way out, he comes forth with the clincher: "Yes, I know you are not a good speaker, so just come along and sit on the platform or at the speaker's table so that the workers can see you there."

In short, every person and every group which the party believes can contribute to its propaganda battle is mobilized, little by little, in one way or another. And few can really hope to remain neutral or apolitical.

Communists Call the Tune

Responsibility for carrying out Communist propaganda aims is vested in *Agitprop* (as noted earlier, this is an abbreviation of the words agitation and propaganda), a section of the party's Central Committee. It is charged, in the broadest sense, with fulfilling the ideological-educational tasks facing the Communist political strategists. Not only does *Agitprop* issue a steady stream of confidential directives to guide responsible officials in the various informational and cultural media, but it also supervises and oversees the actual preparation of much of the textual material which finds its way into print or over the air waves.

That the press and other organs of public opinion are expected to play a role dictated by the party and the government was graphically illustrated when in 1949 Tito had a long conference with Yugoslav press correspondents. In sharp contrast with democratic practice, he openly and frankly told them what role journalists were expected to play. Among other things, he said that it was incumbent upon them to be careful not to hinder the activities of Yugoslav politicians and diplomats.[5]

When one takes into account the vast scope of the Yugoslav Communist-directed press and other publications, the number of organizations having their own official organs, the radio stations and theaters, the vast number of meetings where agitation is primarily oral, the ideological work in the armed services, it can be seen that *Agitprop's* is a far from simple task. At the Sixth Party Congress, Tito asserted that *Agitprop* had tried to do too much, with the result that local party organizations had become inactive and neglected elemental propaganda tasks.[6] In the future, he said, local party units would exercise more and more initiative, with, of course, constant guidance from *Agitprop*.

One relatively recent development deserves at least a passing note. In the years immediately after the war, Yugoslav Communists imitated the Russians in their rigidity of approach to writing, acting, music and other arts. In the past year or two, however, there has been some debate among Yugoslav Communists, chiefly in two literary newspapers, as to how much ideological direction and dictation artists, writers, et al. should have to accept. One group has propounded the view that whatever does not harm the development of socialism should be permitted. They have held that there is some merit in "art for art's sake," and have sharply condemned "Zhdanovism"—a reference to the late Andrei Zhdanov, the Russian leader who in the post-World War II period set himself up as judge of the ideological purity of Soviet literature, music and art.

Although the results of this debate are still inconclusive, it may be significant that the views of this group have been sharply attacked by no less a figure than Milovan Djilas, one of the six top Communists in Yugoslavia and head of *Agitprop*. It can be

[5] *Borba,* November 12, 1949.
[6] *Borba,* November 4, 1952.

assumed, therefore, that, a crackdown is possible at any time. Yet it may serve Yugoslav international interests to permit some discussion of this type, for the question of tolerating the espousal of Western democratic views is not involved. Non-Communists have no means of expressing their views publicly, and the Communists whose views unwittingly become "corrupted" by Western influence will receive stinging rebukes from the party. Art, at least in some of its forms, may in the future be able to retain a modicum of unhampered initiative, but it will continue to be under unremitting scrutiny. Yugoslav Communists can be counted upon to man the literary ramparts against the infiltration of "bourgeois decadence," as well as against the "Soviet-Cominform heresy."

Chapter 13:

Mobilizing the Masses

To ASSIST in harnessing the masses to the dictatorship, the party has spewed forth a welter of organizations, stemming like roots from the central branch, spreading in all directions, dividing and subdividing. To be sure, there is a limit to which such growth can proceed; some organizations are stillborn and others die in infancy. And it is safe to conclude that neither the Yugoslav government nor the Yugoslav Communist Party knows how many such organizations exist at any one time.

Nearly all of these organizations are like parasites—they are economically unproductive, but all have their budgets which dip into the state treasury. No one really knows how much they eat up in the course of a year. Most of them are hungry, ambitious to expand, and consequently need additional material resources. They publish newspapers and magazines, organize special outings, assemble for various congresses, and in general find a hundred and one ways to eat their way through what, for Yugoslavia at least, must be fantastic sums of money.

The Mass Organizations

In imitation of the Soviets, the Yugoslav Communists had from the beginning a strong penchant for mass organizations. The most notable of these was the People's Front, now renamed The Socialist Alliance of the Working People of Yugoslavia. Ostensibly a coalition of political parties and other groupings, at one time allegedly proving that Tito's Communist regime was "broadly representative," the People's Front turned out to be an appendage of the Communist Party. It became a dues paying association to which nearly all adult persons were obliged to belong. Counting some eight million members, its branches and activities are to be found throughout the country.

Among the other mass organizations, all closely related to or under supervision of the People's Front, are the People's Youth, the Association of Anti-Fascist Women, and the Labor Syndicate Federation. Like the People's Front, these groups are nationwide, but a large part of their activities are confined to the urban centers.

Supplementing and often duplicating the larger mass organizations, are a score of lesser associations designed to encompass war veterans, factory workers, government employees, teachers, students, writers, journalists, "religious" workers, drama groups, sports associations, scientific workers, and even peasants (who are the least organized). Consequently, one person oftentimes finds himself a member of several organizations—e.g., People's Front, Anti-Fascist Women, War Veterans, Journalist Association, Labor Syndicate, and perhaps others.

The basic reason for the existence of this welter of organizations is to be found in the conviction of the Communist Party that through them the people can be mobilized to carry out its program. At the same time, a people so mobilized serve two other purposes. They become a captive audience to whom Marxian propaganda is served in liberal doses, and, when so intensively engaged, they have little time or energy to focus their thinking upon the injustices of the regime.

Communist Party members constitute the decisive core in all of these organizations. It is not surprising, therefore, that such associations take their cue from party decisions. In 1948, for example, the People's Front of Macedonia promised "to engage all its forces for the successful accomplishment of all the tasks set for it by the Fifth Congress of the CPY." [1] Other mass organizations performed in similar fashion. More recently a youth paper wrote: "All of our mass organizations have begun the study of the materials from the Sixth Congress of the League of Communists." [2]

[1] *Politika,* August 28, 1948.
[2] *Narodni student* (Belgrade), December 17, 1952.

Mass Organizations in Action

Fundamentally, the mass organizations have engaged in two types of activity. They have performed some useful physical tasks in the postwar reconstruction period. More importantly, however, they have served as additional vehicles by means of which the party has sought to spread the Marxian gospel and at the same time has agitated for an ever-increasing effort to achieve the goals of the economic plan. On one occasion, for example, Mosha Pijade,[3] a leading regime theoretician, referred to the People's Front as a "mass organization . . . which gathers within itself all the other mass people's organizations and the democratic citizens who actively participate in the development of socialism." At the same time he characterized the labor syndicates as "the mighty lever for the development of the socialist economy."

Other officials of the Yugoslav government have from time to time stressed the economic importance of "voluntary" labor recruited for various projects by the People's Front. In 1948, for example, the amount of "voluntary" labor contributed was reported to be worth nearly ten billion dinars,[4] and in 1949 the autonomous region of Vojvodina alone was reported to have contributed nearly forty-two million "voluntary" work hours.[5] At the Fifth Congress of the People's Youth it was reported that youth had taken part in the construction of scores of the most important projects of the Five Year Plan and had contributed approximately sixty million "voluntary" work days.[6]

Such work was rarely voluntary. At one time no university student could expect to be permitted to continue his studies unless he spent at least a month on some youth work project. Effective pressure was brought to bear upon peasants to volunteer not only their labor but also that of their oxen or horses. In the cities, branch organizations of the People's Front vied with one another to see which group would contribute the greatest number of "voluntary" work hours. Each person was asked to pledge a

[3] *Borba,* June 12, 1948.
[4] See Blagoje Neshkovich's report to the Third Congress of the People's Front, *Borba,* April 11, 1949.
[5] *Borba,* January 21, 1950.
[6] *Ibid.,* March 8, 1953.

certain number of hours for the year. Those who pledged some small amount, like ten hours for example, would be asked to pledge more, because, they would be told, "Ward 'X' has challenged us in 'socialist competition,'" and their pledges are averaging fifty hours per person."

While mobilization of the masses for "voluntary" work by the People's Front seems to have declined, many Yugoslavs told me that essentially the same ends were being served in another way. Men of virtually all ages are being called into the army, ostensibly for periodic training of two months, but they are actually employed to perform the same type of work for which the People's Front recruited earlier.

In an attempt to portray youth enthusiasm for the new order, regime propagandists have devoted a great deal of time to publicizing the so-called voluntary youth work projects. With rare exceptions, there was little enthusiasm in evidence among the youth at such projects. Where it was necessary to impress foreign visitors, however, special squads were provided and told that they must make a good impression. As a reward, they were usually given a dinner that included meat, as much bread as they could eat and cookies for dessert. Sometimes they were also taken to a movie. Within the past two years less pressure has been exerted upon students to participate in these undertakings, with the result that there has been a sharp decline in the number of volunteers, as well as in the number of those who had signed up to work who actually report.

Some of the work engaged in by "voluntary" labor groups was of questionable value, although the number of man hours was statistically impressive. The official organ of the People's Front of Belgrade reported one such venture in 1949.[7] A campaign by some eighteen People's Front organizations to collect scrap iron, glass, cans, bottles, rags, etc. was inaugurated after a staff had been organized and after considerable discussion in the press and in various conferences. For want of a better place, the collected materials were placed in the basement of a large building. In the fall, when it became necessary to heat the building, everything was thrown on the lawn outside. Children used old

[7] *20 Oktobar,* November 18, 1949.

cans to kick as footballs, men picked out pieces of glass, grind-stone, etc., and the janitor burned the combustible items. In the words of the paper, "All that members of the People's Front collected for months went into the fire, was scattered by children or taken away by passersby."

Far more important than the physical labor performed by mass organizations is their employment by the Communist leaders as another means through which to convey their message to the people, and to demonstrate to the outside world the "popular support" which they enjoy, and in the process, put as many people as possible in the compromising position of having actively worked for Communist goals.

The People's Front, like the other mass organizations, has its newspapers, meetings, lectures and congresses. The once in-dependent newspaper, *Politika,* and now the official organ of the front, in early 1949 published elaborate instructions concerning ideological-educational work.[8] These instructions provided for the formation of special commissions, composed of the "politi-cally most enlightened and most agile members of the front," to establish courses, seminars, reading groups; and to organize, oversee and co-ordinate the ideological-educational work of all other mass organizations. These commissions were also to or-ganize conferences to popularize and broaden the party line, to help select themes for lectures and assist in the organization of new branches.

Statistically minded members could, a few months later, read in the official organ of the People's Front of Serbia, that (1) over 269,000 members of the front participated in over two thousand conferences and in eleven thousand meetings of front groups, (2) 5,654 persons enrolled in 144 courses, and (3) 34,000 new members were admitted in the subsidiary organizations of the People's Front of Belgrade.[9]

As important as these figures might be to those charged with the task of ideological transformation, there is nothing particu-larly spectacular or dramatic about them as far as the outside world is concerned. And even the ego of a Communist leader

[8] February 27, 1949.
[9] *Glas* (Belgrade), July 13, 1949.

can rarely be inflated with statistics. Consequently, parades, congresses, demonstrations are also needed, and the various mass organizations are utilized to provide them.

Like Communists elsewhere, the Yugoslav leaders make much ado about the "spontaneous" character of their various and sundry demonstrations. Actually all of them are carefully planned. On July 4, 1949, for example, a protest demonstration against colonialism and imperialism took place in Belgrade near the house where we were living. Next day the newspapers described it as if it had been spontaneous. Yet I had witnessed the formation of various groups at established assembly points (with a leader, flags and banners), from which they marched four abreast to the appointed place—a busy square about three blocks away. When they arrived there, large banners, the full width of the street, had been put up and a public address system installed! And it would be difficult to believe that it was merely a matter of coincidence that the demonstration took place on July 4th and that similar demonstrations took place in other Yugoslav cities on the same day.

The careful staging of one demonstration, designed in part to influence foreigners, was described to me by one of the participants. A "voluntary" youth work brigade was carefully drilled for the performance on a parade field. On the appointed day, with Communist leaders and foreign visitors sitting on the reviewing stand, one of the Communist leaders made a speech to the youth brigade, standing in close formation on the parade ground. The speech was frequently punctuated by seemingly enthusiastic applause, especially when Tito's name was mentioned. One of the young men told me how they had been instructed to keep an eye on their leader, who during the speech stood some distance behind the reviewing stand. When he raised a little flag, which he held in his hand, they were to applaud. When he waved it over his head in a circular motion, they were to applaud all the more. And when he lowered it they were to stop applauding. To those on the reviewing stand this may have seemed like convincing evidence of Tito's popularity, but, of course, they did not see the cheerleader.

It would be a mistake, however, to assume that the Communist leaders have had no difficulties in the utilization of mass organizations or that they have been able to maintain the tempo of the early postwar years. On the contrary, there has been a sharp decline in the number of parades, political conferences and demonstrations of a massive nature. Attendance at more and more meetings has become voluntary, with fewer and fewer individuals appearing. Except for a few times in the year, like May Day, a total turnout is rarely ordered. The demonstrations concerning Trieste in the spring of 1952 and in the autumn of 1953 constituted a reversion to the older practice of getting a full turnout by a house-to-house and an apartment-to-apartment canvass.

Tito's major speeches, of course, are always assured a large audience. This was particularly noticeable during the electoral campaign of 1953. On one occasion the Yugoslav press itself admitted that some forty trains and over 1,000 trucks had brought nearly 200,000 people to hear one of Tito's speeches.[10]

The decline in the number of massive conferences is perhaps chiefly attributable to a conviction in the minds of the Communist rulers that the time and energy required to organize them and to struggle against popular inertia could be more profitably utilized in other ways. They have admitted that their methods, especially in the rural areas, have not been overly effective. Labored speechmaking must give way, they now believe, to less imposing local meetings, lectures and printed presentations in language as simple as possible.

At its Sixth Congress, in November 1952, the Yugoslav Communist Party assigned to the People's Front (which it at that time decided should in the future be called the Socialist Alliance of the Working People of Yugoslavia) an additional task. It was to become the main vehicle for extending Yugoslav Communist influence abroad.[11] Little has been revealed as to how this new task is to be performed, except that close co-operation is to be established with "progressive movements," principally socialist parties, independence movements in colonial areas and socialist-controlled trade unions and similar organizations.

This is not to suggest that the Communist propaganda strategists are losing sight of their domestic objectives, or that they

[10] *Politika,* October 5, 1953.
[11] *Borba,* November 4, 1952.

contemplate a letup in their efforts. Circumstances may force them to neglect certain tasks for the time being, but that they do not intend to forget about them is attested to by Tito's report to the above-mentioned Sixth Congress,[12] when he said that the party must augment its politico-educational activities, particularly among the peasants, without neglecting its other functions. A few months earlier, the party's official organ, *Borba*,[13] had declared editorially: ". . . there is no locality or town or village in the country where political and cultural-educational work is not being carried on. There is a big question, however, whether the forces which are engaged in this work are sufficient."

[12] *Ibid.*
[13] June 14, 1952.

Chapter 14:

Accent on Youth

IN ALL their efforts to harness the masses to the regime, the Yugoslav Communists have devoted more of their energies to youth than to any other segment of the population. The importance of youth to them is evidenced by party proclamations, by the fact that the main task of young Communists under twenty-four years of age is to work in youth organizations and with youth, and by the constant, systematic and widespread purposive efforts of the Communist Party and its subsidiary organizations to win the allegiance of youth.[1]

It is not unexpected, therefore, that Communists should concern themselves with the fate of children from an early age. Before reaching adolescence, children enter organizations whose basic aim is to condition them "in order that they may be educated and prepared as future builders and governors of their socialist homeland."[2] Upon reaching adolescence, they join associations whose "general political task" is "to educate youth along the line of our rich revolutionary and heroic past and present" and to explain world events, "particularly the struggle of our Party against the imperialist policy of the USSR as well as against reactionary influences from the West."[3]

To achieve these aims, Yugoslav Communists, while still in the process of attempting to seize power, revitalized their prewar underground youth organizations. Long before they had solidified their control over the country, party leaders had established a variety of associations for young people, largely modeled after

[1] See statement by Rankovich, *Omladina* (Belgrade), June 14, 1952.
[2] *Nasha deca* (Belgrade), No. 2, 1952, p. 56.
[3] Rankovich, *Omladina,* June 14, 1952.

those in the Soviet Union. Since Tito's break with Moscow, however, these associations have undergone some organizational and functional changes, although fundamental aims have remained unchanged.

Children's Organizations

While the Union of Pioneers is, at this writing, still in existence, indications are that it never achieved any notable successes and is therefore being superceded, or at least supplemented, by a more loosely federated network of children's associations in the seven to fourteen age group. Ostensibly, these are to enjoy some individuality, as their names suggest: "Our Children" (Croatia); "Society of Friends of Children and Youth" (Slovenia); "Society of Friends of Children" (Serbia). To co-ordinate their efforts, however, the Council of Societies for the Education and Concern for Children has been established.

But unlike the original Pioneers organization, this council, according to its secretary, Branka Savich, will not endeavor to operate these organizations from above. It will not attempt "to run" anything, but "it will hold meetings, discuss various common questions, publish an official organ, and offer its advice when deemed appropriate." Children's organizations, she believes, should have more autonomy and their activities ought to conform to children's interests, the material resources at hand and the quality of persons available for work with children.

In our conversation, Mrs. Savich asserted that in her opinion Soviet organizations had erroneously assumed that "you could put a child in a glass case and then influence him in the way you like, whereas we all know there are other influences." Without expressly saying so, she clearly implied that the Yugoslav Communists had reached the conclusion that in order to be effective with children it was imperative to harness these "other influences" (e.g. teachers and parents), and to appropriate or duplicate those of their activities which have attracted children away from the Pioneers (e.g. church-sponsored sports events, picnics, etc.). And conversely, to suspend those Pioneer activities which have been unpopular (e.g. lectures and study courses).

Yugoslav Communist leaders have apparently become convinced that "sixteen-year-olds cannot be effective educators of pioneers" (reference to youth organizations), and that it was necessary to enlist the services of many adults rather than leave the work to a few supposedly trained specialists. In addition, according to Mrs. Savich, it is "more important to teach a child things like obedience" than to establish such practices as "the election of leaders among the children, as is done in the Soviet Union." At this age (seven to ten), she continued, "children have little interest in the electoral process; they are interested only in play."

Responsible Communists are assigned to edit a number of publications for children. These include weekly newspapers (e.g. *Pionirske novine*), monthly magazines (e.g. *Poletarac*), yearbooks (e.g. *Pionirski godishnjak*) and other publications. Great care is exercised in precensoring materials intended for children and youth. Even Communist publishing houses cannot print such materials without prior permission from ministries (councils) of education of the republics in which the publishing takes place.

Youth Organizations

Unlike the Union of Pioneers, the Union of Communist Youth was designed to have a greater degree of ideological purity. Since it was to be the training camp from which future Communists would be recruited, membership was restricted to potential Communists. Likewise, the program, the organizational framework and the operational procedures were patterned after those of the party. And full-fledged party members held the key offices in the organization.

As indicated in a previous chapter, the Yugoslav Communists, while in the process of seeking to seize power had considered it tactically wise to avoid the impression that their movement was in reality Communist. To convey the notion of wide popular support, they had established the Liberation Front, later renamed the People's Front. Similarly, they created an appendage to the Union of Communist Youth called the Anti-Fascist Youth, later renamed the People's Youth Organization. Following the Tito-Stalin break, however, Yugoslav leaders threw off the mask and fused "the two organizations into one, with the program and under the leadership of the Communist Party," [4] adopting the name "People's Youth Organization of Yugoslavia."

The People's Youth is supposed to be composed of "the most active and to socialism most devoted young men" [5] between the ages of fourteen and twenty-five. The People's Youth leaders claim for their organization a total membership of around 1,400,-000, which in their words, "represents between 80 and 85 per cent of the total Yugoslav population in this age group." Allegedly, young people must indicate their desire to belong, but the organization is not obligated to accept them.

Like other organizations in Yugoslavia, the People's Youth is organized on a hierarchical basis. The lowest unit is the so-called *aktiv*, or basic unit of organization. Membership in an *aktiv* may range from five to two hundred, but most of them have between fifteen and thirty-five members. These primary units are set up where youth happens to be—in divisions of government enterprises, in factories, in schools, or in peasant settlements.

Above the primary units of organization are placed the youth committees, encompassing towns, counties and regions. And, of course, there is a committee for each of the republics, and at the top, the People's Youth of Yugoslavia, whose governing body is the Central Committee, as in the case of the Communist Party itself. A national congress, held once every four years, chooses the Central Committee.

Members of the Central Committee with whom I talked were frank to admit that their organization is composed of the most active youths who accept the political program of the Communist Party and who seek to gain acceptance for that program among the youth. They do not limit their activities to their own organization, however, but also seek to work in all other organizations, such as cultural clubs, sports associations and other groups. Confirmation of this was also to be found in the official organ of the party, *Borba*,[6] when it declared that not only must more young Communists be active in youth groups, but also

[4] Statute of the People's Youth Organization of Yugoslavia (Belgrade, 1949), p. 14.
[5] Rankovich, *Omladina*, June 14, 1952.
[6] July 31, 1952.

"every Communist should at the same time also be an active member in other social organizations, a way in which the Party exerts its influence and indirectly runs those organizations."

In pursuit of their aim to gain acceptance for the party's program, the People's Youth, its numerous branches, and the subsidiary organizations which it sponsors edit and publish a large number of newspapers for youth of varying age groups. The weekly *Omladina* (Youth), organ of the People's Youth of Yugoslavia, sets the tone for the editors of the other publications. It prints the main political pronouncements which the party's *Agitprop* believes should be brought to the attention of youth, as well as various types of ideological commentary, news of youth activities and features of interest to youth. Associations of students (component parts of the People's Youth) at Yugoslav universities publish their own weeklies, e.g. *Studentski list* (Zagreb), *Narodni student* (Belgrade). A monthly, *Za Otadjbinu* (For the Fatherland), is published by the Yugoslav army for university students as part of their obligatory premilitary training. The Central Committee of the People's Youth issues a monthly (*Narodna omladina*) devoted primarily to ideological questions and discussions of problems concerning work with youth.

In addition, the People's Youth organization stimulates and supervises the sponsorship of lectures, speeches, film showings and study seminars. Seeking to escape the sterility of excessive seriousness which characterized its earlier activities, the People's Youth is now also stressing the development of social life through "outings, comradely suppers, and various other meetings." [7]

Moreover, the People's Youth serves as a recruiting agency to mobilize young people for "voluntary" work projects, chiefly during the spring, summer, and early autumn months. The younger ones are expected to serve for one month, others for two. They get no pay, but the government furnishes food and work clothes. Lodging presents no particular problem, since they sleep in the open air or in temporary dwellings, frequently tents. A planned political indoctrination program accompanies all youth work projects.

In the early years of the Tito regime, the principal emphasis

[7] *Borba,* July 31, 1952.

was placed on the construction of the Belgrade-Zagreb highway; New Belgrade, on which all construction ceased in 1950; the so-called youth railways; and buildings on state and collective farms. Within the past year or so, however, virtually all "voluntary" youth work has been concentrated on certain "key objects" of the Yugoslav Five-Year Plan, such as dams, power plants and steel mills. As previously indicated, however, there is nothing really voluntary about engaging in an activity which becomes a prerequisite for staying in school.

Nevertheless, more and more students have found ways of justifying their abstention from "voluntary" work projects—illness in the family, a weak heart, anemia, or some other likely reason. More important, however, is the fact that many simply did not appear, even though they had volunteered to go, thus making it difficult for punitive action to be taken because of the large number involved.

At one meeting of the youth organization in Belgrade University, for example, it was brought out that some students were openly unco-operative. One girl, when approached by a young Communist recruiter, had replied that she would go provided he went first. This and other examples of nonco-operation brought laughs from the assembled students, but from the secretary of the youth organization the following stern retort: "These students should be identified by name. They have no place in our midst, and should be kicked out of the university." Yet this type of threat does not seem to have nearly the effect it once would have had.

In conversations with foreigners, Yugoslav youth leaders seek to minimize and even to deny the deep-seated apathy and indifference which exists among the youth of Yugoslavia. These leaders contend that the lack of material means to carry on their indoctrination of youth constitutes their greatest difficulty. They lack clubhouses, sports stadiums, cinema projectors, youth homes and youth restaurants.

On the other hand, they admit freely that religious training, especially in some areas, constitutes a considerable handicap, because priests organize sports events, picnics, etc. in an attempt "to keep the youth from being patriotic." Yet, in typical Communist double-talk, they maintain that no pressure is exerted on any of the People's Youth members to give up religious beliefs or church going and that a young person can be both religious and a good member of the People's Youth. In the same breath they acknowledge that in the various and sundry lectures which they sponsor, a conscious effort is made "to expose mysticism and religious fables." And in the official journal of the People's Youth, an article attacking religion says, among other things, that the "People's Youth as an organization has the right to demand of its members a scientific outlook upon the world, a dialectic concept of natural phenomena and relations between men, and to call reactionary priestly humbug by its right name." [8]

Moreover, these youth leaders reflect the concern which is felt in high Yugoslav Communist circles about the impact of Western ideas. Following the Yugoslav-Soviet break and the arrival of Western aid it was inevitable that at least some Western ideas would filter through. While not admitting defeat, some Yugoslav Communists convey the impression that they are fighting a losing battle. Yugoslav young people are just too eager to grasp at anything from the West.

Communist publications, on the other hand, continually assert that the Communists themselves are not exerting sufficient effort. It was brought out, for example, that in one enterprise where twenty-five young Communists worked only four were devoting their efforts to youth,[9] despite the fact that this was supposed to be one of their most important duties. Reports of similar situations are not infrequent in the Communist press, with the ever-present observations about "lessons for the future."

[8] *Omladina,* June 7, 1952.
[9] *Ibid.,* July 19, 1952.

Chapter 15:

Schools in a Strait Jacket

COMMUNISTS look upon schools as another means, perhaps the most important one, of harnessing the masses to the dictatorship. Along with youth organizations, schools are destined to be the main instruments for shaping new generations, in the expectation of producing what Communists longingly call "the new socialist man."

Achieving this aim, Yugoslav leaders have discovered, is no easy matter. In nearly a decade of their rule, they have not seen much progress. The problems which they encountered were many, and new ones have continued to arise.

When they first came to power, Yugoslav Communist leaders faced several school problems. First of all, in some areas the physical facilities had been destroyed in the war. Secondly, many of the most able teachers had been killed during the conflict or fled when it became evident that the Communists would take over. Thirdly, the Titoists seriously aggravated the teacher shortage by shooting, imprisoning or expelling many teachers whom they considered political enemies. Finally—and most important of all —the Communists faced the enormous task of reshaping a people's mode of thought and behavior, of revising their national, cultural and spiritual values.

To meet these problems, the Communist Party sought to copy the Soviet school system. The establishment of fundamental ideological goals, and the creation of bureaucratic machinery to make sure that they would not be lost sight of, seemed to take precedence over the erection of school buildings and the training of teachers. As in the Soviet Union, the party's Central Committee formulated educational policy. Its basic decisions were to guide the government's Committee for Schools and Science, now called the Council for Science and Culture, as it passed on directives to the ministries of education (now called councils) in each one of the six republics. Similarly, in all discussions of educational problems, these basic party decisions constituted the authoritative text to which all speakers were expected to pay homage and from which no speaker was expected to deviate.

Yugoslav Communists now claim that they have departed from Soviet experience. The Council for Science and Culture, they contend, does not dictate to those in charge of education in each of the republics, although they do not disavow the existence of a number of national laws dealing with education (e.g. compulsory education for eight years or until age fifteen). Nor do they deny that basic party decisions serve as the real guideposts for all that is done in the field of education. In substance, therefore, all that has been changed consists of the elimination of minute instructions and detailed supervision of all educational activities from the top. Local school officials and local party officers are now given greater responsibilities for putting into effect fundamental party decisions and for working out solutions to local problems with less frequent reference to the central authorities for concrete guidance in individual cases. The basic aim of education, however, remains the same.

That the central government will continue to determine basic educational policies is not open to doubt. In September of 1953, for example, the Federal Executive Council handed down an edict prohibiting universities and some other schools from limiting the enrollment of students in any way.[1] Even pleas from the executive councils of the republics of Serbia and Croatia to be allowed to postpone the implementation of this decree for one year, because of an alleged lack of physical facilities, were rejected. Moreover, this was acknowledged as "one step" among many others that needed to be taken. The creation in 1953 of a special parliamentary committee to study the whole problem of the schools was said to be the prelude to further legislation in this field by the central government.[2]

It should be noted in passing that the Communist Party main-

[1] See statement of Mosha Pijade in *Borba,* September 22, 1953.
[2] *Ibid.*

tains so-called party schools. These are primarily for the young party elite who are destined to assume positions of responsibility. Here they receive ideological training commensurate with their promise of leadership and with the responsibilities which are likely to be assigned to them. Secret police functionaries and members of the Yugoslav foreign service, for example, pass through these schools.

Teacher Problems

The Yugoslav Communist leaders were well aware that purging the schools of political enemies would not leave them with a corps of teachers upon whom they could depend. From their point of view, nearly all prewar teachers were really unreliable, but the less dangerous ones had to be retained if the schools were to function at all. Special ideological courses were devised for them, and student informers employed to report on their conduct. Many, fearful of losing their jobs, needed no watching; they were perfectly willing to accommodate the Communists. In the meantime, new teachers, with a Marxian outlook, were to be trained.

Indicative of the importance of the teacher problem is the special emphasis which the party gives to teachers' colleges and to the pedagogical groups (departments of education) in the universities. In the University of Belgrade, for example, two-thirds of the students in the pedagogical group are Communists, which is a considerably higher percentage than in some of the other groups (e.g. psychology, which has less than 10 per cent).

But the Yugoslav leaders have discovered that the task of replacing older and more experienced teachers with Communists was neither easy nor was it likely to be achieved in a brief period of time. Several difficulties have been encountered. First of all, grave doubts exist as to whether the "new type" of teacher can be developed unless the process is begun at an exceedingly early age. Secondly, the necessity of "re-educating" pro-Russian Communist teachers after the Tito-Stalin break has proved to be an extremely difficult problem, and considerable doubt persists concerning the reality of the "conversion" of those who have been "re-educated." Thirdly, and closely related to the second, is the delicate problem of producing teachers who are convinced Marxists, but whose Marxism does not at the same time lead them to the conclusion that Stalin was right in his criticism of Tito.

Moreover, efforts to keep non-Marxists out of teaching have not been entirely successful. The People's Youth organ, *Omladina*,[3] has pointed to the futility of trying to weed out students with nonmaterialistic views by assigning written tests, as was done in some teachers' colleges. The paper went on to point out that in some instances students had been so clever as to become "materialists overnight."

Although the average age of teachers in primary and secondary schools in some areas is no more than twenty-two, indicating that they were trained under the Tito regime, the Communist press continues to stress the existence of "undesirable" teachers.[4] Some of these are Communists who in the immediate postwar years had received jobs primarily because of their political qualifications, but whose professional competence has not measured up to expectations. More frequently, they are teachers whose basic outlook is anti-Communist and who utilize their ingenuity to make difficult the realization of Communist aims. Communist leaders are aware of this fact as was attested to by Tito's remarks at the party's Sixth Congress. After speaking of inadequate textbooks, he said of teachers: "There are among them men who are total strangers to our reality, and who harm society more than they help it." Turning to the universities, he added: "But I must, unfortunately, state that in the universities the situation in this respect [textbooks and teachers] is still worse." [5]

The Communists have been unable to tackle these problems successfully for the simple reason that they have not produced qualified teachers and competent research workers who are at the same time Marxists. They admit that non-Communist students have been superior. It was imposible to keep some of these out of university positions, yet every such person meant subjecting "a whole series of student generations to negative ideological and educational influences." [6] With the refusal of most older professors to produce even textbooks, and with the failure of Marxist professors to meet publishing needs, keeping competent young

[3] May 31, 1952.
[4] See *Borba* editorial (Zagreb edition), September 2, 1952.
[5] *Borba,* November 4, 1952.
[6] See *Univerzitetski vesnik,* January 21, 1953.

non-Marxists out of faculties would be little short of catastrophic for the future of the universities. From the political point of view, however, the situation is intolerable.

Problems of Indoctrination

The Yugoslav Communist Party has openly declared that Yugoslav education must be based on "the one and only true science—the science of Marxism-Leninism." [7] In order to conform with this dictum, prewar textbooks and other teaching materials were purged, and translations of Russian textbooks adopted, some of which, interestingly enough, are still in use. Teachers were expected to hue close to the party line. One professor of physics, for example, was publicly taken to task by an official organ of the Communist Party because he had said that some things in nature could not be explained. "Certainly," said the paper, "he is thinking of some supernatural power." [8] In another instance, teachers were warned that they must avoid such generalities as " 'a democracy is a country without a king' since that would indicate that the United States, which has no king, is a democracy. . . ." [9]

It was insufficient, however, to proclaim that all education must be based on a materialistic interpretation of history. It was also necessary to teach what this new science was. Consequently, a course in Marxism-Leninism was introduced in colleges and universities. In some departments the course was required, in others merely recommended. Few students who hoped to be assigned the better jobs failed to enroll. Currently, however, the course is not required and there is less pressure upon students to take it. Consequently, the student enrollment in it has declined sharply. Earlier, Communist leaders had admitted that they had been unsuccessful in indoctrinating the majority of university students. In an interesting display of frankness, they attributed their lack of success mainly to the shortage of qualified persons to teach Marxism.[10] In the intermediate schools, however, ideological indoctrination in some form continues, in hope of convincing younger

[7] *Borba,* February 16, 1949.
[8] *Partiski radnik,* February 17, 1949.
[9] *Politika,* January 15, 1948.
[10] *Ibid.,* September 16, 1948.

students that Marxism constitutes the only true philosophical approach.

Efforts to bring about a radical transformation of the curriculum, however, have not met with much success, especially in the universities. At the Sixth Party Congress held in November, 1952, Rodoljub Cholakovich, head of the Council for Science and Culture, declared that there was "conscious sabotage" during times when a reorganization of teaching plans and programs had been under consideration. He blasted the professors for tolerating such sabotage. Moreover, he insisted that idealism, as opposed to materialism, was still overly strong in the intermediate schools and in the universities. Something had been done about it in the intermediate schools, he said, but in the universities "practically nothing." [11]

Earlier a student newspaper had reported that "student leaders of the Belgrade Technological Faculty contend that it is possible to collaborate with only 5 per cent of the teachers." [12] And just prior to the Sixth Party Congress, the party organization in the University of Belgrade proclaimed as one of its basic tasks "the earlier realization of a teaching staff imbued in the spirit of Marxism." [13]

Yet, it appears, the non-Communists are not alone to blame. Communists, once in comfortable positions, seemed to have lost some of their earlier zeal, for "opportunism in the Party organization of teachers" was rife. Moreover, "careerism, the worst inheritance from former Yugoslavia, has begun to blossom anew." [14]

Problem of Competing Influences

Initially, the regime underestimated the problem of counteracting the influence of anti-Communist forces (family, church, antiregime teachers). It is now conceded by Yugoslav Communists that a great deal of effort over a long period of time will have to be devoted to this end.

One Communist teacher, in a newspaper article, bemoaned the fact that the teachers "said one thing and the parents an-

[11] *Borba,* November 4, 1952.
[12] *Narodni student,* March 12, 1952.
[13] *Univerzitetski vesnik,* November 1, 1952.
[14] *Ibid.*

other," and "the child does not know whom to believe." [15] A student of philosophy laid even more of the blame upon the family and religion when he wrote in another number of the same newspaper: "Parents are very often out of step with pedagogy, and paralyze it. It is understandable, therefore, why clerical forces with more or less success are carrying out their harmful influence. . . . Frequently, the school (at least for now) is simply impotent before contradictory family influence." [16]

A leading article in the People's Youth organ, *Omladina,* concluded:[17] "If those teachers who take students to church and who do not meet their classes on their *Slava* [patron saint day] are further tolerated; if there is not an energic and decisive rising up against mysticism and idealism—and for science and truth—then much help from the school cannot be expected."

Further tribute to these competing influences was paid by *Borba,*[18] when it declared in a front-page editorial that ". . . we have done very little to see to it that connections between the school and the student are not lost during vacations." Similarly, an army publication reported that men who were "excellent soldiers while in the army" had succumbed to "petty bourgeois influences" after returning home.[19]

Yugoslav Communists have noted that many of their students are "two-faced," particularly students from anti-Communist families. The students, while really anti-Communist, are adept in the use of "socialist phrases," and oftentimes they "know certain speeches of government leaders better than many other students." [20] This type of student may be found not only in the universities but in primary and intermediate schools as well.[21]

It is, of course, perfectly understandable that individuals should develop a dual personality under a regime of fear, suspicion and distrust. People have learned that they must practice deception in order to get along. But the regime fails to perceive the true origin of such behavior, and attempts to place the blame on parents and teachers. How can students arrive at a proper evaluation "of religion and related questions," they ask, "when their

[15] *Politika,* August 8, 1952.
[16] *Ibid.,* June 5, 1952.
[17] July 5, 1952.
[18] Zagreb edition, September 2, 1952.
[19] *Narodna armija,* July 10, 1952.
[20] *Narodni student,* March 5, 1952.
[21] See editorial in *Omladina,* May 31, 1952.

teacher extends Christmas holiday greetings to them and in front of them complains because he has to work on that day." After such announcements, they continue, "are his lectures based on materialism apt to be convincing?" [22]

The answer, needless to say, is in the negative. Whereas the school is supposed to be "the real center of socialist education," some teachers continue to assert objectively that in the case of certain problems the materialists look upon them "this way, the idealists that way." [23] To Yugoslav Communists "such objectivity is in fact idealism," and in direct opposition to the materialistic philosophy which the party seeks to implant in the minds of the young.

No great perspicacity is needed, therefore, to realize that this concept of education is at sharp variance with the traditional notion that schools should be centers of free inquiry. The historic unending search for truth has given way to indoctrination in the one and only truth—Marxism-Leninism.

Students are aware of the consequences of this approach to education as is illustrated by the following incident. In an English class in one of the secondary schools some of the students had established correspondence with student pen pals in England. One morning, after class had begun, some of them interrupted the teacher to tell him that they had received an interesting letter and to ask if they could read it. Suspecting that the students were merely interested in creating a diversion from their studies, the teacher tried to put them off, but finally consented. The letter was read sentence by sentence, with the students translating. Apparently, the section of the letter which they were most interested in reading was that which told about the elections then being held in England. The letter writer observed that British elections "were not like yours behind the Iron Curtain. You do not dare to speak or associate freely, and your papers do not carry criticism of the party in power." With this, the students burst into laughter. When the laughter had subsided, one of the students turned to the teacher, and asked rhetorically, "But what good is it maintaining this correspondence when we dare not write him that what he says is true!"

[22] *Ibid.*
[23] *Ibid.*

Chapter 16:

The War on Religion

THE Yugoslav Communists have steadfastly adhered to the conviction that the masses cannot be successfully harnessed to the dictatorship unless distracting and contradictory influences are neutralized or eliminated. They have unrelentingly continued to act upon this premise. Liquidating fraternal orders, luncheon clubs, boy scouts and similar organizations was not a difficult task. But the struggle against the church and against religion generally has turned out to be much more formidable.

Tito has repeatedly told American visitors that there is "freedom of religion" in Yugoslavia; that "the churches are open and that priests have a right to hold services in them"; that "people can go to church and no one prevents them from doing so." [1]

It can easily be demonstrated that these statements are meaningless and that they do not depict the true status of religion in Yugoslavia. That there is a purposeful, systematically organized and persistent attack upon religion can be seen even from the statements of Yugoslav leaders, including Tito himself. At the Sixth Party Congress, for example, he said: "I must particularly emphasize here that recently there have been many indications that party organizations were insensitive to and inactive against ever-stronger clerical and religious influences in some areas." [2] A few months earlier, the Central Committee of the People's Youth had declared that the "struggle against the influence of religion and priests cannot be separated from the struggle for general education." [3] And it had added a reassuring note to the

[1] See *Borba*, July 30, 1952.
[2] *Ibid.*, November 4, 1952.
[3] *Omladina*, July 5, 1952.

Communist faithful by stating that "in recent months our organizations have joined the organized and constant struggle against priests and the influence of religion."

There are countless similar public pronouncements of their avowed aims and intentions. More telling than these, however, are some of the concrete examples implementing these policy statements, which are discussed in the pages to follow.

In general the assault upon religion in Yugoslavia is aimed at all religious faiths. For the most part, however, world public opinion has heard only about the campaign against the Roman Catholic Church. Yet the Tito regime has more successfully assailed the numerically stronger Serbian Orthodox Church, perhaps because it lacked the world-wide publicity facilities available to the Vatican. Public opinion in the United States, one important Yugoslav Communist told me, was the only thing which stood in their way from shooting the Catholic prelate of Yugoslavia, Archbishop Stepinac (named a Cardinal in 1952) of Zagreb. Although released in the spring of 1952, after having served approximately one-third of his prison sentence as an alleged wartime enemy collaborator, Stepinac has not been permitted to perform the functions of his office. Although having a considerably smaller membership than either the Orthodox or Catholic denominations, the Islamic faith has also been under severe and ceaseless onslaught.

Churches Materially Impoverished

In prewar Yugoslavia, the churches had two principal sources of income: grants from the state treasury and income from church-owned property. The Tito regime destroyed both of these by abolishing the practice of significant state support and by confiscating virtually all church-owned lands and other property. What church property remains is under close scrutiny of the state. Reports concerning income and expenditure must be made constantly, even though the Titoists like to point out that in Yugoslavia there is separation of church and state.

Much church property was destroyed, vandalized or stolen during World War II. This is particularly noticeable in the case of Serbian Orthodox churches in the areas which during the war were under control of the Nazi puppet state of Croatia. In one diocese (Gornjokarlovachka), out of 189 churches only fourteen remain, and instead of over 400 Orthodox clergymen there are at this writing only twenty-one.

Continuing from where the war left off, Tito's regime engaged in destroying or appropriating church property. Priests' residences and monastery buildings were frequently taken over for state purposes. As late as 1951 two Orthodox churches (in Uroshevac and in Duganj) were physically demolished by order of the local people's committees even before their decisions could be appealed to higher authority. Efforts to have damaged churches repaired have not met with success. In the vicinity of Dalj, for example, the peasants collected money to repair a badly damaged church. Authorities in Zagreb granted permission for this undertaking only because the church constituted an "artistic antiquity," but the local authorities disagreed and consequently no materials could be procured for its repair.

The regime has also sought to nullify aid from abroad. In 1947, for example, the Federation of Christian Churches sent the Serbian Patriarchate a set of the *Encyclopedia Britannica*. But at the post office Tito's officials appropriated it, "because the church does not need it." Similarly, the federation has sent food, clothing, paper and other articles, but Yugoslav customs officials insisted upon collecting fees amounting to three times the worth of the goods. Even medicines fall in the same category.

Many more facts could be recited to show how badly impoverished the Yugoslav churches are. Some observers believe that the Roman Catholic Church fares a bit better than the Orthodox because it did not suffer materially nearly so much during the war. And in the postwar period it succeeded in receiving more assistance from abroad than the other religious faiths. Yet this situation may not continue for long if increased taxes are imposed, of which there was some indication in the summer of 1952. In Croatia one small church was assessed a tax of 215,000 dinars ($715) for the year, which is a sizable sum if we keep in mind that the average monthly salary for most workers is about twenty dollars. Another church was not only taxed more heavily than in previous years, but in addition the authorities "discovered" that it had not been taxed sufficiently in the past, and are now adding several hundred thousand dinars in back taxes.

Toward the end of 1952 notice was publicly served upon the church that it cannot expect a return of its former lands "because they have been divided among working peasants"; it could not recover its one-time banks and commercial establishments "because they have been nationalized"; neither could printing plants and newspaper concerns be returned "because that too has become public property." [4]

Obstructing Religious Worship

To the casual visitor today churches in Yugoslavia would appear undisturbed. But such would at best be a misleading surface impression, conveying none of the past or present actions deliberately calculated to weaken and to destroy religion.

Like many persons in other callings, a number of clergymen and other church leaders of all denominations were killed during the war. Tito's post-liberation purge added others to the total. Some may have been guilty of wartime collaboration with the enemy, but many were no more than conscious political opponents of Tito's Partisans. Many were imprisoned on the slightest pretext, often manufactured by Tito's agents, and hundreds are still in jail. Others were maltreated solely because they were clergymen. Archbishop Arsenije of Montenegro, who is about seventy years old, is one of these. He has had to hire a private car to take him from Kotor to Cetinje because the government-operated bus refused him transportation. On one occasion, he was permitted to board the bus, but was put out midway between the two cities.

Moreover, all clergymen and their activities are under close surveillance. Any sign of increased activity in the church brings instant retaliation from the regime. Within the past few years, certain Orthodox priests sought to prepare more attractive services during the Christmas holidays. They prepared the traditional wheat dish, cookies and candy. There were recitations by children and some books as gifts to those who were judged to have

[4] See statement by Edward Kardelj in *Politika*, December 19, 1952.

done well. Following the holidays, however, these priests were attacked and ridiculed at youth conferences and in the schools. They were accused of trying "to fool the children with candy."

Other priests were not so fortunate. In the village of Jasenovo in the Banat, for example, the priest was fined 3,500 dinars because he had taught some children declamations which they gave on Saint Sava Day. In another city, which must remain unidentified, the president of the local people's committee, having heard that cookies and candy were being prepared for a similar occasion, sent for the head of the church and expressly forbade him from going through with his plans.

Ordinary would-be churchgoers are under a slightly different type of pressure and surveillance. Government employees in Bosnia-Herzegovina, for example, have been forbidden to go to church on penalty of losing their jobs. The same is true in the Kosmet area. Other areas differ only in that such orders are conveyed orally. Teachers in the Nish area, for example, were publicly told at a meeting that everyone would be dismissed who was married in church, had a child christened there or had any other connection with church.

Consequently, many persons travel miles in order to have secret church weddings or christenings. Sometimes even Communists give in to their wives. One told his wife that he was going to the office, that she could have the priest come "and get it over with" (i.e. christen the child), but he did not want to know anything about it. One priest, when asked by a friend how things were, replied: "It couldn't be better. During the day I marry and christen non-Communists and at night I marry and christen Communists, and what's more the Communists pay better."

In further pursuit of its determination to obstruct the practice of religion, the Tito regime has not recognized church holidays, such as Christmas, and has compelled workers, students and teachers to carry on as usual. One white-collar worker told me that he was threatened with summary dismissal and no chance of re-employment anywhere else for six months if he stayed away from work on Christmas day. Other workers told me of having received a circular memorandum which each one had to initial, informing them that Christmas would not be a holiday. Similarly, no person is permitted to be away from work or school on his

Slava (patron saint day), a day which in the Serbian Orthodox faith is on a par with Christmas and Easter. Some workers even showed me written decisions handed down against them, which stated that pleading religious freedom was not a valid excuse for being absent, since no government-enacted statute proclaimed Christmas a holiday.

Many workers throughout the country, perhaps a sizable majority, stay home to celebrate Christmas and their *Slava,* paying little heed to government orders. The more defiant ones and those suspected of having an admixture of political motives have been punished. While sanctions against persons who stay home to celebrate religious holidays have in the past been more vigorously enforced in the Serbian Orthodox areas than elsewhere, the regime has found it difficult to impose penalties against large numbers of industrial workers.

Teachers and students, on the other hand, being more vulnerable, have been successfully cowed. Failure of students to attend school on Christmas day or on their *Slava* has brought its penalties. A poor grade in conduct is the least that a student can expect. Sometimes all grades are lowered as a result. Sometimes even expulsion from school is resorted to. And it most certainly means ridicule of him and his parents in front of his fellow students. The same type of mocking derision is visited upon those youngsters who sing in church choirs.

The celebration of Christmas at home cost one teacher in a Belgrade commercial school 10 per cent of his salary for three months. Similarly, the appointment of an able physics teacher as professor in a teacher's college was not confirmed by the ministry of education because he had a habit of not going to school on Christmas day and because he was known as a churchgoer. Slightly different economic sanctions were imposed upon teachers known to attend church, when, during the reclassification of teaching positions in early 1952, they were placed two grades below other teachers of comparable education and experience.

Particularly revealing of the government's attitude toward religion is the recent experience of a teacher in the secondary schools who had been granted permission to take a group of students on an excursion lasting several days. They visited several historic places, camped in the mountains and in general had a good time. One of the historic spots they visited was a famous monastery, where a civilian guide took them through. Upon their return, because the trip had been such a popular success, many other students inquired about similar trips in the future. Everyone was seemingly satisfied. A few days later, however, the teacher who had taken the boys on the trip was called into the superintendent's office. When he arrived there, he was confronted not only by the superintendent but also by the secretary of the Communist Party unit in the school and by the secretary of the teacher's syndicate organization—all of them Communists. The superintendent opened up by saying that she understood that when he took the students into the monastery he had crossed himself and lit a candle. He readily admitted having done this, but saw nothing wrong in having done it. "You know we are Communists," he was told, "and we are trying to stamp out religion. Don't you see that an act such as yours might have the opposite effect upon children?"

Far from being frightened, as they had expected, he came forth with a strong statement. He referred to the fact that the Yugoslav constitution guaranteed freedom of religion. Describing himself as a religious man, he asserted that it was only natural that he should cross himself. He could not find words, he said, to express his surprise and astonishment that he should be called in for this. If they did not want him to practice his religion, he went on, why didn't they forbid it, why didn't they destroy the churches themselves?

To such a defense they could only reply: "Yes, the constitution guarantees freedom of religion, but you know how it is, we have a task to perform with the youth and the example you set is important. When some of the students were asked why they had crossed themselves, they replied, 'Why can't we cross ourselves if professor ———— does?' "

As a parting shot, they said to him: "What is more, when you come to school on Christmas day and on your *Slava,* you come all dressed up in your best clothes!" Teachers in widely scattered areas in Serbia told me that they had been criticized for wearing their best clothes to school on Christmas and on their *Slava* day. To regime leaders, this constituted a particularly insidious way for the teachers to tell their students that they believed in God!

In Croatia, Ivan Leko, Secretary of the Council for Schools, was quoted in a Zagreb newspaper [5] in the summer of 1952 as having said that 100 teachers had been found to be openly pro-clerical in Croatia, and that they were subsequently "liquidated as educators." Moreover, he described the formation of various organizations that had been employed to clear the schools of clerical elements and to reduce to the utmost the influence of priests on youth. A few days later, Mr. Leko found it necessary to write a denial, no doubt for foreign consumption, in which he said that none of "the educational workers was dismissed on account of his religious inclinations." Rather, he said, the dismissals were attributable to incompetence, drunkenness and immoral behavior.

In some areas indirect methods have been employed to impede or make less meaningful the observance of religious holidays. In the Slovenian village of Vinice it was impossible to buy any meat for a whole week prior to Confirmation Day 1952. And, of course, the traditional shooting of guns is no longer possible. Consequently, the populace felt particularly avenged by the unusually heavy thunder which rumbled over their village that day. Other cities and regions have similar stories to tell. In at least some Yugoslav cities in 1952 no lard was available during the week preceding Easter, which appeared as a calculated effort to prevent the baking of Easter cakes.

Taking a page from the Soviet book, Yugoslav Communists sponsor "voluntary" work projects, youth picnics, film showings or other gatherings on Sundays and religious holidays. It is particularly important to divert youth on these days so that they cannot go to church or participate in religious festivals. A somewhat awkward situation developed, however, when they proclaimed a children's holiday which they called "Day of Spring." Inquiring students could not understand why it should fall on a different day each spring. While they could not admit it publicly, the Communists had created this holiday to coincide with *Vrbica*, an Orthodox religious holiday for children which falls on the Saturday preceding Good Friday.

The insidious nature of such artful contriving was illustrated by an occurrence in a Belgrade elementary school in the spring

[5] *Vjesnik,* August 14, 1952.

of 1949. On Friday the children were told that the next day was the "Day of Spring," and that a picnic, a trip to the zoo and an outing in the country had been prepared for the following day. Each child was permitted to choose which of the three he desired, and then all were asked to pledge their word as members of the organization of Pioneers that they would appear at the appointed place. Not being aware of the scheme, all of them did so. But the next day not all of them came. On Monday those who had not come were asked in class to explain their absence. Some said that they had been ill, but a number of them reported that their mothers had wanted them to participate in the children's festivities at church. With an air of contempt, the teacher told them pointedly that it was obvious they did not respect their word as Pioneers. "Publicly, you gave your word in front of all of us that you would come. And you let us down! How can we put trust in you in the future when our country will have much more important tasks with which to entrust us!"

Methods utilized to impede the practice of religion vary from place to place, depending in large part on how local Communist leaders choose to implement the general antireligion directives of the party's Central Committee. Orders limiting the ringing of church bells to a set number of minutes per day and prohibiting the passing of a collection plate may be rare, but in places they have existed. In some Moslem areas, the women were compelled to throw off the veil by being threatened with arrest. In others, they were bribed by making scarce textiles for suit or coat available at a low cost, and sometimes the services of a tailor were thrown in as a part of the bargain.

Proregime Clerical Associations

The Yugoslav Communists initiated the creation of proregime associations among the clergy of each of the major religious denominations as part of their antireligious campaign. They hoped that to the outside world these associations would convey the impression of support for the regime even among religious groups. In this way the widely held notions that the regime was antireligious would be nullified. From the domestic standpoint, the Communist leaders no doubt hoped, these associations would be the instruments of a divide-and-rule policy. Through them the unity of the religious front would be broken. All who refused to participate in them would be labeled as "people's enemies." Similarly, these associations could be employed as ready tools whenever the government needed "recommendations" for the ousting of certain bishops or for other actions in the realm of religion which it might from time to time desire to take. On the face of it, the regime would only be acting upon recommendations of the faithful.

Pressure in various forms has been utilized to get the clergy to join these associations. Initially the government had little success. With the passage of time, however, and as more and more people, out of a feeling of futility, became resigned to the regime, an increasing number of priests have joined. In the Orthodox regions, according to regime officials, over two-thirds of the clergy have joined. In Slovenia, which is Roman Catholic, more than a majority have reportedly become members. In Croatia, also Roman Catholic, the regime did not begin its organization drive in earnest until early 1953, consequently there are no statistics available at this writing. In the Islamic and Jewish faiths the government claims nearly full co-operation.

The government makes financial grants to these proregime associations ostensibly to aid them in the furtherance of religious activities. Members are eligible to social security benefits, which include medical care. This in itself is not an unimportant inducement to join. But even in the eyes of those who join, to say nothing of the rank and file of the faithful, these associations are merely tools of the Communist regime, and as such have little interest in the welfare of religion or the religious life.

Simultaneously with its accelerated drive to gather the clergy into these associations, the regime in May, 1953 promulgated a law allegedly designed to normalize relations between religious communities and the state.[6] It does little more, however, than affirm what has been in the constitution since the beginning of 1946. Government leaders admit that in essence it regularizes hitherto existing practice.[7] The constitution, for example, permits religious schools for the training of priests, under the general

[6] *Borba,* May 23, 1953.
[7] See Rankovich statement, *Borba,* May 23, 1953.

supervision of the state; it provides that the state may extend material assistance to religious communities; and it permits church marriage following the civil ceremony. The 1953 law reaffirms these provisions, but adds that punitive action, in case of misuse, can be taken against schools for training the clergy; it asserts that the state has the right to indicate the purposes for which the aid it might extend shall be used; and it permits a church marriage ceremony only if both husband and wife demand it.

Moreover, the law provides that no one can be forced to be a church member. It permits baptism only if both parents demand it, and if the child concerned is able to indicate his wishes, his consent is required. Likewise, religious teaching outside school hours is permitted, provided both parents consent and provided the child agrees. The law also permits a religious press which, of course, cannot be concerned with mundane problems. Collections of offerings in church and church buildings are permitted; outside these places a special permit is necessary. Finally, the law prohibits interference with the conduct of religious services.

Anti-Religious Propaganda Campaign

No less important than the regime's other actions in its war on religion is the one-sided propaganda campaign which is waged incessantly by the Communists. Continually, antireligious articles appear in the press. Antireligious organizations are encouraged and material means extended to them in support of their activities. Government enterprises sponsor evening courses for their employees to "unmask religion." Satirical magazines poke fun at priests and at religion generally. Even more significant is the oral propaganda purveyed at meetings, conferences and in the schools.

Teachers are told to talk against religion and to prevent children from going to church. Public ridicule is a widely employed technique. A fourteen-year-old son of an Orthodox priest was asked in front of his classmates if his father urged him to go to church. The boy replied in the negative, adding that his father did not mix in such matters. Later the young man confided to his parents that he was ashamed of himself for lying, but he said he just had to do it, because he could not stand the ridicule.

Even the Communist guardians in nursery schools are instructed to speak openly against God. The Yugoslav press continually hammers at the theme that religious teachers are not fit to educate children.[8] Educational periodicals follow the same line, and the accusing finger is publicly pointed at some of these teachers by name. And no matter how unfair or untrue the accusations may be, those who are attacked cannot reply.

Toward the end of 1952 one of the Yugoslav youth newspapers declared, among other things: "An ideological battle against the harmful influence of church and religion has spread throughout our country, a battle for rooting out religious humbug from the people's consciousness. All the more frequently pamphlets, books and scientific works are being published and various lectures held, which light up the dark cave of this ancient ideology. . . ."[9] In this type of propaganda religion is rarely referred to by its true name. Usually it is represented as "mysticism," "superstition," "ignorance," "stupidity" and "unreality."

Against such assaults there can be no defense. Not a single item can appear in the press which would speak in favor of the church or of clergymen. Ironically enough, it was the Tito regime that inserted in the Yugoslav constitution the proviso that "any propagation of . . . religious hatred or discord" is "contrary to the Constitution and punishable."

[8] For example, see *Borba,* August 7 and September 8, 1952.
[9] *Narodni student,* December 10, 1952.

Chapter 17:

The Dead Hand of Conformity

ALL of the above described efforts of the Tito regime to shackle the masses to the dictatorship are characterized by one overriding purpose—to force everyone to surrender his independence of thought and to embrace whatever the Communist leaders offer. Once having yielded their freedom to think for themselves, the people are expected to abandon their independence of action and to accept regimentation of body as well as of mind.

Anti-Intellectualism

Communists never tire of proclaiming that they are scientific, yet all their actions betray them as having nothing but contempt for free scientific inquiry. As audacious anti-intellectualists, they are contemptous of freedom and intelligence. In Yugoslavia, the effects of the intellectual strait jacket are amply in evidence on every hand. Loss of freedom has brought with it a universal disappearance of mental vitality. Discussions are monotonous and devoid of substance. There can be no clash of really basic ideas, no give and take. Uniformity abounds in all meetings and conferences; everything must be in the Marxian context. Communist spokesmen open the discussions, and are usually followed by other party members who reiterate or add to what has already been said. Most persons avoid participating. Again and again, young people of university age said to me, "What fun is there in discussions if you can't take issue with what is said!"

Those who were once naive enough to accept Communist professions of belief in free discussion have learned the truth through bitter experience. Suffice it to mention two examples of many which could be cited. One man was expelled from a professional association simply because he defended a colleague who was under attack. A student in the University of Belgrade, who had criticized the tenets of Marxism at a student meeting, was brought to heel three months later by the student youth organization. He was told that since Yugoslavia and the youth association had accepted the tenets of Marxism, his criticism had been subversive and unpatriotic. His expulsion from the university was not only prompt, but in addition contained a stipulation prohibiting him from re-entering for a period of five years.[1]

The absence of intellectual vitality is to be found among old and young alike, but it is particularly frightening among the latter. In the case of persons whose intellectual development preceded the Tito regime, mental vitality is not so much lacking as it is dormant. But the products of Tito's education, except in rare cases where educated parents nourish intellectual growth, are and will continue to be intellectually stunted individuals. New generations will grow up intellectually deformed and underdeveloped. The mind, not unlike the body, needs certain elemental things if it is to grow and develop. Yugoslav young people, especially in the cities where secret police agents and informers are so prevalent, do not discuss serious political, economic and social questions with one another. If on occasion they do, knowing the dangers involved when conversations are repeated, their observations are apt to be something less than full, frank and sincere.

The Yugoslav Communists make much of having battled against illiteracy. But the desirability of teaching a man to read cannot be evaluated without some appreciation of the uses to which such training is to be put. It seems fair to ask: Is teaching a man to read an unmixed blessing when it is done with the avowed purpose of enslaving his mind?

There are many illustrations of Communist anti-intellectualism at work in Yugoslavia, but none more illustrative than that involving Dr. Alexander Kostich, professor of histology in the Belgrade University Medical School. For those who may be inclined to believe that Tito is building a new type of Communist society, less repugnant than that in the Soviet Union, no commentary could be more instructive.

[1] *Narodni student,* March 5, 1952.

First a word about Dr. Kostich, who is no stranger to the Who's Whos of American and European medicine. As a promising young Serbian doctor, he was given the herculean task at the end of the First World War of building a medical faculty in the ruins of Belgrade. He not only succeeded in getting able young Serbian doctors, then in residence in various medical centers of Europe, to join the faculty, but in addition, through his personal achievements and his scholarship, attained considerable recognition in medical circles throughout Europe. The Histology Institute which he founded enjoyed a deserved reputation. Moreover, it was he who organized the School of Pharmocology, the Veterinary Institute and the Photo-Film Institute. Dr. Kostich has written extensively in his field, and is the author of the principal textbooks in use in Belgrade in histology, in embryology and in histological technique.

In March, 1952 he attended an "open party meeting" of the Communists on the staff of the Belgrade Medical School, to which all teachers had been invited. The meeting was held pursuant to directives from the Central Committee of the Communist Party, which had decided that "open party meetings" should be held in various governmental institutions and enterprises, ostensibly for the purpose of getting party and nonparty people closer together, enabling them to hear each other's views and consequently working more harmoniously together.

With some 175 persons present, including Milka Minich as a representative of the Central Committee of the Communist Party of Serbia, the meeting was opened by the secretary of the Communist Party organization within the faculty, on the subject: "How Democracy Is Conceived and How It Is Carried Out in the Medical School."

It was immediately evident that this was to be an attack upon Dr. Kostich, who had drafted for the medical school the various rules and bylaws concerning scholarships, faculty travel abroad, rules for faculty government, and principles governing the recruitment of new teachers. All of these had been accepted overwhelmingly, even by the Communists on the staff. But Communist Party bosses resent any initiative which stems from non-Communist sources, and their feeling of inferiority in this case caused them to lose their heads. One of the things they resented most was the secret voting clause in the rules on choosing new teachers, for in this way it would be difficult to substitute political for professional qualifications. Throughout her speech, the party secretary not only uttered various untruths about Dr. Kostich, but also contended that secret voting in the choice of new teachers was undemocratic.

Dr. Kostich arose, and in a brief statement addressed to the party secretary, said that everything which had been alleged about him constituted the most ordinary untruths, and challenged her to prove the contrary. He was surprised, he said, at a "democracy" where ordinary lies could be leveled at a person without one man's daring to get up to defend a colleague and his thirty years of useful work.

The secretary whispered to Mrs. Minich, asking what to say, but Mrs. Minich decided to make the reply herself. Her chief contention was that Communist Party members could not get on the faculty under the rules drafted by Dr. Kostich.

Kostich broke in to say: "Madame Minister, I will not allow you to utter such untruths!"

In this charged atmosphere, Mrs. Minich continued. She said that it was clear that two groups existed in the medical school— the one constructive, democratic and friendly (here she paused to name those she considered loyal), and the other hostile, undemocratic and destructive. "Dr. Kostich," she continued, "perhaps unintentionally, had become the leader" of the latter group, and she wanted him to know that they were not afraid of this group.

When she finished, Dr. Kostich took the floor and began a measured criticism of political domination in the school. He was building his case from the lesser offenses to the more repugnant ones. As he was approaching a climax, Mrs. Minich gave the chairman the sign that he should be stopped. Thereupon the chairman broke in to say that since this was a meeting of the party organization she wanted to ask the party members if Dr. Kostich should be allowed to continue.

For Dr. Kostich this was the breaking point. "What did you say?" he shouted. "You asked us to come here, you wanted to hear our views, and now the handful of you want to forbid me to talk. In this type of democracy there is no place for me." And with that parting shot, he picked up his hat and left the meeting.

The next day he was dismissed!

Technically and officially he was retired because he had served the requisite number of years. Yet throughout institutions of learning a retired professor is known as professor emeritus—honored and permitted to carry on scientific research if he so desires. But Professor Kostich, able and vigorous at 59, is denied all access to the medical school and to the various institutes that he headed. He has no laboratory, and the Academy of Science has notified him that his resignation has been accepted, although he had not submitted one.

Moreover, he was denied a farewell meeting with his advanced students. He had placed a notice on the bulletin board, inviting the advanced students to meet with him in a university classroom. The notice was soon torn down (but not until many students had seen it), and he was expressly told not to hold such a meeting. He decided to comply, especially when he learned of the organized groups of hoodlums who had been assigned the job of preventing such a meeting.

Six months later, people in Belgrade were still talking about this case. Dr. Kostich, I was told, has accepted his fate philosophically. He reads at home, plays the piano, and walks the streets of Belgrade. And the medical school, falling more and more into incompetent hands, continues its downhill slide. A pharmacist, for example, was chosen to take over Professor Kostich's job as head of the photo-film laboratory, although he did not have the least idea of what it was all about.

Ironically enough, the Communist Party continues to stress the need of training cadres in all fields, and persists in emphasizing the need for party and nonparty people to come into closer association and to work harmoniously together.

A slightly different type of case resulting from the same anti-intellectualist philosophy involved a professor in another Yugoslav university. In planning a summer seminar (1952) for teachers of English, Yugoslav authorities had turned to the American Information Center in Belgrade for English language materials. The Americans responded generously with a good assortment of documentary films, magazines and booklets, taking care not to include materials which would be clearly offensive to the Yugoslav regime. The professor in charge of the seminar, however, was explicitly warned that "it would be his neck" if he used any materials containing items critical of Yugoslavia. Since even a news item that someone had escaped from Yugoslavia or a critical letter to the editor would fall in the forbidden category, and since the task of minutely screening all the materials was well-nigh impossible, most of the contributions of the American Information Center were left in a heap on the floor to gather dust.

Conformity But Not Consent

Communist actions and methods such as those described in the preceding pages can bring about conformity, but it is doubtful that they can ever create consent. They can crush the people's spirit so completely as to produce despair and resignation, but they cannot evoke enthusiasm or induce support.

Wherever one goes in Yugoslavia, usually excepting the Communists who make up less than 5 per cent of the population, one finds apathy and indifference toward regime propaganda. The people get the same story—in a thousand contexts—in the press, over the radio and in political meetings. They are aware that it is at variance with reality, but most of it passes them by and evokes little or no response. Experience has taught them that it is safer to be apolitical—an attitude which envelops the whole fabric of Yugoslav society.

Hostility toward the regime and contempt for its leaders abounds everywhere, but it is accompanied by frustration, by a feeling of impotence and utter helplessness. There is confidence in victory over Communism in the long run, but also the belief that for the most part the matter is out of their hands, that their fate hinges on the outcome of the struggle between the Soviet Union and the West.

The attitude of youth is little different from that of the other age groups in the population. Once in part enthusiastic about the future under Tito, young people have been completely disillusioned. Many promises of a better life were made, but few if any have been realized. Obligations in the form of "voluntary" work, acting as informers, and participating in propaganda demonstrations have been many and unromantic, while rewards have been conspicuous by their absence. And their gradual realization of the enormity of the injustices heaped upon their parents has had a telling effect on their attitude toward the regime.

Communist leaders, on the other hand, continue to operate on the principle that there should never be a letup in their efforts. Party members must be everywhere to guide all public, and many private, activities along desired lines. People's time should be managed. They are to be kept occupied, involved and exhausted. And the local party functionary, intoxicated by his newly found self-importance, welcomes new and different assignments, for they help him, like anesthetic injections, to forget the pains of past failures, apathy and popular hostility.

This psychological side of life in a Communist paradise—this effort to build up a drab and colorless new man, an applauding machine which approves or rebukes things as it is told—is difficult for a free man to conceive of. When a free man is tempted to choose Communism, he must understand that he is not choosing between two political systems. He is not even choosing between freedom and slavery. He is choosing between his own existence and nonexistence, for in a Communist state the individual exists only to the extent to which they will let him exist. If they decide to liquidate him, move him, use him as a stooge, promote him, issue proclamations in his name, there is nothing he can do but conform. This assault on the dignity of the person is difficult to describe and more difficult to visualize, unless one has seen it with his own eyes.

Erosion of Moral Principles

The character of a people does not change rapidly, but it is interesting to observe that the Communist dictatorship seems to be having a negative effect upon once recognized moral principles. This is particularly noticeable in the cities, the peasant areas perhaps being little touched by it. Even if we should accept the argument that erosion of moral principles in the cities antedated the Communist regime, there is evidence on every hand that it is more widespread and proceeding at an accelerated rate under Communism.

By and large, this question cannot be divorced from recent history. It should be noted that the Yugoslav people passed through two world wars within a short time. In the midst of the second, gestapo terror and Communist-led revolution conspired to make life cheap. Heads rolled easily, and the people's moral fiber was seriously weakened. After World War II, instead of freedom and hope there was tyranny and despair. Among the results were anti-intellectualism, loss of vitality, drabness and a further weakening of moral standards.

The results of Communist-imposed conformity are not simple or always clearly definable. But there are indications that mental stagnation, opportunism, bewilderment and emotional conflict to some degree stem from it. In the hope of satisfying regime pressures and in the expectation of acquiring more of the material needs of life, many individuals have turned informers even on their best friends. Unbearable pressures have transfomed many persons into rank opportunists. This alone has made for inner conflict, bewilderment, and rationalization. People behave not in a manner they believe to be right but in a way that is required or expected.

Under such conditions one cannot expect sincerity. A foreign visitor, for example, asked a well-known Yugoslav university professor if they could sit down for a sincere and frank discussion. The answer constituted a revealing commentary on intellectual life in Tito's Yugoslavia. "I don't know," replied the professor with a sardonic grin, "I have not been sincere for seven years now."

The absence of sincerity is manifested in other ways. Students, for example, who desire to make good marks know that they must do well in assigned tasks. But to do well in assigned projects means being able to turn out what is wanted and not what the students sincerely believe. An assignment, therefore, to write a paper on the wartime achievements of the Partisans, if it is to be rated high, will require skill and ingenuity. Consequently, young people—twelve, fifteen, seventeen years of age—learn to put down what is wanted, to practice deception systematically and cleverly.

Parents are apt to ask what impact such training will have on the youngster's reliability in adulthood. Moreover, a delicate problem faces the parents when they are aware that their children are being taught lies and nonsense. If they do nothing, the youngster grows up dwarfed and uneducated. If, on the other hand, an attempt is made to correct errors, the result may be an unhappy child (e.g. the child of a man who fought with the Chetniks against the Germans is told in school that the Chetniks were traitors).

Not all persons can be easily beaten down. But even among those who are made of sterner stuff, the dead hand of conformity takes its toll. Refusing to compromise principles in return for increased material comforts, these individuals have gone through material privations only to suffer even more from mental anguish as, with Western aid to Tito, the day of hoped-for liberation recedes. Many a pro-Western Yugoslav has told me that his pains of the spirit are more intense and more difficult to bear than those resulting from the lack of material comforts.

It would be erroneous to assume, as do some individuals in the West, that those positive attributes of Western civilization and culture with which Yugoslav society was endowed can be preserved indefinitely under Communism. It would be equally erroneous to believe, as do some ex-Stalinists, that the Yugoslavs will accept only the more positive attributes of Marxism. There is more reason to believe that, with the continuation of Communism, Yugoslav society will acquire and retain the worst aspects of both.

PART FOUR

GOVERNMENT

AND

THE ECONOMY

DISRUPTION, confusion and change have been the principal characteristics of the Yugoslav economy under Communist rule. Determined to establish a collectivized economy, the Yugoslav Communists
turned to Soviet experience for guidance. In employing Soviet methods, however, they did not wish to traverse the full length of the
Soviet path. Rather, they wanted to profit from Russian experience,
taking the shorter route while at the same time avoiding the failures
and disappointments. But their efforts, instead of producing a functioning collectivist economy, resulted in disruption, chaos and confusion. Yet, they always displayed an assurance of knowing where
they were going, and seemingly had no doubts about their ability to
get there. Their one answer to repeated failures has been to change,
to improvise, to try anew. This involved a steady stream of decrees,
instructions and directives, amending, repealing or re-enforcing previous regulations. That this made for costly mistakes, incomprehensible confusion and intolerable waste did not seem to be of grave
concern to Stalin's imitators.

In self-defense, the Yugoslav leaders have at times attempted to
explain their economic failures by insisting that they inherited a war-
devastated economy. Without minimizing the war damage, it is only
fair to point out, however, that the economies of other European
countries suffered far more (e.g. Greece, Italy and Western Germany,
to mention only three). Moreover, the industrialized nations were

more deeply hurt by the war. Yugoslavia's economy, being primarily agricultural, for the most part retained its functional powers. Finally, non-Yugoslav economists familiar with the Balkans point to Serbia's rapid recovery after World War I, by way of contrast, although her economy was considerably more devastated at that time than was the case after World War II.

In short, Yugoslavia's economy was wrecked by the attempt of her Communist rulers to emulate the Russians. Some three years after their expulsion from the Cominform family, these same rulers began taking steps in an attempt to salvage it—a process that is still going on—through the technique of a controlled market economy. In its broader aspects it is still a planned economy, but allegedly one in which economic laws operate more freely and state-owned enterprises are managed more independently by actual producers. Moreover, those actually engaged in production purportedly share in the economic policy making process at all levels, through the various councils of producers which in 1953 were made part of the governmental structure. Although all sectors of the economy are represented in the councils of producers, industry has the predominant voice.

Private property outside of agriculture, it should be noted, plays no significant role in the Yugoslav economy. Except for domestic dwellings and a few other buildings, whose utilization is rigidly controlled and allocated by the government, everything is owned by the state. Barbers, watch repairmen, and artisans generally continue to practice their occupations, but the government forced many of them to organize into state-controlled co-operatives, or otherwise mobilized them to work for the state. Doctors and dentists are permitted to practice privately after their regular day at state clinics. Some privately operated taxis are also allowed but, like all other persons receiving a private income, their owners are taxed almost out of existence.

While this and the following sections are devoted in large part to a study of the Yugoslav economy, the primary approach is political. The main emphasis is more on the role played by the government and upon some of the results, rather than upon a technical and detailed analysis of the purely economic factors in the functioning of the economy.

Chapter 18:

Yugoslav Economy and Marxism

WHEN Karl Marx and his principal collaborator, Friedrich Engels, developed their Communist theories in the second half of the last century they viewed capitalism as part of an historical process. Like other economic systems which preceded it, capitalism would, in their opinion, develop internal contradictions which would bring about its downfall. This would come about in the latter phases of capitalist development—in a highly developed industrial society, with its concentration of wealth on the one hand, and the existence of a large and exploited class-conscious proletariat on the other.

Yugoslav Economy Agricultural

The Yugoslav economy, however, was neither industrially developed nor did it have a wage-earning class of any consequence. Approximately 85 per cent of the population was engaged in agricultural pursuits and less than 5 per cent in industry. The Yugoslav Communists, however, were not bothered by the fact that their country did not fit the Marxian formula. To them the Soviet Union was everything. After all, its economy had also been primarily agrarian when the Communists seized power. Moreover, Soviet theorists had made the necessary doctrinal elaborations to provide for Communist revolutions in states whose economies were primarily agricultural.

Prior to World War II Yugoslavia had little heavy industry. Industrial capital was in large part foreign controlled, and domestic industrial growth was proceeding gradually. At the end of the war, however, Yugoslavia had fewer prerequisites for industrial development than she had possessed in 1941. The war had wrought destruction of physical facilities in some areas, but far more serious was the marked depletion of an already small skilled labor force. Many workers had been compelled by the Nazis to join labor battalions in Germany and many more were killed in guerrilla warfare and in internal civil strife.

In theory, however, Yugoslavia has a fairly good industrial potential. She has considerable quantities of copper, zinc, bauxite, lead and other raw materials. Her water power resources are sizable. She has iron ore, but her known resources of coal are not such as to warrant much heavy industry, a fact which the Communists refuse to recognize. Yugoslavia has little or no petroleum. Moreover, her roads, railroads and other transportation facilities which industry needs are little developed, especially in the areas where they are most needed.

Towards Collectivism

The lack of an industrial base, the shortage of skilled workers, the absence of significant class cleavages and the virtual nonexistence of managerial know-how did not dampen the determination of the Yugoslav Communists to build an industrial society on the Soviet model. Nor did they wait for the establishment of the new constitutional order, which would endow them with appropriate legal authority, before plunging ahead.

During World War II, while assuring the Western Allies that private property would be respected in the postwar period, Tito's Partisans were busy confiscating industrial enterprises which were within physical reach. They now admit that during the war much property "passed into the hands of the revolutionary organs of the people's government [sic] chiefly through confiscation. . . ." [1] By the end of the war, they assert, "over half (54 per cent) of industry was under state control. Twenty-seven per cent was foreign property under provisional state management and the remaining 19 per cent was still in private hands." [2] But

[1] Jovan Djordjevich, "Essential Characteristics of the New System of Managing State Economic Enterprises and Higher Economic Associations," *New Yugoslav Law*, I (June–September, 1950), p. 13.

[2] Vlajko Begovich, "Our Unique System," *United Nations World*, 6 (August, 1952), p. 45.

since "the state took direction not only of the nationalized sector of the economy but of the nation's entire economic life" [3] as well, private property, except perhaps in land, lost its traditional meaning from the outset.

A sweeping nationalization law in 1946 for the most part merely ratified what had already become an accomplished fact.[4] Other laws were quickly enacted to take care of unforeseen circumstances.[5] A supplementary nationalization law in the spring of 1948, for example, brought virtually every remaining economic enterprise, most land holdings excluded, under government ownership.[6] This included resort hotels, the few remaining restaurants, garages, second-hand bookstores and other small business establishments. Moreover, the owners had no advance warning of the supplementary law. Even members of the parliament knew nothing about it until late one afternoon the chief of the Yugoslav economy, the late Boris Kidrich, asked special consideration for its introduction and immediate passage. The Federal People's Assembly obliged. Contrary to the usual wording that a law comes into effect when published in the official gazette, the supplementary nationalization law specified that it would go into effect when passed by the assembly. The next morning agents were at the doors of the establishments to be nationalized. The owners were not permitted to take anything. Even the money in their safes and cash registers was nationalized. This was certainly true in Belgrade, for I saw it happen. It is possible, however, that regime agents acted with less alacrity in some other parts of the country; at least there were scattered reports to that effect.

Although the nationalization laws provided for compensation, the owners were merely given a slip of paper as a receipt. Years later they were to receive only a fraction of the real worth of their properties, and ironically enough, in highly inflated currency and in government bonds of questionable value.

Property which was not nationalized, such as most private landholdings and residence dwellings, came under rigid government control. Efforts were made to force peasants and artisans into state-controlled collectives and co-operatives. Prices were

[3] *Ibid.*
[4] *Sluzhbeni list* (official gazette), No. 98, 1946.
[5] *Ibid.,* No. 28, 1947.
[6] *Ibid.,* No. 35, 1948.

fixed on most services and commodities, including rents. Full power to allocate housing space was assumed even in private homes which did not desire tenants. Owners were told how much space they could have in their own homes. Transfer of real estate was forbidden even as a gift without prior authorization.[7] In the event of violation of this decree, both the giver and the recipient could be held criminally responsible, and the real estate in question was subject to confiscation. It was stipulated, however, that no authorization was required if a person desired to give his property to the state!

Several months following the first nationalization law, the Yugoslav Communists launched a Five Year economic plan. Following in the footsteps of Soviet planners, the Yugoslav Planning Commission placed major emphasis on industrialization and electrification. The Titoists were determined to emulate the Soviets even if in the process they should set the country back fifty years. They sought not only to transform Yugoslavia into a collectivist planned economy, but also to cut her traditional economic ties with the West and to orient her trade toward Eastern Europe.

Some Consequences

It does not seem to have occurred to the Yugoslav planners that their ambitious industrialization plans, having taken little account of the prerequisites and conditions necessary to industrialization, were destined to run into difficulties. By seeking to accomplish much, they succeeded chiefly in dispersing money, materials and manpower with few concrete achievements in evidence. Partially completed projects dot the Yugoslav countryside as monuments of this colossal waste. Many of the completed plants were built with no calculation of cost, probable markets or the availability of qualified personnel to man them. To make matters worse, most of the goods produced in Yugoslav factories have been of substandard quality.

The results of emulating the Russians for five years have been nothing short of catastrophic. Many industries have been shattered, public utilities are in a decrepit state, agricultural produc-

[7] *Sluzhbeni list,* March 24, 1948. Also see *Politika,* June 25, 1949.

tivity has declined, and the standard of living has been lowered. Furthermore, these negative achievements of the Yugoslav Communist economic experiment have been bought at a tremendous cost. Priceless natural resources, such as forests and coal, have been consumed at an increasingly rapid rate. Much manpower was utilized in unproductive activities. Yugoslav financial reserves have been depleted, to say nothing of hundreds of millions of dollars which the Western Powers have poured into Yugoslavia since World War II. Some improvements, such as construction of roads and hydroelectric projects, are of more permanent value even if achieved at a high cost. Much industrial capacity and equipment will, however, deteriorate prematurely, or wear out completely, for lack of proper care and adequate maintenance.

Moreover, the Yugoslav economy was seriously dislocated by its orientation toward Eastern Europe and away from its prewar Western European trade. The full extent of this dislocation became known only after Yugoslavia's expulsion from the Cominform. From time to time, after Tito's break with Moscow, the Yugoslavs have revealed the amazingly exploitive nature of their onetime trade arrangements with the Soviet Union. The full cost to Yugoslavia, however, can only be estimated.

While a more detailed consideration of the varied consequences of Yugoslav Communist economic policies must await subsequent chapters of this and the following Part, it should be noted here that none of the developments described above seems to have had any noticeable impact upon the basic Yugoslav policy of driving toward Communism. Yugoslav Communist leaders have lost no opportunity in pointing out that while circumstances may force them to delay the completion of certain projects there can be no retreat from the fundamental objective. Every change in tactics or tempo of development has been accompanied by doctrinal assurances that the changes in question, far from constituting a deviation from ultimate goals, were in fact designed to accelerate the movement toward their attainment. Private enterprise, on the other hand, has certainly made no gains.

Chapter 19:

Planning and Directing the Economy

THE monumental scope of planning and directing a country's entire economy is difficult to visualize. Planning requires much factual data, e.g. availability of raw materials, productive facilities and their capacity, transportation potential, manpower in all phases, and distribution (domestic and foreign), to mention only a few of the major items. An erroneous estimate at one point is certain to result in dislocations at many other points. Moreover, performance must live up to the plans if serious disruption is not to ensue. The rate of production, the Yugoslav planners discovered, was also important. In one coal mine, for example, the workers were in the habit of speeding up production toward the end of the month in order to meet planned output. But the factories needed coal at an even rate, to say nothing of the sacrifice in quality which resulted from such speedups. Moreover, there were insufficient railway cars to transport the coal toward the end of the month, while during the first part many of them were idle.[1]

In order to ascertain the extent to which the plans are being fulfilled, voluminous and detailed records must be kept, a corps of inspectors engaged, statistics compiled and analyzed and, where necessary, corrective measures taken. At one time the Yugoslav inspectorate consisted of a national control commission, control commissions in each of the six republics, control commissions in each county, each city and each ward. The basic task

[1] *Borba,* February 10, 1949.

of these agencies was to investigate the operation of economic enterprises and other government agencies and to insist upon improvement where it was needed. As if this inspection corps was not enough, the government at one time established the so-called People's Inspectorates, supposedly composed of ordinary citizens, to check upon "failures, deficiencies, illegality and the masking of failures." These were to be created in enterprises, villages and various state institutions.

Yet all of this is but the briefest indication of the scope of the economic tasks which face the governors of a planned economy, to say nothing of the noneconomic problems with which they must also grapple. Within the past two years the nature of Yugoslav economic planning and the manner in which the economy has been directed have been undergoing significant changes. These will be discussed in the pages to follow, but first a word about their earlier experiences.

Historical Note on Yugoslav Planning

The characteristic feature of initial Yugoslav economic planning was, in the words of the onetime principal planner, Boris Kidrich, "that almost everything was planned from above, and the enterprise had almost nothing to plan. . . . The earlier so-called basic plans entered deeply into the details of production and distribution." [2]

In addition to the Five Year Plan, there were annual, quarterly and monthly plans. Each industry and each enterprise had its own plan. In every enterprise each person was expected to have a daily plan of work. Inspectors made periodic inquiries into these plans. On one occasion, for example, three men from the now defunct Control Commission appeared one morning at the office of an enterprise and asked to see the daily work plan of each person. When they came to the stenographer-typist she did not have a plan. Her superior immediately took responsibility, arguing that it was impossible for her to have a plan since her work depended upon the amount of dictation she would receive, the length of the letters she would have to type, etc. This, however, did not satisfy the inspectors, who steadfastly maintained

[2] *Borba,* August 26, 1951.

that she must have a daily work plan. Similarly, a mechanic in a transport enterprise was required to have a daily work plan, but unforeseen developments, such as going to the suburbs to perform emergency repairs, forced constant revision of his plan.

✳ In general, it can be said that until 1951 the trend was toward more and more centralization in planning, direction and actual operation of the economy. Since 1951, however, the trend has been toward having the central government determine the basic direction in which the economy should develop, and to assure its moving in that direction, principally through the employment of indirect controls. In other words, the basic planning is centralized, while the more detailed planning, actual production and distribution have for the most part been left to the governments of the republics and to the individual enterprises.

This change was described by Kidrich [3] as "a decentralization which is in its essence not antagonistic to an essential centralization of the socialist plans." The role of the state has been changed from that of the "proprietor of the basic means of production" to that of "socialist regulator of the nation's industry, a consistent defender of the achievements of the socialist revolution." Edward Kardelj, who seems to have been devoting a great deal of time to economic problems since Kidrich's death, stated more recently that they needed to develop a system which "will reconcile the necessity of maximum independence of the working collectives in enterprises with the necessity of satisfying the general needs of society, and especially with the necessity of the planned development of our economy as a whole." [4] On another occasion, he spoke of the need to facilitate "natural economic development" [5] (in a planned socialist economy!).

Elements in Basic Planning

The responsibility for basic planning is vested in the Federal Planning Institute, which is attached to the Secretariat for Economic Affairs. Its basic policy directives come from the party, through the Federal Executive Council and the secretariat to

[3] "From State Socialism to Economic Democracy," *The Yugoslav Review* (February, 1952), p. 14.
[4] *Politika,* April 8, 1953.
[5] *Ibid.,* March 29, 1953.

which it is attached. In carrying out these directives it relies heavily on the Federal Institute for Statistics, and upon its own record of past plans and past performances in relation to those plans. Moreover, it works through planning agencies in each of the six republics, to which requirements are submitted. These agencies in turn submit them to, and receive comments from, industries and enterprises within their respective republics.

In addition to the Federal Institute for Statistics, each republic and each county has its own statistical bureau. They collect statistics from enterprises, co-operatives, municipalities, and individuals. They are supposed to be compiled in some meaningful fashion for planners to use. The work of statistical bureaus is enormous. In the republic of Serbia, for example, it is said that "they collect data concerning production, achievements, stocks and activities of 770 industrial enterprises; they check trade for 12,000 shops; they record labor for 8,000 enterprises and collect data concerning agriculture in all of the 2,250 municipalities, etc. In addition, each year they collect data about prices, about family budgets, about peasant labor co-operatives and co-operatives of the general type, about educational, cultural, social and other institutions, about population, etc." [6]

Contrary to past practice, planning by the central authorities today is supposed to be concerned only with *"basic proportions of production and distribution."* [7] The basic plan, known as the social plan, by establishing the basic proportions in production and distribution, "determines the direction of development of material productive forces, and effects the basic division of the national income. . . ." [8] In other words, the central government (party) determines in a general way what should be produced, at what rate to produce it, and how to distribute the national income.

Yugoslavia's late economic chief, Boris Kidrich, described this more recent planning as envisaging two spheres—a minimum sphere determined by the central authorities, and a more extensive sphere which economic enterprises will develop in order

[6] *Politika*, August 20, 1952.

[7] Kidrich, "From State Socialism to Economic Democracy," *The Yugoslav Review* (February, 1952), p. 5. Also see Kardelj's speech, *Politika*, April 8, 1953.

[8] *Borba*, August 25, 1951.

to utilize their productive and commercial opportunities.[9] The chairman of the Federal Planning Institute, Vlajko Begovich, in a conversation with me, described the state's planning functions in slightly different words. He said that the state would continue (1) to establish production goals for each enterprise (2) to plan the amount of capital construction in key areas and industries (3) to fix the rate of investment for individual enterprises, and (4) to determine the extent to which these enterprises should contribute to general social needs.

In implementing these plans, however, the central government was after 1951 determined to employ fiscal and monetary policies instead of direct controls. The most important of these has been the rate of accumulation, a tax calculated on the basis of the wages paid out in any given enterprise. In determining this rate, which varied greatly in different branches of the economy, the government in effect decided how the sum total of the net product was going to be divided between the workers and society in general. According to the 1952 plan,[10] for example, the rate of accumulation in forestry was 146 per cent, which meant that for every one hundred dollars paid out in wages one hundred forty-six dollars went into the government treasury. In mining and industry the rate was 582 per cent, or for every dollar paid out to a miner in wages five dollars and eighty-two cents went to the government.

This tax has constituted the principal source of government revenue. Kidrich referred to it as "a sort of monopoly rent collected by the state." [11] But contrary to the surplus value of labor which capitalists siphon off for their private gain, said Kidrich, the "socially accumulated surplus of labor in the hands of the socialist state" is used "for socially useful purposes." The fact remains, however, that these funds have been exacted by the state (party) to be used for the needs of the country, and in order to channel economic activity in desired directions. Certainly the funds have not been a free-will offering by the workers to society.

During 1953, however, the government announced that it would eliminate the rate of accumulation as no longer appropriate, perhaps by January, 1954.[12] It is being replaced by some

[9] *Ibid.*, August 27, 1951.
[10] *Predlog drushtvenog plana* (Belgrade, 1952), p. 7.
[11] *Komunist* (Belgrade, 1952), No. 1–2.
[12] *Borba*, June 18, 1953.

of the well known institutions of a market economy: (1) interest
on fixed and circulating capital (2) a so-called tax on rent (e.g.
a charge for the natural wealth of a mine) (3) a tax on profits
and (4) a sales tax. To facilitate the fullfillment of its economic
plans, therefore, the government will employ these techniques
not only to control credit and profits but also to fix wages. "The
control over wage funds," said Kardelj, "represents one of the
most important instruments of the social plan." [13] Hence, workers
will continue to share with society the surplus of their labor.

In addition, it is important to remember that the central government will continue to exercise a substantial control over foreign trade, and to determine the extent of defense and other national expenditures. Moreover, it has reserved the right of direct
intervention where the basic plans are being violated. Finally,
the Central Committee of the party can at any time bring about
changes in the governmental structure so as to incorporate any
other techniques it may deem desirable in the pursuit of its fundamental aims.

Local Planning

Within the scope of the basic proportions of the social plan
and other laws and regulations, the more detailed planning is
done in the republics and in the individual enterprises. Since the
national government sets the basic goals and determines interest
and wage rates, local planning tends to be narrowed down to
devising the means of achieving a predetermined end. But,
contrary to past practice, local planners now have many worries
with which they were not plagued before.

In the past, local enterprises did not have to worry about
credit, about raw materials, or about costs and prices. They were
told what to produce and were paid for their output by the appropriate ministry. Now, however, local planners have to be concerned about all of these. The more they can cut costs, the more
money they can retain for their enterprise, which can be used,
within limits, for additional investment, supplemental wages or
other expenditures.[14] They must now pay heed to production
costs, for these will determine the extent of the profits of the en-

[13] *Politika,* April 8, 1953.
[14] See Kardelj's speech, *Politika,* April 8, 1953.

terprise. They must also concern themselves about the existence or nonexistence of a demand for the particular product. And, of course, quality will be important, for it may in large measure determine if the goods will sell.

To meet these problems, individual enterprises have been granted permission to fix their own prices and to vary the type of production, provided, of course, that the minimum requirements of the social plan are met. But this should not be construed to signify a return to individual enterprise. In the first place, the bulk of the output of any enterprise will be pretty well determined in advance. Secondly, the government will in large measure determine costs and prices through its power to manipulate credit, wages and taxes. In the final analysis, the latter can be utilized to encourage enterprises or to put them out of existence.

The practical effect of the changed situation in local Yugoslav planning would seem to be that (1) local economic units will have more operational autonomy than heretofore in seeking to achieve the main targets or goals set by the central authorities (2) local planners will now in most cases have to concern themselves as to whether their goods are of the appropriate type and quality to sell (3) local enterprises which can cut costs will have at least some money to spend locally, in supplemental wages, in investment, in housing or in social services generally. Party policies and local party men will no doubt determine in large measure how it is to be spent. Should the workers succeed in having a large part of it diverted into supplementary wages, however, the government has provided a progressively steep scale of taxes to take care of that eventuality.

These changes in economic planning were apparently motivated by: (1) a realization that in the past planning was conceived too broadly, that there were too many unreal aims and too many failures, and that for the time being, therefore, the major effort should be concentrated on certain minimum objectives (2) a determination to place greater responsibility for detailed planning, as well as actual plant operation, on local authorities and economic enterprises (3) a decision to provide some tangible rewards to successful local enterprises (4) a resolution to employ indirect controls, instead of direct, where intervention is deemed necessary.

Chapter 20:

Management and Operation
of Industry

THE years of Communist rule in Yugoslavia have been characterized by constant changes in the governmental administrative organization charged with the management and operation of industry. In launching their economic experiment, the Yugoslav Communists created a whole host of economic ministries, in part comparable to those existing in the Soviet Union. Some ministries were set up even before there were industries for them to manage. Failures, serious economic dislocations, and general turmoil led to the abolition of some ministries, reorganization of others, and the creation of new ones. In addition, commissions, directorates, and other agencies were established to take charge of what were considered to be unique industrial and technical problems. The net result was a top-heavy federal bureaucracy, characterized by duplication, inefficiency, and failure to secure expected accomplishments.

By 1950 the Yugoslavs were convinced that centralized control and operation of industry was a failure. As noted earlier, they decided that decentralization in some form was the answer. There were two general steps which they believed needed to be taken. First of all, it was necessary to transfer to the republics more and more authority to manage and operate industry. Secondly, it was imperative to accord the individual enterprises and the workers a greater voice in management.

To accomplish the first step, most federal economic ministries were abolished and federal councils created to control groupings of related industries. The basic task of these councils was to advise and co-ordinate, while the tasks of actual management were assigned to republican ministries. At one time there were eleven councils, one for each major sector of the economy. With the constitutional changes of January, 1953, which established only five federal secretariats of state (economic affairs and budget among them), these councils were abolished. With that, at least in theory, the last phase of industrial management by central authorities passed from the scene.

To increase the role of individual enterprises and of the workers, a new managerial system at the factory level was inaugurated. According to this system, a plant manager, appointed by the state or a parent economic organization, had to share at least some of the functions of management with a management board, to be elected by newly created workers' councils. The latter, representing the workers, was also to have a voice in management, thus symbolizing control of industry by the workers themselves. And this, in the words of Yugoslav Marxian theoreticians, was as it should be.

Government as Manager

Without minimizing the fact that actual management functions have passed from the central government, it should be noted that basic economic decisions have not. Nor can there be any doubt about the central government's possessing sufficient power, exercised indirectly for the most part, to enforce its decisions. Government leaders have in recent years often publicly stated that they intend to employ indirect controls to guide economic development in the desired direction. They have openly asserted, for example, that the tax on wage funds, although "quite misunderstood" in many enterprises, will be utilized to control prices and to stabilize the market.[1]

The provision for councils of producers at all governmental levels, however, has in theory given industrial workers a voice in economic and other important policy making. Because these councils have few representatives from agriculture, although the

[1] See *Borba,* June 2 and 18, 1953.

overwhelming majority of the population is engaged in agricultural pursuits, industrial workers are accorded a voice all out of proportion to their numbers. But the Titoists argue that this is in accord with good Marxian doctrine, which stresses the greater importance of the industrial proletariat. But no one in Yugoslavia is apt to get worked up about this matter, for all Yugoslavs realize that the councils of producers are but a psychological propaganda measure, or at most an administrative device, with little likelihood of having a significant bearing on Communist Party decisions.

The execution of the federal government's fundamental economic policies is exercised through the Federal Executive Council, and more specifically by the State Secretariat for Economic Affairs. With the aid of the State Secretariat for the Budget, the National Bank and other federal agencies, the State Secretariat for Economic Affairs issues in its name, or in the name of the Federal Executive Council, the basic decisions affecting the economy. Rather than a number of federal ministries or councils directing or supervising the management of the economy, there is now the equivalent of a general staff, planning the objectives and issuing the orders for their realization.

The more detailed orders are issued through the executive councils of the republics, and more specifically through their respective secretariats of state which are responsible for different sectors of the economy. Moreover, these secretariats are charged with the task of general supervision of economic performance within their field of responsibility. In most instances, the local people's committee, with its newly created second house (the council of producers), has been given the immediate responsibility for assisting in and of overseeing the work of enterprises within its geographical jurisdiction. This, of course, in no way minimizes the ultimate responsibility vested in the respective republican secretariats of state.

The party, it is understood, exerts its influence at all levels of administration, in an effort to create and to preserve a certain unanimity of aim and high achievement. To do this, it not only utilizes its own organization and the agencies of the government, but also the vast network of mass organizations, such as the

Socialist Alliance (People's Front), the Federation of Syndicates, and the youth organizations. All are directed to dedicate their efforts to the fulfillment of planned output.

Workers as Managers

Since mid-1950 the Yugoslav Communists have proudly been telling the world that they have turned the factories over to the workers. But they have been careful to point out to their own people that this did not imply ownership by the workers. The workers were merely entrusted with managing economic enterprises on behalf of the people as a whole. Moreover, such management must be effected in conformity with basic laws, orders and instructions from competent governmental authorities.

Concretely, the responsibility for managing each factory or enterprise is vested in a workers' council, elected annually by the workers of the factory or enterprise. But the workers' council, averaging between 15 and 120 members and meeting infrequently, is not expected to perform the actual work of day-to-day management. The workers' council does, however, elect a management board which assists the manager in performing the day-to-day managerial tasks. The manager is chosen either by the responsible republican secretariat or the local people's committee, or, if the factory is a subsidiary of a larger economic association, by the parent organization. He is responsible both to the management board and to competent state organs. Presumably only the latter can remove him, for the management board and the workers' council have power only to propose his removal.

The substantive work of management is, by and large, performed by the manager. The members of the management board, of which the manager is an ex-officio member, draw up proposals for plans of the enterprise, prepare operational plans, and make other decisions to facilitate the smooth and productive functioning of the enterprise. For the most part, however, they neither have the time nor the know-how to enter into the technical questions of management. First of all they serve for only one year, and no more than a third are eligible for re-election, and in no case can a person serve for more than two consecutive years. Secondly, three-fourths of them must be workers who are actually engaged in production, and they are expected to carry on with their regular duties while serving as members of the management board. Under such circumstances, they can hardly be expected to have much time for over-all management problems. Finally, the manager is obligated to postpone execution of management board decisions where he believes them to be contrary to law or executive orders, and to report this fact to higher authority.

The members of the workers' councils, being even more removed from the actual scene of management, can expect to be even less prepared to pass judgment on the ways in which the enterprise is managed. At best, they can hope to hear reports, discuss proposals, and voice dissatisfactions. One highly placed Yugoslav Communist told me that the fundamental job of the workers' councils was to increase production and to improve the quality of the goods produced, thereby cutting costs and improving efficiency, which he said would result in a higher standard of living. Similar statements have also appeared in the Yugoslav press.[2]

Workers' Councils at Work

Making an estimate of the performance of Yugoslav workers' councils is far from easy. First of all, they have been in existence only a brief time. Secondly, sufficient facts about their functioning are not yet available. In the summer and fall of 1952 I was permitted to sit in on meetings of two different workers' councils, and I had an opportunity to talk privately with members and presidents of other workers' councils. The following estimate, therefore, is based principally on these firsthand observations.

When the workers' councils were first organized in 1950, lists of candidates were prepared by chapters of the Labor Syndicate Federation and the elections conducted by them, which means that the members were hand picked by Communist Party leaders. One worker, who referred to the workers' council as "a joke," told me that when the workers in his enterprise were assembled, the presiding officer called for nominations. A known party man arose and read off a list of names. Whereupon every-

[2] See *Borba,* September 4, 1952.

one applauded and that was the "election." At the Bor mining and smelting enterprise, the printed list of candidates was presented over the name of the local labor syndicate organization. One president of a workers' council pointed out to me that while Communists were in a minority among the workers, they often have a majority on the workers' councils—or at least representation all out of proportion to their numbers.

According to subsequent and amended instructions,[3] promulgated in 1952, future elections were to be conducted by an electoral commission chosen by workers' councils, and voting was to be for individual members instead of by lists. More than one list of candidates, either partial or complete, may be presented. Workers are to have all lists in front of them and may vote for candidates on all lists by circling the number in front of the names of the persons for whom they wish to vote.

Most Yugoslavs with whom I have talked about their workers' councils frequently made two observations. First, they contended that workers' councils did not have the power to make significant decisions. Secondly, they doubted that workers, even the more advanced American or Western European workers, had the ability or general training required for successful management. The Yugoslav press itself, while not granting the validity of the second point, has alluded to it numerous times. It has done so by pointing out that members of workers' councils were not sufficiently versed in financial affairs, and that special courses in economics were being organized for the workers.[4]

There can be little doubt that as of the present Yugoslav workers are far from qualified to shoulder the responsibilities of management. But from my observations, in most enterprises they do not yet possess the power to manage. They can discuss problems; they can offer suggestions; they can voice complaints, provided they are careful not to state or imply that political authorities are at fault, or that the tenets of Marxism or the program of the Yugoslav Communist Party are unreal; and they can make those decisions which the party believes wise or wants adopted. Many an ordinary worker can expect to be consulted occasionally, but he need not think that his opinions will be re-

[3] *Narodna drzhava* VI (Belgrade, No. 1–2, 1952), pp. 77–80.
[4] *Borba*, June 15, 1952.

spected. For the time being, his principal hope is that by working harder, conserving materials and producing better goods, he may perhaps earn a maximum of 10 per cent over his basic wage, although this is by no means assured.

In the meetings of the workers' councils which I attended, discussion was general and specific, and many suggestions and proposals were made. But there was no attempt to find out how the majority of the workers' council felt about any specific question or proposal. There were no formal motions, and no proposal was put to a vote. At the end of one discussion, the secretary briefly summed up what he judged to be the sense of the meeting on the basis of the discussion he had heard, although no more than one-fourth of the members had spoken. He then asked if it was acceptable. After a few scattered members declared, "It is accepted," the president turned to other matters. In another enterprise the procedure was the same, except that the president asked if anyone disagreed, but there was no dissent.

My observations were reinforced by what members of other workers' councils told me. One member, referring to the workers' council as a "comedy" and a "circus," asserted that the management board did not permit them to vote yes or no on proposals, and in some instances even consideration of a proposal was not allowed. A member of the council had pointed out, for example, that a certain commodity could be purchased from private sources for 1,500 dinars each, while their enterprise was paying another state enterprise 5,000 dinars for the same commodity. The manager told the workers' council that this implied proposal could not be considered, for it would be "contrary to the State Plan" and "not in harmony with the building of socialism."

The ex-president of another workers' council reported that when he was elected he considered himself "really somebody." But when one day he voiced his thoughts on the subject under discussion, men whom he knew to be Communists spoke up to say that his views were not in accord "with the directives we have received." When he persisted in his views, he was dismissed as president within twenty-four hours.

Similarly, the president of still another workers' council said that in his enterprise—and he believed this to be true elsewhere—actual management was still "in the hands of a few Communists."

When, for example, a manager had gone contrary to the wishes of the workers' council he told him that it was the manager's job to make decisions, and it was sufficient to report to the workers' council what those decisions had been.

The Yugoslav Communist press has on occasion criticized the arrogant managers and management boards who do not pay much attention to workers' councils.[5] They have been charged with making decisions without consulting the workers' council, and to have failed in reporting their decisions to the workers of the enterprises involved. Such official criticism is one way of dealing with recalcitrant party members in local enterprises who think they know more than their party superiors. It is, of course, also a way utilized by the party to tell rank-and-file workers that the party has their interests at heart.

In other instances, party leaders have noted that certain workers' councils assumed an independent attitude to the point of resenting all outside interference. New regulations, in preparation at this writing (summer, 1953), make it quite explicit that economic enterprises are responsible to society for the way in which they operate the facilities put at their disposal. Financial inspection commissions will act as overseers, and, in case of gross abuses, may recommend to the appropriate county or district people's committee the dismissal of the workers' council and the management board, or the ousting of the manager.[6]

Workers as Employees

Workers in Yugoslavia play a dual role. They are told that they have been chosen to manage their respective enterprises on behalf of society as a whole. But they are also workers, to whom food, clothing, shelter and other material elements in life are of no small consequence. Communists argue that there is no fundamental conflict in these two roles. If there were an abundance of material needs for all, perhaps their case might have some validity. But under present conditions, the conflict is very real, except that the workers are in no position to do anything about

[5] See *Borba,* June 7 and 14, 1952; *Politika,* April 8 and June 13, 1953.
[6] *Borba,* July 30, 1953.

it. If this conflict did not exist, the system would not require a tyrannical dictatorship to preserve it.

Yugoslav workers are organized, but not in the traditional trade union sense. Prewar labor unions were snuffed out and replaced by Soviet-type Communist syndicates. Yugoslav sources report that the total membership approximates 1,700,000, or nearly 80 per cent of all industrial and white-collar workers. Yugoslav officials insist that membership is voluntary, pointing out that only about 60 per cent of the workers in the mines, the forests and in the building trades belong to syndicates. One syndicate official told me that many of the workers in these pursuits were peasants who have only recently joined the ranks of the proletariat, and have not yet seen the need of joining syndicates.

In the metal and textile trades, however, this same official asserted, "proletarian consciousness" has resulted in a syndicate membership ranging from 90 to 96 per cent. Among the white-collar workers, he said, membership averages 95 per cent. All syndicate members pay dues amounting to about 1 per cent of their earnings.

As in the case of other Communist groupings, the organization of the syndicates is hierarchical, culminating in the National Council of Syndicates of Yugoslavia. Although no more than one worker out of ten is a member of the Communist Party, it is not unexpected that the Communists should play the major role in syndicate organizations. Or conversely, as Yugoslav officials put it, the "best members" of the syndicates become the leading candidates for party membership.

The traditional trade union functions, such as striking for higher pay and shorter hours, are not to be found in Yugoslav syndicates. This is not unexpected, the Communists point out, for since the people "own" the means of production, such activities would be aimed against the people themselves. It was interesting, however, that whenever non-Communist Yugoslav workers referred to this matter, their remarks always took a sarcastic twist.

Yugoslav syndicate officials with whom I talked were quite frank in stating that the principal function of the syndicates was to convey to the workers the general political line of the party.

Sometimes this function is euphemistically referred to as politico-ideological activities or educational-cultural work. One syndicate official, however, foresaw the need of a watchdog function should workers' councils, in their efforts to attain profits for their respective enterprises, violate such legal provisions as those which require certain safety standards and which prohibit discrimination against women and older men.

Some Facts and Problems of Management

Under the system which the Yugoslavs copied from the Soviet Union, management was concerned almost solely with producing the planned output. To do this, plants and enterprises had chiefly to worry about procuring sufficient raw materials and maintaining a labor force. They did not have to worry about the costs or about markets. The government supplied the raw materials, fixed wages, and took delivery of the finished product. Management did not trouble itself particularly about the quality of the goods produced, for it did not have the responsibility of selling or distributing them. Nor did management need to worry about an excessively large labor force or about maintaining large inventories of raw materials, where these things were possible, even though shortages resulted elsewhere as a consequence. And there was no need for concern about credit or interest rates.

During the first five years of the Tito regime, the government sought the answer to these problems in increased regimentation and centralized control. It is interesting to note how one of these problems — labor — was handled. From the outset, Yugoslav Communists were beset by a fluctuating labor supply, creating manpower shortages in certain sectors of the economy and thereby raising havoc with the economic plan. In order to stabilize the labor supply, the government embarked upon a series of measures.

Every worker was required to have a work booklet, without which he could not be employed.[7] This booklet would show if the laborer had left his previous job in accordance with regulations, and if not, he could not be employed. Every employer was

[7] *Politika,* March 17, 1949.

required to conclude a written work agreement with the prospective worker, and this agreement had to be registered with the manpower office within five days of its conclusion.

This effort, accompanied by decree after decree, reached its height in 1950 with the introduction of long-period labor contracts. Even "socialist competition" was introduced, with worker competing against worker to increase the length of their respective contracts. The press reported that in the motor industry contracts were concluded for periods of five, six, and even ten years.[8] "At the height of the competition," one paper reported, "it happened that workers destroyed contracts concluded earlier in the competition for briefer periods and entered into contracts for longer periods." [9]

Communist leaders stressed the "voluntary" nature of these contracts, but the Serbian ministry of labor, by announcing that workers who failed to sign written labor contracts by a specified time would not receive ration cards until they had done so,[10] revealed that compulsion was involved. The press joined to warn workers that "all violations of this contract on the part of the worker will be considered as economic sabotage." [11]

While the fact was not publicized, these contracts contained a clause permitting the transfer of workers. The reason was twofold. It was foreseen that workers would flock to sign labor contracts in locations they considered more desirable, while certain factories or enterprises for their part would grab up more manpower than they needed. Yet the complete control of manpower, which these contracts provided, not only proved unwieldly but also contributed to the growth of a largely unproductive bureaucracy.

Other decrees concerning labor made this fact even more evident. At one time, for example, elaborate measures were devised to deal with labor discipline problems. Unexcused absences from work were punished with progressively severe reductions in food and textile rations for the following month. An unexcused monthly absence of three to five days, by way of illustration, meant the loss of bread coupons for as many days as the worker

[8] *20 Oktobar,* February 18, 1950.
[9] *Ibid.*
[10] *Politika,* February 19, 1950.
[11] *20 Oktobar,* February 5, 1950.

was absent, all of his coffee ration for the month and one-fourth of his meat, sugar and fats ration.[12]

In dealing with labor problems, however, the government did not confine itself to decrees. It also maintained a persistent campaign in the press and through other propaganda channels. Skilled workers were reprimanded for wasting their talents in jobs which did not require their skills. Local enterprises were singled out and criticized for holding more men than the plan called for, and thereby denying them to heavy industry and mining. Private persons (e.g. makers of ashtrays) were accused of paying high wages and thereby attracting skilled workers from the socialist sector. This was said to constitute "speculating in manpower" and being engaged in "disloyal work against the interests of society." [13]

Similar stories might be recounted concerning the government's efforts to channel raw materials, to establish prices, and to solve the problem of distribution. Yet the above discussion of some of the government's efforts in dealing with the question of labor constitutes, it seems to me, a graphic illustration of the regimentation and the bureaucracy that are so much a part of centralized management.

This situation has been considerably altered by the changes which the Yugoslavs have made since 1950, and especially by those introduced during 1952 and 1953. Now management has to concern itself with most of the problems to which it devoted little or no attention in the past. This does not mean, however, that management has been left free, for it must continue to function within specified limits. The declared basic principle is that an enterprise is expected to make a profit. But various national and local taxes, interest rates on capital, etc., will serve to narrow the possibility for net profits. On the other hand, the government assures a certain stability in the cost structure by determining in large measure the basic wage scale and a certain constancy in the price of raw materials. What the new system means, therefore, is that the factory or enterprise, by cutting costs, producing good quality goods and in general operating efficiently, possesses the possibility of making a limited profit.

[12] *Politika,* May 12, 1949.
[13] *Politika,* February 14, 1949. See also *Partiski radnik,* April 1, 1949.

In calculating planned costs, industries and individual enterprises must take into account manpower and materials costs, interest on fixed and circulating capital, depreciation and national and local taxes. Some of the more detailed information which Yugoslav authorities have handed out about these problems is not always clear or consistent. In the summer of 1952, for example, the price of raw materials was declared to be decontrolled. Yet a highly placed Communist in the Economic Council told me that individual enterprises, in making their plans, could put a price tag on the needed raw materials, for they would be in a position to know what the price would be.

Moreover, when I sought to find out what rate of interest economic enterprises would have to pay for credit extended to them by the National Bank, I received varied answers. One responsible official in the Economic Council told me that the general interest rate was low, "about one and one-half per cent." Another official in the same Council told me that it was between 2 and 3 per cent. When I asked the first official if enterprises had to pay a "penalty interest" on credit funds requested but not used, he appeared surprised that I should ask such a question. After regaining his composure, he replied in the affirmative, explaining that a charge of this type was justified on the ground that such funds "were blocked and consequently denied to other potential users." When I asked about the rate of this "penalty interest," he said it was 3 per cent. The second official to whom I had talked told me that it was "six per cent or so."

On the other hand, a member of one workers' council insisted that the normal rate of interest in his enterprise was 7 per cent. And on credits not used up at the end of a month, they had to pay a "penalty interest" of 22 per cent. Consequently, the last few days of every month found them scurrying to spend their unused credits in order to avoid the penalty.

In the matter of wages, however, the picture is much clearer. In theory, the workers' council in each economic enterprise determines the basic wage rates. It prepares a set of so-called "wage rules," which must have the approval of the responsible labor syndicate committee. What this means is that the party-controlled Yugoslav Labor Syndicate Federation has established a fairly uniform country-wide wage scale for various types of jobs. And its subsidiary committees will certainly reject any set of "wage rules" which attempt a significant departure from it. In enterprises which have jobs that have not lent themselves to the establishment of a uniform wage scale, however, the workers' council will possess greater authority in setting the wage rates.

Some Yugoslav workers are paid by the hour, others in accordance with piece rates, and some by the month. All administrative personnel is paid on the basis of a monthly salary. Provision is also made for overtime pay, with the normal work week, as a general rule, being forty-eight hours, based on 208 hours as the normal work month.

Enterprises making a net profit may distribute any amount of such net profit to the workers as supplementary wages. But if the total wages received by the workers exceed the national average by more than 10 per cent, the enterprise must pay a progressively steep tax on that part which exceeds 10 per cent.[14] The national monthly average in the summer of 1952 was declared to be 9,000 dinars per month. For the purposes of calculating this tax, however, the minister of finance (in agreement with the Economic Council) was empowered to increase this average by as much as 25 per cent in certain branches or groups of enterprises. If, on the other hand, an enterprise should have insufficient funds to pay its workers, after it has met its other obligations, the government undertakes to guarantee 80 per cent of the basic wage to which the workers are entitled. This, however, is in the form of a loan from the national bank which the enterprise is obligated to pay back as soon as its wage fund rises above the 80 per cent minimum.[15]

Management also needs to be concerned about income. Preliminary contracts with prospective buyers, chiefly other state enterprises, provide the basis for calculating planned income. Contrary to past practice, supply and demand are supposed to determine prices. But it would seem evident from what has already been said that the government, by and large, determines costs (including wages), and thereby to no small degree controls supply and demand. The government is also the largest buyer. Moreover, Yugoslav enterprises have not been permitted to

[14] *Sluzhbeni list,* June 27, 1952.
[15] *Borba,* July 30, 1953.

engage in price competition with one another either domestically or in foreign trade. When enterprises have offered different prices to foreign buyers they have been severely taken to task.[16]

Unsold goods also present a problem to management, for large inventories mean large interest payments for added working capital which is needed. Some managers who in the past had no idea of how much money their respective enterprises were spending, in 1952 complained of large inventories.[17] Yugoslavia's economic chiefs have told them publicly that insofar as the reason was not poor quality they should not worry, because a satisfactory inventory of goods was desirable. In 1953, government leaders were still insisting that reserves of goods were low. In view of the fact that production was not increasing, they said, the government would seek to increase them by decreasing purchasing power through the tax on wage funds.[18]

Decentralized management has also created other problems. "Particularism" has reared its head. Republics, cities and localities are jealously watching each other for signs of favoritism. In the more wealthy areas resentment has been in evidence even among some Communists against being taxed to aid the economically poorer regions. Although government leaders have spoken out against such manifestations of local selfishness, it is interesting that "particularism" was to be found among party members, to say nothing of the population at large.

Decentralization of economic enterprises has also given rise to the problem of responsibility in cases of bankruptcy. Under centralized management the national government prevented bankruptcy by subsidies from the state treasury. Since enterprises have been put on their own, however, the creditors (other state enterprises) have suffered, while directors and the workers' councils of defunct enterprises have apparently escaped responsibility.[19]

The decision to abandon the rate of accumulation as a means of guiding economic development along desired lines will without doubt result in many new problems yet unforeseen. It has already been admitted that perhaps the most immediate problem

[16] See *Naprijed* (Zagreb), August 29, 1952.
[17] *Borba,* August 17, 1952.
[18] See interview with Svetozar Vukmanovich-Tempo, *Borba,* June 9, 1953.
[19] *Borba,* June 29, 1953.

will be that of revising the whole accounting and bookkeeping system in state economic enterprises. In view of past difficulties with the present involved and complicated system, this is likely to be anything but a simple matter.

Direct Government Intervention

It hardly need be said that direct governmental intervention at any point is always possible. Yugoslav Communist leaders can always find a legal peg, or if need be make one, on which to hang desired decisions. This becomes strikingly evident under abnormal conditions, such as those created by the drought in the summer of 1952. Under the system then prevailing, prices were supposed to be determined by the producers. Yet a highly placed Communist in the Yugoslav foreign office told me that reductions in the price of bread in the late summer of 1952 were ordered by the government as a "psychological measure," designed "to quiet fears which might arise as a result of the drought." Three months later the Yugoslav Economic Council not only raised the price of bread, flour and other food products but also decreed that only one grade of flour could be milled for bread.

Similarly, when the price of meat began to fall as a result of increased slaughtering of livestock by peasants who did not have sufficient fodder, Yugoslavia's economic chief, Kidrich, declared: "We must keep the price of meat at the present level." [20] To accomplish this, the government decreed a ban on the export of fodder, lowered freight rates for the internal transport of stock feed, and resorted to a number of other measures.[21] Nonagricultural enterprises were told, for example, that they must seek to increase their exports. Nearly all of these activities of the national government could be expected to upset the calculation of the local managements affected.

That government regulations about economic decentralization may be misleading was also dramatically illustrated in the case of foreign trade in general. In the summer of 1952, economic enterprises were told that they might independently spend

[20] *Borba,* August 17, 1952.
[21] *Naprijed,* August 29, 1952.

45 per cent of the foreign exchange earned as a result of export-ing their products.[22] Elaborate customs regulations, however, narrowed the choice of products for which the money might be spent. If, for example, a factory was tempted to buy a passenger automobile, it would have to pay a customs tax equivalent to four times the price of the car. The same was true of refrigerators. The customs fee on trucks, however, was one and one-half times the price of the truck.

But the government could evade even these regulations. In October of 1952, the Economic Council, in order to overcome the serious effects of the drought on Yugoslavia's foreign trade balance, declared a six-month import ban on some one hundred items. In effect, the government was nullifying its own previously established regulations concerning foreign trade. More recently a promise has been held out to enterprises that in the future they could independently spend approximately 30 per cent of their foreign exchange earnings.[23]

In seeking an explanation to the workings of their economic system, my questions did not always evoke illuminating replies from Yugoslav leaders. I was several times amused, for example, by statements of important Yugoslav Communists that the various segments of their economy operated not unlike American corpo-rations with their officers, boards of directors and annual meet-ings of stockholders. But one Communist in the Economic Coun-cil was quite candid. He said more and more initiative was being given local units, for otherwise "you would need a perfect sys-tem," and this they did not have. No doubt there will be much hit and miss, he observed, but "through trial and error enter-prises will need to discover how to manage."

It would be unreal, therefore, to expect that the economic arrangements described above will remain in existence for long. In an effort to extricate themselves from the economic morass which they have created and in which they constantly find them-selves, the Yugoslav Communist rulers are engaged in making frequent changes. One of the things which they stressed most in 1951 and 1952, for example, was that enterprises should be solvent, that they should make a profit. In mid-1953, however,

[22] *Politika,* June 20, 1952.
[23] See Vukmanovich interview, *Borba,* June 2, 1953.

one of Tito's close collaborators asserted that enterprises engaged in commerce and trade should not attempt to make money.[24] Rather, they should "strive to give the consumer cheaper goods." They should just cover their expenses. Wherein lies the incentive, one might ask, for workers engaged in commerce to improve their lot, at a time when workers in other enterprises are told that their one hope for higher wages is for their enterprises to make a profit?

Similarly, Yugoslav Communist leaders have since 1950 made much of having turned the factories over to the workers. They have said that the principal incentive for efficient management was the possibility of the enterprises' using some of their profits as supplementary wages. By mid-1953, however, there were a number of indications that pressure was being exerted to have enterprises spend such funds elsewhere. The press reported that various enterprises in the Tusla basin had, in response to appeals from the people's committees, relinquished their rights to funds from 1952 profits which had been intended as supplementary wages.[25] Instead, the money would be spent for the purchase of machinery and similar other needs of the enterprises.

The Communists can argue, as they no doubt will, that since the workers are represented in the people's committees, through the councils of producers, the wishes of the people's committees are the wishes of the workers. Could it be that the councils of producers were devised as a technique for preventing the workers' councils from asserting the authority which they theoretically possess? It seems fairly clear that workers' councils will be free to make decisions as long as the party thinks they are the "right" decisions. Otherwise there will be interference to prevent or to change decisions which the party deems "incorrect." [26]

Recent developments tend to confirm the party's continuing active and predominant role in the economic field, as in all others. The failure to take sufficient account of this fact has led some students of the Yugoslav economy astray. Experts of the International Monetary Fund, for example, predicted that under Yugoslavia's "new" economic system "the state will have a less

[24] See Vukmanovich interview, *Borba*, June 9, 1953.

[25] See *Politika* and *Borba*, July 2, 1953.

[26] See the economic commentary in *Borba*, July 4, 1953. For some concrete examples, see *Borba*, September 29, 1953 and *Politika*, October 2, 1953.

significant role to play," that the "government will not interfere with the current performance of an enterprise, but will . . . exercise a general, though infrequent, control," and that "a large share" of the profits of an enterprise will go into wages.[27] Items appearing in the Yugoslav press, to say nothing of unofficial private sources, would seem to contradict these conclusions. Such studies are to be criticized, however, less for their conclusions than for their admitted, seemingly uncritical, acceptance of "official estimates" and official versions of the facts. It is stated, for example, that the "supply of consumer goods was reduced by the consequences of the 'blockade' of Yugoslavia by the Cominform countries. . . ." [28] Anyone who spent some time in Yugoslavia before as well as after the break with Moscow knows that the shortage of consumer goods was, if anything, more acute *before* the Cominform "blockade." It is hoped that studies currently being made by members of the United Nations technical assistance mission will employ a more critical approach and be less ready to accept at face value the statements of Tito's "experts."

[27] J. V. Mladek, E. Sturc, and M. R. Wyczalkowski, "The Change in the Yugoslav Economic System," *Staff Papers,* II (November, 1952), pp. 407–38.
[28] *Ibid.,* p. 421.

Chapter 21:

Agriculture

RELATIVELY small private landholdings have long characterized Yugoslav agriculture. A country the bulk of whose people are even today engaged in agricultural pursuits, Yugoslavia has had few feudal landed estates. Most of these were to be found in areas formerly under Austro-Hungarian rule, and, by and large, broken up by the agrarian reform laws which followed the establishment of Yugoslavia as a nation, following the First World War.

Although Yugoslavia has suffered from agrarian overpopulation, land was fairly evenly distributed. The pre-World War II Communist position was that the bulk of the land was in the hands of the *kulaks* and the church and that the man who worked the land did not possess it. After being in power for a time, however, they did not hesitate to admit that less than 25 per cent of the land had been in parcels of fifty acres or more. Or that less than 10 per cent had been in holdings exceeding 125 acres. In their own words, "over 50 per cent of the land belonged to the poor or middle peasant who had less than ten hectares" [1] (approximately twenty-five acres).

Nevertheless, Yugoslav Communists have not let these or any other facts interfere with their determination to collectivize agriculture. While they may execute strategic retreats, modify their tempo or vary their methods, the party's policy of ultimate collectivization remains firm.[2] This is the central point to remem-

---

[1] See Kidrich's report to the party's Fifth Congress, *Borba,* July 27, 1948.
[2] See Mijalko Todorovich's article, "Concerning the Labor Co-operative," in *Komunist* (Belgrade), No. 1–2, 1952, (in Serbo-Croatian). Also Tito's speech, *Politika,* September 28, 1953.

ber about Yugoslav agriculture so long as the Communists remain in power. In the unlikely event that this basic policy is
reversed, it will then be possible to speak about an ideological
transformation in Yugoslav Communism.

Early Agricultural Policies

As in other spheres of activity, so in agriculture, impatient
Yugoslav Communists were resolved to telescope Soviet experience. They did not want to wait until some ten years after
the revolution, as did the Russians, before embarking upon full-
scale collectivization. Perhaps—aware that the task was not to
be an easy one—they nevertheless set in motion a whole series of
measures, implemented with utter ruthlessness, calculated to
propel Yugoslavia rapidly down the road to Soviet-type collectivized agriculture.

As a first step, the Titoists confiscated many acres of fertile
land belonging to the German minority (Volksdeutsche), some
of whose members had fled with the retreating Nazi forces, while
those who remained behind were "resettled," presumably some-
where in the Soviet Union. This step was justified on the ground
that the Volksdeutsche had collaborated with the enemy, and
some no doubt had. Many additional fertile acres were confiscated from other alleged collaborators, but often the charges
were unproved, and sometimes no effort was made to prove them.

Augmenting the confiscation of land, a Communist agrarian
reform law relieved the churches of most of their lands, as well
as the agricultural holdings of absentee owners. Moreover, approximately eighty-five acres was fixed as the maximum size of
private landholdings. Since this maximum was considerably
above the existing average, and in view of the fact that land was
already fairly widely distributed, it was evident that the Communist agrarian reform was not aimed at a more equitable distribution of land. Rather, it was motivated by a desire to take
what the churches and a few wealthy men possessed, with the
intent of rewarding some of the deserving Communist Partisan
supporters.

On the lands acquired through confiscation and through the
agrarian reform law, the government established some state

farms and a number of so-called labor co-operatives (collectives). The former, with the state as owner and the peasant as wage earner, were patterned after state farms in the Soviet Union. Similarly, the latter were an imitation of Soviet collective farms. Most of the peasants who came to work on these farms were settled there by the government. First priority went to deserving members of Tito's Partisan army, to orphans of those who fell while fighting for Tito and others who had in some way contributed to the Communist successes. Most of these people came from the mountainous regions of Bosnia-Herzegovina and Montenegro where arable land is scarce and of poor quality.

The most impalatable of Tito's early agricultural policies was the system of compulsory deliveries. Under this system, the private peasant was obligated to sell his surplus produce to the government at the latter's price, which was so pathetically low as to constitute confiscation. What was worse, government agents determined the extent of each peasant's surplus, which often exceeded actual yield. This was particularly true in the case of the more well-to-do peasant, who, in typical Soviet fashion, was labeled a *kulak*. In actuality, many peasants thus labeled were not well to do at all. They merely possessed a few more of the necessities of life than did some of the others. Tito once said that the amount of land possessed by a peasant was not a good criterion for deciding if he were a *kulak* but rather whether he is "for a socialist Yugoslavia, whether he wants to work sincerely in a labor co-operative." [3]

In assessing surpluses, local Communist functionaries paid no attention to that provision of the law which stated that a man was supposed to be left sufficient produce for his own family needs. Time after time, peasants had to turn over their whole yield to the government, and where the yield was insufficient to meet the government-assessed "surplus," they had to sell a cow or in some other way procure money, in order to buy additional grain on the open market, at fantastically high prices, only to turn it over to the government at a small fraction of its cost. That is, of course, if they wanted to stay out of prison. And after this obligation was met there was still the problem of buying food on the open market to feed their families.

[3] *Borba,* August 6, 1949.

Surplus quotas were proclaimed on all sorts of farm produce —bread grains, meat, fats, potatoes, wool, grapes, honey, sugar beets, and even such things as horsetails, pumpkin seeds and cow horns. Local Communists in large measure determined the "surplus" of each peasant on the basis of personal whim. They knew each peasant from the past. If they knew a peasant to have been poor, they might assess him low. If, on the other hand, they knew a peasant to have prospered through hard work, frugality or whatnot, they would purposely assess him beyond any possible yield, forcing him to sell his belongings in order to meet his "surplus quota." Peasants were even assessed "surplus quotas" of products which they did not grow or produce.

Typical of the way the Titoists worked was their seizure of "surplus" hogs in the summer of 1948. Early one morning government agents came to the peasants in each village and took all pigs in excess of two. The peasants were given receipts, and the hogs were to be paid for at later date, at prices set by the government and, as it turned out, in highly inflated currency. The bane of the Yugoslav economy, Kidrich, described this action unashamed when he said in parliament, "we *took away* over 300,-000 hogs from the kulaks." [4]

In addition to the system of compulsory deliveries, private peasants were beaten down in other ways. They were told what and how much to plant, and when to plant it. And where compulsory deliveries were not impoverishing the peasant rapidly enough, exceedingly high property taxes were imposed, and often made retroactive. All of these measures were carried out with impunity and with no regard for due process, the privacy of the home, or any other commonly accepted standards of decency. The object of these actions was to impoverish the peasant, bring him down to a common level, degrade him and destroy him morally—and then collectivize him.

Some Consequences of Early Policies

As might be expected, these policies met with peasant opposition. It was obvious to the peasants that so long as compulsory deliveries continued they would, in effect, be producing food for

[4] *Borba,* December 29, 1948. Italics mine.

the government with no compensation. Since there was no motive to produce, they reasoned, why plant above a bare minimum? Consequently, acreages were sharply reduced and the total agricultural yield for the country went down markedly.

The Communists, not willing to recognize their errors, reacted to peasant opposition in a typically arrogant and ruthless fashion. They continued to impose high "surplus quotas" which further infuriated the peasants. While permitting the authorities to take their total yield, many of them refused or were unable to raise money to buy grain to meet the remainder of the quota. The government's answer was chains, imprisonment, and forced labor camps. Those who sought unsuccessfully to hide some of their produce received even harsher treatment.

Many a peasant in forced labor camps died from cold, exposure and a starvation diet. Countless others suffered untold miseries and indescribable hardships. There is scarcely a peasant household in all of Yugoslavia that has not felt the cruel hand of Communist injustice, either directly or indirectly through close relatives.

Through it all, however, most of them have assumed a stoical attitude. They were convinced that in the long run they could not lose. Illustrative of this attitude is the case of a peasant who was serving a prison term for having failed to deliver as much grain as he had been ordered to do. When his cellmate asked him the length of his sentence, he replied, "Life." His astonished fellow prisoner inquired how this was possible. It was very simple, the peasant observed, he had been sentenced for a year, but since he was not working his land and since his wife could do very little, he was sure that the next year's quota could not be met and he would again be sentenced to another year—and so on for the remainder of his life!

But the Communists were not content with punitive actions against "unco-operative" peasants. The decline in agricultural output had to be faced. To meet it, the Communists decided to accelerate collectivization at all costs. Peasants were promised everything under the sun if they would create collective farms. Those in difficulties with the authorities, because of failure to deliver grain or other "surpluses," were told that their "sins" would be forgiven if they would agree to join in creating the so-called labor co-operatives. In some areas threats of and/or actual imprisonment were utilized. In some cases physical beatings and threats against life and limb were freely employed. In other instances, families who refused to set up collective farms were driven from their land without being allowed to take anything with them.

To make the lot of the independent peasants more difficult, local Communist functionaries required them to participate in various so-called voluntary work projects. Often they were taken away at critical periods, when it was time to sow or when their crops needed attention. If they had work horses, oxen or mules, they were requested to bring them. Peasants who lost draft animals on such jobs (through broken legs, etc.) were, of course, in no way compensated.

Most of the methods which the Yugoslav Communists have utilized to implement their agricultural policies, although their existence was vehemently denied during the years when they were most frequently employed (1947–1951), have more recently been admitted, either directly or inferentially.[5] These admissions came, in the main, after the agricultural crisis of 1951 had been weathered.

Collectivized Agriculture in Operation

By the end of 1952 between 25 and 30 per cent of Yugoslavia's agricultural lands were within the "socialist sector" of the economy. Approximately four-fifths of this acreage was in the so-called peasant labor co-operatives (collectives), while the various state farms constituted about one-fifth of the total. In addition, local people's committees controlled nearly four million acres of pasture lands.

The state farms are owned and operated by the government. They are worked by farm laborers who are ordinary wage earners. As in the case of their Soviet prototypes, Yugoslav state farms aimed at introducing and popularizing mechanization and systematic fertilization. They sought to develop new and better plant varieties. They were also designed as showpieces of Communist planning. Large sums of money were expended in the

[5] See Vladimir Bakarich's speech, *Naprijed*, April 18, 1952.

erection of model buildings and other improvements. At the same time, there was a serious deficiency in trained personnel to operate the farms. Consequently, few of the state farms are going concerns in the sense of making a profit. Most of them are in the red, but the government is in a position to cancel their debts at any time it sees fit to do so.

The peasant labor co-operatives were declared to be the ultimate goal for Yugoslav agriculture. Ostensibly, they were designed to be flexible in order to fit the regional environmental needs as well as the temperament of the different peasant groups. Four categories were established, each progressively approaching the Soviet *Kolkhoz* (collective farm), of which category four was an exact copy. In the first three categories the peasant theoretically retained title to his land, and in the case of the first two he was to receive land rental.

In practice, however, enthusiastic local party functionaries pushed for full and complete collectivization along the lines of category four. Few co-operatives were created of the types prescribed in the first three categories. Moreover, in the case of those corresponding to the first two, rent was either not paid or only a token rent payment was made.[6] Hence, all peasant labor co-operatives, of whatever category, were essentially alike in practice.

They were alike, too, in that most of them were created against the will of the peasants, although Yugoslav leaders were at the time insisting that they were being set up on a voluntary basis. As in the case of so many other of their programs, Yugoslav Communists at a later date admitted what we who were there knew to be taking place at the time. No less a figure than Tito has admitted that even the poor peasants to whom they gave land did not want to form collective farms. Even they, according to Tito, "wanted to live a while first." [7]

In a peasant labor co-operative land, except for domestic plots of an acre or two, is held in common and decisions concerning its operation are allegedly made by governing bodies selected by the membership. A popularly elected assembly theoretically makes the basic decisions, although an examination

[6] See *Borba* editorial, July 20, 1952.
[7] *Borba*, February 27, 1950.

of the minutes of some of them did not reveal that they had exercised this power. Testimony from members of different labor co-operatives tended to confirm the hypothesis that the assembly does no more than rubber-stamp the decisions of the management board and the director of the co-operative. More recently there have been official admissions that these assemblies have in the past been "only a formality." [8]

The assembly "elects" the management board. The director of the co-operative, in the words of a responsible Communist dealing with agriculture, "is the commander who carries out the decisions of the management board." In addition, there is a supervisory committee, whose job it is to keep an eye on finances and on co-operative operations in general.

Specific statutes and decrees prescribe the manner in which labor co-operatives are to function. It was no secret, however, that they were in the main run by Communist Party members in accordance with party instructions which they received. While some of these were in the form of secret directives, many of them were issued publicly through official government channels. Their nature is partially revealed by listing the names of a few of them:

"Decree on granting credits to and supplying of peasant labor co-operatives."
"Decree on wages of workers on state-owned and co-operative-owned agricultural estates."
"Order on the regulation of livestock slaughtering."
"Decree on disciplinary and material responsibility of the employees of co-operative organizations."
"Instruction on keeping of books by labor co-operatives."
"Decision on the alterations in and amendments to the decision governing the sale and purchase of wine, potatoes, olive oil, rice and dried cherries — 1948 crop."

These are but a sample of literally thousands of orders, instructions, decisions and decrees governing some aspect of Yugoslav economic life, most of which have been either repealed or replaced by subsequent directives.

As in industry, so in agriculture, the central government formulates the basic plans and sets the general targets. Individual co-operatives, however, have more independence than heretofore

[8] *Politika,* April 5, 1953.

in planning their output and in the adaptation of management and production techniques. Yet agricultural planning is in some ways more precarious than planning in industry. More factors have to be taken into account, one of which is, of course, the weather. The yearly, quarterly, and monthly plans consist of the following four general plans: production plan, price plan, financial plan, investment plan. The production plan includes livestock and plant production, as well as auxiliary activities (blacksmithing, carpentry, etc.). Included are such items as a feeding plan for livestock, a wine production plan, etc. In the price plan are included such items as an estimate of the cost of one tractor work day, an estimate of livestock production costs, an estimate of warehouse costs. The financial plan includes plans for distribution of products, wages, income and expenditure. The investment plan involves both material and financial costs.

As one reads the instructions for preparing agricultural plans which are sent to labor co-operatives, one cannot but be impressed by the all-embracing and detailed nature of the plans, to say nothing of the bewilderment they no doubt create. Occasionally, there is an amusing note. Livestock plans, for example, include not only milk production, breeding, and estimated weight accretion of young animals, but also the production of manure by work horses, including accretion in manure production as young horses continue to grow.

While labor co-operatives were being told in late 1951 and in early 1952 that they would have more independence in planning and in the operation of their establishments, they were also informed that they must go on a profit and loss basis. For most of them this would have been difficult because they were in considerable debt to the government for capital construction loans. To make their burden easier, and in a way to give them a fresh start, the government in the late summer of 1951 canceled these debts, amounting to eight and one-half billion dinars. Thus one great hurdle was removed, but that co-operatives would continue to need financial assistance from the government was evident to all.

In the fall of 1952, the Yugoslav Economic Council reported total credits to co-operatives for the year would amount to over ten billion dinars.[9] Four billions of this total were for the purchase of agricultural machinery, and nearly three billions were earmarked for completion of capital construction projects, including dwelling units. Most of the remainder was set aside for buying livestock. These would be long-term credits with an interest rate of 2 per cent. Loans to buy livestock are to be repaid in five years, while loans for the development of orchards and vineyards would be due in twenty years. Building construction credits need not be repaid for thirty years. To make sure that the loans would be repaid, the government has instructed each co-operative to set aside in a special fund a certain portion of its annual earnings.

Labor co-operatives were instructed in 1952 to abandon the Soviet methods which they had "inherited" and which were admittedly a failure. Instead of having the brigade leader appointed by the management board, for example, they were told that the results would be more satisfactory if he were chosen by the farm workers. Also discouraged were references to brigades, with the term "labor group" used in its place.[10] Moreover, labor co-operatives were told to pay their members in wages. Instead of waiting until the end of the year to be paid, as heretofore, each co-operative member is given a monthly advance on his basic wage. At the end of the year he receives the balance plus a share of the net undivided profits in proportion to his basic wage. Simultaneously, the previous plan of extending all sorts of loans to members was abolished except in special circumstances.[11]

Finally, labor co-operatives in all four categories were told that hereafter they must pay rent,[12] ranging between 15 and 30 per cent of their income after deduction of the amounts which go into the various funds. Although admitting the capitalistic nature of rent, Yugoslav Communists defended their decision on practical grounds. First of all, many older members who can no longer work would be provided social security in the form of rent, instead of being neglected and forced to "beg for aid." [13]

[9] *Borba,* September 3, 1952.
[10] *Ibid.,* September 5, 1952.
[11] *Ibid.*
[12] *Ibid.,* also see *Politika,* August 17, 1952.
[13] See *Borba* editorial, August 7, 1952.

Also private peasants who otherwise might be inclined to join co-operatives will be deterred from doing so if rent is not paid. In addition, nonpayment of rent would have the effect of slowing down the development of socialist relations in the co-operatives. In other words, the payment of rent might appease at least some of the dissatisfied co-operative members.

This decision, although it may have pleased some members, met with considerable opposition from others. Party members objected to it on narrow ideological grounds, while the poorer peasants asserted that they had joined the co-operatives "in order that we should all be equal." [14] If rent is paid, they argued, the richer peasants who brought in more land would "live on someone else's labor." A "fair number of co-operative members," according to the party press, simply "look upon the paying of rent as a loss of acquired privileges." [15] Party leaders attributed these attitudes to the "remnants of the *kolkhoz* theory" which was widely known, while the "theoretical elaboration of our road to socialism has not made strong headway in the villages." [16]

The opposition was apparently strong enough, however, to get the government to modify its stand. Co-operatives were subsequently told that "a portion of the rent" would be paid into "the co-operative's basic fund," while the balance would be divided among the members in proportion to the land which they brought into the co-operative.[17] What proportion of the rent would go into the basic fund and what part would be distributed was not revealed.

Independent peasants who sought to comply with the government's collectivization policy, while at the same time seeking to avoid everyday Communist interference in their affairs, were in for a rude shock. By taking the initiative in creating labor co-operatives on a truly voluntary basis, they succeeded in infuriating the Communists, who viewed this as an effort on the part of "the rich peasants" to create co-operatives "without poor peasants and of course without Communists." To them a labor co-operative without Communists was "a purely capitalistic or-

[14] *Ibid.,* also see *Borba* editorial, July 20, 1952.
[15] *Borba* (Zagreb edition), August 27, 1952.
[16] See *Borba* editorial, August 7, 1952.
[17] *Borba,* September 5, 1952.

ganization" and, warned the minister of agriculture, "we will never permit their organization anywhere." [18]

Strategic Retreat—1951–52

During most of 1951 the Yugoslav Communists faced an acute agricultural crisis. Thousands of peasants, after being members of collective farms for three years, petitioned to leave, as was their legal right under the terms of the agreements by which they joined. The government, of course, could not see its basic agricultural policy collapse, and therefore sought to prevent disruption of the collectives. The peasants, as a consequence, refused to work or did so little work as to endanger the whole season's harvest. Private peasants, too, joined in what seems to have been a country-wide effort to impede or slow down the grain harvest. Only after the critical situation was well past did the Communists admit the seriousness or the widespread nature of the threat to their whole collectivization program.[19]

That the Communist leaders would not permit withdrawal from the collectives was already evident in 1948. In that year many peasants sought to withdraw from the collective farms created by impatient local party leaders immediately at the end of World War II. In one such collective the peasants were told that they could withdraw, provided they paid their individual shares of the collective's indebtedness (credits for capital construction, cost of seed for three years, taxes which individual peasants would have paid if they had not been members, etc.). Since each peasant's share was calculated to be over 100,000 dinars, and since no peasant could hope to have even a fraction of this amount, none was able to withdraw.

The 1951 attempt of peasants to leave collective farms, although legal, was cruelly suppressed. Many peasants, as well as the lawyers who drew up their petitions, were arrested, tried and convicted on charges of antistate activities. In some instances peasants who desired to withdraw were physically beaten by Communist goon squads. In others they were told to take their

[18] *Borba,* March 2, 1949.
[19] See *Naprijed,* December 14, 1951.

withdrawal petitions to the local UDB (secret police) office! Lawyers were publicly warned that they would be considered enemies of the people if they persisted in drawing up petitions for peasants who desired to leave collectives.[20] In July of 1952, a number of lawyers were given prison terms simply because they had advised peasants as to their legal rights in the matter of withdrawing from collectives.[21]

In the summer of 1952 I asked the man in charge of agriculture in the Yugoslav Economic Council about peasant efforts in the preceding year to leave collective farms. His answer was brief and to the point. With perfect equanimity, he said: "We forbade it by administrative measures." Without denying that the government had violated its promise to the peasants that they could leave at the end of three years if they wished, he argued that the government could not permit the destruction of something which was desired and which was just in the process of formation.

After reflecting upon the crisis, the party high command adopted what appeared to be at least four rather distinct decisions.[22] First, the policy of extending collectivization was reaffirmed. Secondly, it was determined that existing collectives should be strengthened by abandoning Soviet-type management and making other internal reforms, by permitting them to acquire, through a type of eminent domain power, adjoining private lands judged to be necessary to the efficient functioning of the collective, and by disbanding those where conditions were not favorable. Thirdly, the decision was made to resurrect the so-called general-type co-operative, which they had previously condemned, as a useful way station to ultimate collectivization. Finally, it was decided to abolish compulsory deliveries, and to concentrate upon punitive taxation as the most effective weapon in the war against the private peasant.

These decisions constituted at once a reaffirmation of the ultimate goal and a strategic retreat. But party leaders were quick to point out that there was no retreat, only the utilization of different methods. They were no less convinced than before in

[20] *Borba*, August 24, 1951.
[21] *Ibid.*, July 13, 1952.
[22] *Naprijed*, April 18, 1952. See also the dispatches of M. S. Handler, *New York Times*, November 18 and 19, 1951; January 3, 1952.

the wisdom of ultimate collectivization. They were not going to permit withdrawal from collectives, although they would take the initiative in dissolving or reorganizing those in the unproductive areas. They recognized that Soviet-type management had proved to be extremely unpopular, and they would inaugurate the necessary changes to eliminate the sources of dissatisfaction within collectives.

The decision to abolish compulsory deliveries was a retreat, at least psychologically, for it was perhaps the most hated of Tito's agricultural policies. For the peasant this was more of an illusion than a reality. Psychologically, he felt better, but since there could be no private trading in agricultural produce his only substantial market was the government.

The general-type co-operative was the institution through which the peasant would market his produce. It was also the place where he would purchase the merchandise which he needed. Although principally a buying-marketing institution, the general-type co-operative was designed, as one important party leader said to me, "to help the peasant see what is good for him." To do this, the co-operative would engage in developing seed cultures, in improving stock breeding, and perhaps in sponsoring such common endeavors as a creamery, a flour mill, and agricultural machines for general use.

Rather than a retreat, the general-type co-operative, although permitting private ownership of land, livestock, etc., emphasized collective effort. It was, in essence, an experiment to ascertain whether agricultural production could be increased through this type of collective undertaking. Certainly, it could not be considered more than a way station on the road to complete collectivization. Circumstances, such as the need of a market outlet, have forced most private peasants into at least a nominal membership in the general-type co-operative.

A responsible Communist in the Yugoslav Economic Council told me quite frankly that it was a mistake to make any sharp distinctions between their co-operatives, i.e. between the general-type co-operative and the peasant labor co-operative (collective). They are all moving along the same road, he declared, and there is one common goal—the collective nature of agricultural production. He did not believe that this necessarily implied uniform

collective farms or an identical type of farm organization
throughout the country. But it did mean, he emphasized, collective farming of one type or another as opposed to individualized
private farming.

Most private peasants, however, interpreted the changes as a
sign of weakness. Some believed that the changes were the result
of pressure exerted by the Western Powers who were extending
aid to Yugoslavia. Others viewed the changes as an indication
of the inevitable collapse of the Communist system. For most of
them, their heavy burden was psychologically lifted, but only
momentarily. The government tax assessors did not let them
forget that the party was uncompromising and determined in its
efforts to liquidate them as private producers.

Some local party bosses interpreted the instructions on punitive taxation a bit too literally, and in many areas in early 1952
sought to put independent peasants out of business with one
single tax assessment. One peasant told me that his taxes had
been raised from 20,000 dinars in 1950 to 120,000 dinars in
1951. And in spite of the severe drought in 1952, the government had made three quarterly collections of his 1952 taxes at
the 1951 rate. Another peasant related how his taxes had been
increased from 75,000 dinars to 450,000 dinars in one year.
Comparable reports were given to me by scores of other peasants
in widely scattered areas throughout Yugoslavia. Leading Yugoslav Communists have admitted the widespread use of punitive
taxation against the private peasant.[23] Some of them, however,
have publicly questioned the wisdom of employing it as a technique with which to extend collectivization. The party, nevertheless, retains it as a weapon against the peasant, and there is
every indication that it will continue to utilize it.

In effect, therefore, their enmity toward the private peasant
has not decreased, but they are somewhat bewildered as to the
effectiveness of the weapons which they have used against him.
Consequently, they resort to the trial and error technique; they
improvise; they experiment. Sometimes they publicly criticize
the execution of unpopular policies, in order to divert attention
from the policies themselves. While tangible evidence is lacking,
there are indications that at times secret instructions to local

[23] See Bakarich speech, *Naprijed*, April 18, 1952.

party leaders are at variance with the party's public pronouncements.

New Retreat—1953

By early 1953 party leaders realized that the reforms of
1951–52 would not remedy or even alleviate the steadily deteriorating agricultural situation. Peasants in collective farms,
more and more demoralized as a result of the government's
ruthless suppression of their legal attempts to withdraw, worked
less and less in the collective effort. Many withdrew entirely
from participating in the work of the collective, devoting their
time to working their private plots of an acre or so all the more
intensively. Much collective acreage went to weeds. Similarly,
peasants remaining outside labor co-operatives, rebelling against
punitive taxation, produced less and less, and, following the
abolition of compulsory deliveries, brought less and less produce
to market.

Faced with a rapidly deteriorating state of affairs, Yugoslav
Communist rulers in March, 1953 issued a decree permitting
reorganization or liquidation of labor co-operatives, as well as
individual withdrawals from them.[24] On the surface this seemed
like the end of collectivization, but the provisions of the decree
were designed to facilitate reorganization and not liquidation.[25]
Land, buildings, inventory, livestock and other resources attained
through collective means could not be distributed to the members in case the collective ceased to exist. Land which peasants
had received as a result of the agrarian reform, but which had
been taken directly into labor co-operatives, was declared to be
public property. In addition, a person who would withdraw was
obliged to reimburse the collective for improvements made on
property which would be returned to him. Moreover, he had to
assume a part of the co-operative's debt, in the proportion as the
worth of the property returned to him would be to the total
worth of the co-operative's property. Pending such payment a
mortgage would be placed on his property.

In spite of these provisions and in the face of party declara-

[24] For text of decree, see *Borba,* March 30, 1953.
[25] *Ibid.,* see articles 7, 19, 26 and 27.

tions that the aim of this decree was to strengthen collectivism rather than to weaken it, the response was immediate. The vast majority of members, convinced that they should strike while the iron was hot, surged to get out, to liquidate the labor co-operatives. One of Tito's closest collaborators admitted privately that he thought most of the labor co-operatives would be abandoned.[26]

Among the small minority of party functionaries who had been running the labor co-operatives veritable panic broke loose. Most of them had brought nothing into the co-operatives, except themselves and their good connections with the party and regime. As co-operative officials they had good jobs. Since they nominally worked the year round they received steady pay, in contrast to the ordinary members, who worked only in response to seasonal needs and orders from the officers, and who were paid only for the time that they worked. These landless party adherents were prepared to do anything to save their good and enduring sinecures, except, of course, to start for the fields with plow and hoe.

The party's main concern turned to the question of what to do with these landless peasants, its adherents and agents. How would they make a living? Even where the government had given them land, buildings, livestock and tools, it had not at the same time bestowed upon them a desire for work. The party resolved the issue by reducing the maximum landholding of all peasants to twenty-five acres each.[27] Thus a person who had taken eighty-five acres into a co-operative could now get less than a third of it. Those outside the co-operatives were also reduced to twenty-five acres. Those who thus lost their land were promised compensation over a period of twenty years. And so the Communists, whose main prewar criticism of the status of agriculture was that the bulk of the peasants owned less than twenty-five acres of land each, now made this the maximum!

Landless peasants, however, were not to receive land as individuals from the land fund thus created. It was made available to them only as they became members of labor co-operatives or other collective groups. The government was careful not to

[26] Tito has admitted that well over half of the labor co-operatives have dissolved, *Politika*, September 28, 1953.
[27] *Politika*, May 23, 1953.

create the impression that it was making property owners out of the landless peasants.

This was one way of reassuring the party rank and file, among whom excitement and confusion had reached almost panic proportions. Understandably, in view of the fact that in the past they had been told that labor co-operatives were the highest form of Communism in the countryside, party members had been quite openly asking, "What remains of our whole system if we let collectivization go by the boards?"

On the propaganda front, too, Communist leaders sought to assure the faithful that collectivization in some form was still the ultimate goal. The aim of the decree permitting withdrawal from and liquidation of collectives, said Kardelj, "was not dissolution of labor co-operatives, nor was it an abandonment of the line of socialist transformation of agriculture." [28] Socialist aims in agriculture must be pursued, he said on another occasion, by different means than heretofore.[29] Tito voiced his assurance to youth that they would "not stop half way." [30] A few days earlier he had declared: "We will build socialism even if the whole of world reaction should be against us." [31] Another party leader reminded Communists that they must never forget that the "aim of the decree is reorganization and not liquidation of peasant labor co-operatives." [32]

Moreover, Communist leaders let it be known that the independent peasant was to have no respite. Tito in effect said that pauperization of private peasants was the party's consistent policy. Speaking of the twenty-five acre limit on private holdings, he said: "From this it can be seen that capitalist elements in the peasant areas are constantly withering away politically and economically, that this is a consistent policy of the socialist buildup of our agriculture, that this law will help that process." [33]

Kardelj echoed the same sentiments when he referred to taxes as "an instrument . . . of class policy." [34] A few days later, he said it was their aim to leave the peasant "free," but "to create

[28] *Politika,* April 8, 1953.
[29] *Ibid.,* March 29, 1953.
[30] *Omladina,* May 27, 1953.
[31] *Politika,* May 18, 1953.
[32] *Ibid.,* April 9, 1953.
[33] *Ibid.,* May 18, 1953.
[34] *Ibid.,* March 29, 1953.

such conditions as to prevent the development of capitalist elements, conditions which will all the more economically tie individual peasant production to the socialist economy . . . and
which will, in the final analysis, constantly strengthen the economic power of the socialist forces in the peasant areas." [35] Another member of the party's Central Committee declared: "It is
impossible to build socialism in industry and to permit capitalism
to develop among the peasantry." [36] More recently, it has been
revealed that the tax system was being revised to further impoverish the independent peasants and thus force them to bring
their produce to market.[37]

The Future

A continuing crisis in Yugoslav agriculture is a certainty,
unless there should be a radical revolution in Communist Party
policy. There is no reason to believe that collectivized agriculture
will be any more successful than in the past. On the other hand,
the opposition of the independent peasant to punitive taxation
and other hostile acts of the regime is not likely to diminish.

Tito graphically depicted the failure of their agricultural
policies when he said: "That which we wanted to achieve—that
there would be more bread, that there would be more agricultural products—we did not achieve, rather it turned out that there
was less." [38] At the same time, he appealed to the peasants to
turn over to the state as much agricultural produce as possible.
"Do not permit," he added, "that each year we import bread." On
the one hand, he admits that collectivization has been an economic failure. On the other, he wants increased production. But
who will step up production, the new collectives to be created
from the land confiscated from those having more than twenty-
five acres, or does he expect those from whom the land was taken
to increase their output?

Kardelj added his voice when he said that labor co-operatives,
in spite of material means that had been extended to them, had

[35] *Borba,* April 28, 1953.
[36] See speech of Petar Stambolich, *Politika,* April 10, 1953.
[37] See interview with Vukmanovich, *Borba,* June 9, 1953.
[38] *Politika,* May 18, 1953.

not increased production.[39] In many instances, he asserted, production actually went down. He attributed this in part to the peasant's entering collectives in order *"to get more from society, i.e. in order to give less to it, and not so much that he would produce more and better. . . ."* [40] Granting economic privileges to labor co-operatives, he said, only "educates man in parasitism. . . ." If the labor co-operatives were a failure economically with considerable government aid, one wonders how they can be expected to succeed without it.

Throughout the discussion of the decree permitting liquidation of labor co-operatives it was revealed that there was a surplus of manpower in many of them. The regime has wanted this surplus to go into industry, but has apparently been unsuccessful in persuading peasants to leave the land. In one instance Kardelj sought to demonstrate the failure of a labor co-operative because it had refused to become mechanized.[41] Because there was a surplus of manpower, farm machines were locked up in sheds in order to give the members work. Instead of the men resting, he said, the machines rested while the men worked. Another top party leader, Vladimir Bakarich, told of a different co-operative which had decided to dissolve, ironically enough, for the reason that, from Kardelj's point of view, it had succeeded.[42] It accepted mechanization, but after it became mechanized the co-operative could employ less than 300 of its 1,400 able-bodied men, resulting in some 1,100 to 1,200 being thrown out of work. Understandably, these men became dissatisfied and succeeded in dissolving the co-operative.

The government has indicated that it will seek a different solution to this problem. If the peasant will not leave his land to go into industry the government may bring the industry to him. No concrete plans have yet been announced, but the indications are that initially the government intends to build processing plants for different agricultural products at or near the source of supply.

In view of the developments discussed above, the independent peasant, if he ever had any doubts about the labor co-operatives,

[39] *Politika,* March 29, 1953.
[40] *Ibid.,* italics his.
[41] *Politika,* April 8, 1953.
[42] *Borba,* April 6, 1953.

has none now. Everything that he has learned and everything that the government has done has reinforced his belief in private ownership. Yet the Communist policies call for some form of collectivization in the long run. How can Communist leaders meet this problem? Tito has often said that they would not use force even when force was being employed. Moreover, he has often made unequivocal declarations that collectivized agriculture in some form would have to come. According to him, the peasant must be persuaded, but his definition of persuasion is broad enough to include such things as punitive taxation. The attitude of the independent peasant, however, was dramatically expressed by one of them when he said: "They won't create another one [labor co-operative] without bayonets!"

PART FIVE

DECADE
OF COMMUNISM

THE Communist philosophy promised to liberate the workingman from the evils of capitalism and to provide for him and for society as a whole a greater measure of social justice. In the Communist society, according to Marx, every man would be expected to contribute according to his ability and he would be rewarded in accordance with his needs. This ideal situation has not only failed of realization in the Soviet Union, thirty-six years after the Bolshevik Revolution, but in addition holds no promise of being realized there in the foreseeable future.

In Yugoslavia, Stalin's imitators have been in power nearly a decade. Although they did not enter Belgrade until October of 1944, they officially date their regime from November 29, 1943. It is the aim of Part Five to attempt an evaluation of the results of these years—to focus attention upon the more important economic aspects of Yugoslav Communism in action, and to indicate the impact upon the individual's standard of living and upon his outlook for the future. In view of the fact that the political impact of the Communist dictatorship has already been described in earlier chapters, particularly in Part III, and since political prospects for the future will be discussed in Part VI, the appraisal in Part V will be limited largely to the economic aspects of Yugoslav Communism.

In 1945 Tito told the Yugoslavs: "We cannot give you all you need at once. We will do this gradually . . . if not within one or two years, then within three or four. . . ." [1] In a speech to parliament in

[1] See his Kragujevac speech, *Borba,* October 23, 1945.

the spring of 1947 one of his closest collaborators, Milovan Djilas, reasserted an earlier declaration that within ten years they would catch up with England, and added: "Perhaps within ten or within eight years, the question of getting ahead of America will be posed." [2] As we survey the results of their rule, therefore, it may be well to keep before us the question: how well has their performance matched their promises?

[2] *Stenografske beleshke* (treche redovno zasedanje, March 26–April 28, 1947), p. 438.

Chapter 22:

Factors in Evaluating Communist Economy

ANY attempt to evaluate the Communist experiment in Yugoslavia must inevitably run into some difficulties. The situation there is far from static, and predictions are hazardous. The best that one can hope for is that his analyses will correspond to the past and the present. Certain factors which may shape one's judgments or influence the future of the Communist experiment need to be carefully noted and remembered.

Doctrinal Shortcomings

Unlike the main philosophical systems which preceded it, Marxism does not recognize any unknowns. By applying the dialectic method, the answers to all problems can be arrived at, and consequently everything becomes more or less possible. Marx virtually drew a blueprint of how his system was to be achieved. He developed the notion of the proletarian revolution, the tactics required to bring it about, and the positive steps in the building of the Communist society. In such a closed philosophical system it is impossible to admit that socialization of industry, collectivization of agriculture and other requisites of Marxian dogma might be impossible of attainment.

It is not surprising, therefore, that in Yugoslavia, as in other Communist countries, all problems are attacked with religious zeal. The word impossible never enters the Communist vocabulary, for it is determined in advance that all obstacles must give way under pressure of the Marxian dialectic. For that reason many difficult problems receive little or no detailed study in advance of attempted solutions. Is it any wonder, under such circumstances, that errors multiply as one unsuccessful attack is followed by an equally determined frontal assault? Is it surprising that Communist economic systems are constantly in readjustment and reorganization?

In addition to suffering from philosophical limitations, Yugoslav Communists who have been directing the economy, particularly their late chief, Boris Kidrich, were further handicapped by knowing virtually nothing about liberal-classical economics. Moreover, a not inconsiderable number of men assigned to economic positions were not sure that they even understood Kidrich's Marxism. His speeches and statements lack clarity and conciseness. They are involved, complicated and highly technical. To rank-and-file members of the Yugoslav Communist Party most of his statements must be utterly incomprehensible. Even economists were not sure they understood him. On one occasion, for example, an intelligent Yugoslav friend of mine was complaining to an economist friend, who holds a relatively important position in the Yugoslav government, that he could not understand Kidrich's speeches and statements. To which the economist replied, "I understand him to the same extent as you do!"

The doctrinal shortcomings of Marxism make for rigidity and inelasticity. In practice this leads to authoritarianism. Able non-Communists in economic enterprises are afraid to disagree with party men and inevitably defer to Communist managers. The latter are frequently hesitant to accept advice from non-Communist technicians when that advice seems to be contrary to Communist dogma. They are only too well aware that their future in the hierarchy will in large part depend upon the extent to which they are able to please their party superiors.

Frequent Changes and Unreliable Statistics

The theoretical shortcomings of Marxism and the lack of practical experience among its Yugoslav adherents have led to frequent failures and equally frequent changes. Decree piled upon decree, usually leaving many uncertainties about the

validity of past decrees. In the summer of 1952, the Yugoslav
government admitted that there were some 3,500 economic
decrees, orders, regulations and instructions still in force, many
of them contradictory.[3] Because of the rapid changes, it is often
difficult to assess the impact or the significance of certain steps
which the government has from time to time taken. Nor can one
always be sure in the case of certain problems of the exact status
of government regulations concerning them.

Adding to the general confusion is the Yugoslav government's system of statistics. Communist leaders seemingly never
tire of stressing the importance of "evidence" (record keeping)
and "control" (power of overseeing and directing). Record keeping is said to be the basic indicator of the fulfillment of planned
goals. Party men have emphasized the importance of keeping
records in all fields of activity, e.g. attendance at special courses,
voluntary work, etc.[4] Non-Communists, on the other hand, maintain that the result is "mountains of paper." Individuals in different enterprises have told me that the vast amount of paper work
that must be done constitutes "one of the big drains on the
economy." Moreover, there is a widespread impression among
employees of enterprises that "no one looks at all this evidence
and bookkeeping."

In any case, Yugoslav Communist statistics are highly unreliable. There are several reasons why this is so. First of all,
there is a great deal of guesswork. Often precise records are not
kept, and when figures are entered in the books they are only
rough estimates. There is a tendency to use round numbers, for
few Yugoslavs are scientifically trained or have an appreciation
of exactness. Although most of the record keeping is done by
party men, Communist newspapers have recognized that they
are oftentimes "unqualified, uninformed and half-literate comrades." [5]

Yugoslav statistics are also unreliable because the party has
insisted on manipulating them in order to depict its undertakings
in the best possible light. In making comparisons with prewar
Yugoslavia, for example, no one year is utilized as a standard.

[3] *Borba*, July 17, 1952.
[4] *Politika*, March 16, 1949.
[5] *Partiski radnik*, February 17, 1949.

For each field of endeavor the prewar year which is most favorable from the Communist point of view is chosen. Sometimes they use production figures, and at other times prices are employed as standards of comparison. Moreover, party leaders have not hesitated to engage in outright falsification of statistics when they considered it prudent to do so either for domestic or foreign reasons. The father of one government statistician told me that his son had been asked to prepare certain statistical tables on economic production which were desired by a foreign government. When he had done so, his superior, seeing that the statistical information would put the regime in a bad light, said: "I just will not give them these!" Thereupon, he instructed the young statistician as to what type of statistical report he wanted him to prepare.

Yugoslav statistics are unreliable for a third reason: incompleteness. As in the case of other Communist governments, the Yugoslav regime regards much economic information in the category of a state secret. Only the briefest financial information is published. There is no indication, for example, as to how much money is spent by the foreign office, the secret police or the various propaganda agencies.

Secrecy, however, is not the only reason for the incompleteness of statistical information. Ignorance and the failure to publish vital information also play their respective roles. The Yugoslav government, by way of illustration, as late as 1951 did not know how much money there was in circulation, nor did it have an estimate of the value of fixed capital, physical plant, factories, etc. Likewise, there was no estimate of the rate of depreciation, the cost of maintenance, or the cost of replacement. Moreover, evaluating Communist claims with respect to fulfillment of plans is made difficult when one knows that, in establishing norms in some instances, night work has been calculated at three times day work, although this fact was not published.

Yugoslav Communists have been under considerable pressure during the past two years to establish a system of more meaningful statistics. This pressure has come primarily from the United States economic assistance mission in Belgrade, and to a lesser extent from the United Nations technical assistance mission and from the field representatives of the International Bank.

In some instances (e.g. estimate of fixed capital, amount of money in circulation, etc.), the Yugoslavs have made some progress. Yet it would be little more than wishful thinking to believe that reliable statistics will be available any time soon. Many record keepers will continue to guess and to be inexact. The party will continue to conceal at least the more unpleasant facts. And secrecy will continue to compound ignorance and deliberate manipulation.

Unofficial Sources of Information

Without unofficial private sources of information it would be futile to attempt an evaluation of Yugoslav Communism in operation. I have come to this conclusion after spending three years in Tito's Yugoslavia. There are countless significant facts which simply cannot be obtained otherwise. But there are limitations in the information obtained from private sources. First of all, in a country so hostile to Communism one needs to be on guard against exaggerations. Secondly, one needs to exercise care in the use of any sampling of information. Finally, one needs to remember that many persons are afraid to speak frankly, although under appropriate circumstances (usually when no third person is present) this does not present much of a problem.

In gathering and analyzing my information I have tried to take careful note of these factors. I have sought to discount prejudice, to verify information through independent sources, to develop corroborating evidence, to seek firsthand information where possible, and to concentrate on persons in whom I had confidence. I attempted to obtain information and opinion from experts. Where, for example, I did not know economists but knew lawyers or political scientists, I posed certain questions and asked my acquaintances to obtain expert information from economists whom they knew and trusted. Sometimes they personally knew men in the party who in private talked to them with considerable frankness.

If I had doubts about information which I obtained, I discarded it. If private sources were in disagreement, which was rarely true, and I could not obtain fairly certain verification one way or the other, I did not make use of such information. It seemed remarkable to me that there was such general agreement among private sources and so little disagreement. Wherever possible I tried to find confirmation in government sources for information obtained privately. Information thus confirmed, and this was not infrequently, I considered most reliable.

The Impact of Aid from the West

Aside from significant UNRRA assistance, the Western Powers, principally the United States, have extended to Yugoslavia grants and loans amounting to several hundred million dollars. This aid has been forthcoming chiefly in the years since Yugoslavia's expulsion from the Soviet bloc. In addition, United Nations technical assistance to Yugoslavia has in the past few years exceeded that extended to any other European nation. It would be erroneous to minimize the influence of this outside aid upon the future of the Communist experiment. If the Yugoslav regime should succeed in making a going concern of their economy, it will in the main be due to the financing and other assistance which the experiment received from the capitalist West.

Chapter 23:

Results in Industry

PRIOR to World War II Yugoslavia had approximately 800,000 industrial workers. The present regime claims that this number has been doubled. Reliable non-Communist sources argue that this cannot be so unless all those who have been mobilized to build dams, railroads, highways, etc. are included in the category of "workers." They maintain that during the duration of World War II the skilled labor force was sharply reduced by Nazi mobilization and transportation of workers to Germany, by losses in battle during the enemy occupation of the country, and through natural deaths. Immediately after the war, moreover, the Communists took the most politically conscious and able workers into the government apparatus (secret police, people's committees, etc.). In the meantime, they argue, new workers have not been trained on anything like the prewar scale.

It is true that the Tito regime placed its major stress on industrialization, but the above, not to mention other considerations, would suggest that there was some reason to be skeptical about Communist claims. It is certainly true that much manpower has been utilized in the construction of roads, factories, dams and other projects. Even if Communists statistics concerning their progress in industrialization are accepted, there is little reason to believe that they have the skilled workers necessary to operate their newly constructed plants. If we were to assume, however, that they did have the necessary workers, their output per man hour would be even lower than it now appears to be.

Unreal Aims and Uneconomic Production

The ambitions of Yugoslav Communist rulers at the outset knew no bounds. Once in power, they embarked upon rapid industrialization and electrification. While stressing heavy industry, they were determined to manufacture nearly everything under the sun. Their calculations, however, had not taken sufficient account of money, materials or manpower. Fortunately for them, they ran desperately short on all of these just about the time of their break with the Cominform countries. Although initial aid from the West would have been forthcoming in 1948 and 1949 for other reasons, they were able to secure continued and subsequent aid, at least in part because they were successful in getting influential circles in the West to accept the explanation that their economic difficulties stemmed from the economic boycott instituted against Yugoslavia by Russia and her satellites.

That such an explanation is patently false is not difficult to demonstrate. Traditionally, the bulk of Yugoslav trade was with Western Europe and very little with the Eastern European states. Moreover, the Titoists have in effect admitted that their postwar trade with the Soviet bloc was disastrous. They shipped minerals, wines and other products at prices which were many times below the actual cost of production. On the other hand, the items which they bought from the Soviet Union had to be paid for with scarce dollars or other hard currency. Moreover, there can be little doubt that the initial grants and loans which Tito's regime received from the West in 1948 and 1949, to say nothing of subsequent and increasing assistance, were in excess of anything which they would have received from the Soviet bloc if they had not been expelled from it.

The real reason for Yugoslavia's economic difficulties under Communism can be found in such fallow and wasteful objects as New Belgrade, and countless other projects about the country, which have been abandoned, for the time being at least, but which consumed immeasurable quantities of raw materials, money and manpower. It is also to be found in such unproductive ventures as the welter of propaganda organizations and their manifold activities. It stems, too, from various economic undertakings which are of questionable value.

While it is true that some of the more grandiose and unreal projects have been abandoned, modified or set aside, there are any number of them which are uneconomic but which continue to absorb large expenditures. After the war, for example, the Tito regime was going to show the world that Yugoslavia could produce motion pictures. Film companies were founded, costly film cities were built, expensive equipment was bought and producers, writers and actors assembled. All of this required money, men and materials which Yugoslavia could ill afford, for box-office receipts would pay only a small percentage of the cost. Although considerably modified, this venture continues to be a drain on the state treasury. In early 1953 the press reported that the republic of Serbia alone spends approximately 100 million dinars a year for film production, adding regretfully that after all these years not "one good propaganda film for the village" (peasant area) had been produced.[1]

Even in the case of a more practical venture, like the building of a tractor, the results have not been encouraging. It took the Yugoslavs four or five years to produce a tractor, which is of such poor quality that even their own collective farms have refused to buy it. Among other things, it is powered by a truck engine and it requires frequent overhauling. In an effort to sell it, the government had made two significant price cuts on it by midsummer of 1952. Despite this experience they were at the same time engaged in producing a passenger automobile.

One of the best illustrations of an uneconomic venture is a factory in Nish, one of whose principal products is supposed to be radio and X-ray tubes. Some 120 German technicians were brought to Nish on a three-year contract to build this plant. They were provided with homes to live in and paid salaries of 30,000 dinars per month at a time when the average Yugoslav worker was earning no more than 4,000 dinars. When the three-year contracts had expired the plant was not yet finished. The German technicians were offered more attractive terms by Philips radio as well as by the Siemens Company to work in projected plants in Latin America. To keep them, the Yugoslav government had to double their salaries. According to government reports, the plant was completed in 1953. The really pertinent question is not

[1] *Politika,* April 10, 1953.

so much the cost of the plant, but rather the market outlook. Within a year or two the plant should produce enough radio and X-ray tubes to satisfy Yugoslav needs for years and years to come. The prospects of its being able to continue in production by competing with Western European or American companies would seem to be dim indeed.

In some cases factories are well designed and well run. Oftentimes, however, bad designing, poor engineering and undue haste have resulted in parts of plants being torn down and rebuilt several times. Errors are sometimes discovered after considerable waste. One plant engaged in making bearing castings had many molds set out in the open air. Workers would grab a huge dipper of molten metal and run with it as fast as they could to pour it into the molds. The metal, of course, cooled on the way, but the men in charge of the plant were for a long time puzzled why there were so many rejects among their castings.

One of the most costly ventures is a plant which is supposed to make coke out of lignite. Although apparently proved feasible in the laboratory, nowhere in the world is it done on a large-scale commercial basis. Although it may be too early to pass judgment on this undertaking, it was interesting to note that some twenty billion dinars have been invested in it, and that it was widely reported that Tito himself had said that heads would roll if it were a failure. It may be significant, too, that one of Yugoslavia's top Communists, who was in charge of the project, Svetozar Vukmanovich-Tempo, was moved about six months prior to its completion, hence making it possible to save him from suffering the consequences if the project failed. There has been a reluctance to put the plant to a test. As of this writing (mid-1953) the Yugoslavs were still engaged in the economically questionable practice of producing coke through liberal additions of imported coking coal as well as domestic coal. There has been no report, however, as to the quality of the coke thus produced.

Certain projects, although costly, seemed to make sense. One of these was the copper cable plant at Svetozarevo. Yugoslavia has good resources of copper and there is a good market for copper products. Likewise, hydroelectric plants were desirable, since potential Yugoslav waterpower resources are considerable. The tempo of industrialization, however, even in the case of justifiable projects, was usually in excess of what the circumstances would prudently permit.

Local pride has at times influenced the location of industrial enterprises. A highly placed Communist told a Yugoslav friend of mine that the only reason they were going through with the building of an aluminum plant at Strnishche (Slovenia) was because Kidrich, at that time chief of the Yugoslav economy, was from Slovenia. Similarly, through the influence of Communist leaders from Montenegro, a large modern hotel was built in Titograd. Operating at only one-fifth capacity during its first month, it lost one and one-half million dinars "not counting amortization and some other costs," and government economists estimated that it would go on losing money at the rate of two million dinars per month unless some solution was found.[2]

It would be unfair to say that the Yugoslav Communists have not learned anything from their quest for unreal aims and from their ventures into uneconomic production. After several years of experimentation, they have learned some lessons and have made certain adjustments. They are determined, however, that their basic ideas are sound and that a functioning Communist society can be built. Consequently, experimentation will no doubt continue, and the Yugoslav people will remain the unwilling guinea pigs.

Inefficiency

Whatever disagreements there may be about the Yugoslav Communist economy, there can be no question about its being inefficient and wasteful. If a person conscientiously follows the party press, he needs no other evidence. Yet the press reveals only carefully selected examples which are designed to be instructive for other enterprises. The worst examples are never brought to light publicly.

By 1951 Yugoslav Communists were forced reluctantly to admit that inefficiency in the economy stemmed primarily from the impossibility of devising and executing a perfect economic plan. Perfect synchronization, on which the whole economic setup depended, could not be achieved. Dislocations of all sorts took place. In some instances storehouses were full of goods, but

[2] *Politika,* July 25, 1953.

distribution generally failed or resulted in too much in some areas and not enough in others.[3] Materials needed in winter were delivered in summer and vice versa. Metallurgical coke was delivered to a cafe, while an industrial plant received poor coke.[4] Bricks needed by a co-operative in Vojvodina were shipped all the way from Macedonia, although plenty of bricks were made in Vojvodina.[5] In one case workers were told that they must unload a carload of cabbage because that particular freight car was needed for other purposes, only to discover a few hours later that they had been given the same car to reload the cabbage. Oftentimes warehouses lacked appropriate instructions and hence did not dare ship badly needed materials.

Some government agencies were able to accumulate more than they needed. In 1949 it was discovered that the ministry of agriculture had a quantity of ordinary pencils which would last over seven years, at a time when school children were begging for pencil stubs. In the same year, the construction ministry had sufficient envelopes which at the current rate of use would last forty-six years.[6] In the American Embassy in Belgrade I was at that very time receiving official correspondence from Yugoslav hospitals in envelopes that had been made from prewar used hospital ledger sheets, entries fortunately having been made only on one side. Simultaneously, propaganda agencies were consuming tons of paper daily.

Since the government decreed in 1952 that economic enterprises were being put on a profit and loss basis, inefficiency in another form became evident. Hundreds, if not thousands, of enterprises were found to be operating at a loss. One accountant who had examined the books of scores of enterprises in the summer of 1952 told a friend of mine that he did not find a one operating at a profit. The Communist press admitted that twenty-two hostelries had a deficit of ninety million dinars in the first six months of 1952.[7] Hotels and restaurants in Zagreb alone had an operating deficit of sixty million dinars in the first quarter of 1952.[8]

[3] See *Borba* editorial, December 8, 1948.
[4] *Borba,* March 24, 1949.
[5] *Ibid.,* June 16, 1949.
[6] *Borba,* February 15, 1949.
[7] *Ibid.,* August 2, 1952.
[8] *Borba* (Zagreb edition), August 31, 1952.

Government operated taxicabs were in a similar position. The city taxi enterprise of Belgrade was dissolved in the summer of 1952 after a nine million dinar deficit was discovered. Private cabs, on the other hand, continued to operate in spite of extremely heavy taxes, expensive gasoline and costly tires. "We will continue to operate," said one cab driver, "at least until these old wrecks wear out." A similar situation prevailed in Zagreb. Private cab drivers in both cities agreed that deficits in the government taxi enterprises resulted from an indifferent attitude of the drivers toward their vehicles, theft of gasoline and oil, and the cost of maintaining a large office force.

A member of a workers' council, in response to my query, voiced the opinion that many enterprises had operating deficits because they "had to pay too many engineers, too many office workers and other nonproducing personnel." Moreover, government purchasing policies have resulted in increased costs. One enterprise, for example, was compelled to buy chemicals from another government enterprise although it could buy better quality English chemicals at one-fourth the domestic price. Unexpected high costs have sometimes forced end-users to return the product. This in turn has caused the selling enterprise considerable difficulty. It has sometimes been compelled, in order to pay workers' salaries, to seek advances on goods to be shipped the following month.

In their haste to exceed planned output, party functionaries have frequently contributed to the production of poor quality goods and to excessive waste of materials and manpower. The glass in the mirrors in the best hotel in Mostar, for example, had waves in it and was otherwise imperfect. When he saw me examining it, one of the hotel employees said with a sly grin, "Well, you know they had to be ready for the announced opening of the hotel." A striking case of inefficiency was revealed by the official party organ, *Borba*.[9] It reported that during 1948 the coal mines had produced, in addition to coal, 630,000 tons of rock, which was transported on the average a distance of 200 kilometers and after burning moved as waste. The total damage as a result, it said, amounted to over 500,000,000 dinars. This did not take into account damage to locomotives nor the fact that the econ-

[9] February 7, 1949.

omy had been denied the use of 60,000 railway cars for the transport of other goods. The minister of trade and supplies, Osman Karabegovich, reported that the "quality of supplies from the socialist sector was bad." [10] Spoilage, long waiting for transportation, improper storage facilities and waiting for prices had often resulted, he said, in a complete loss.

A Communist bureaucracy, by virtue of its considerable size and by virtue of the rigid discipline which the party imposes upon it, tends to be not only unwieldly but also to lend itself to confusion and general uncertainty. Because there is no free speech or press, errors go undetected for long periods of time. An example or two can serve as instructive illustrations. A Belgrade hospital sent a bloodtesting apparatus to be repaired by the makers of medical instruments, and received an itemized bill for 9,915 dinars, more than half of which was "accumulation" (tax). Yet a new blood-testing apparatus sells for 3,800 dinars.[11]

While rationing was still in effect, all sorts of abuses were prevalent.[12] Some persons were able to get several cards. A man who butchered two hogs was able to get a ration card for fats, while an old pensioner with no independent source of supply did not get a card. While these and similar abuses were often the result of deliberate effort, more often than not they were attributable to untrained and inexperienced bureaucrats who simply did not know what was going on.

Undoubtedly many mistakes and inefficient practices have been remedied, but it should also be noted that costly errors in other forms perpetuate inefficiency. In 1952, for example, a man stopped by a government agency to collect a month's rent on property leased to it. The amount was 1,500 dinars, but the man in charge insisted that according to their books they owed 6,000 dinars and could not pay less. In another instance a man in one agency called another government enterprise, asking to be billed for goods purchased. He was told that his agency did not owe anything, yet it developed that the agency owed some 600,000 dinars.

[10] *Broba,* January 22, 1950.
[11] *Politika,* October 26, 1952.
[12] *Borba,* April 18, 1949.

Both the state and the individual have often suffered from Communist red tape. On one occasion an expert engineer devoted two years in training two young men to become plastics experts. Then one day they were transferred to do work that had nothing to do with plastics. The engineer went to several ministries, even saw General Kocha Popovich, present secretary of state for foreign affairs, but all to no avail. Finally, two new men were assigned to him. In a system which treats people as so much furniture it was not surprising that the individuals were not considered. No one in authority seemed to appreciate the fact that this was also society's loss.

Corruption

That corruption has existed in modern-day Communist states is not open to doubt. Its extent and nature, as well as the reasons for it, have not always been revealed. It is widespread in Yugoslavia as may be proved by a number of sources. The party press reveals a great deal, although it can safely be assumed that much more remains hidden than is disclosed. Individual citizens learn about it from their friends. Communist leaders admit a great deal in private conversations. In the summer of 1952, the chief public prosecutor of Yugoslavia, Brana D. Jevremovich, told me quite frankly that the principal problem facing the prosecutor's office involved the malpractices in various economic enterprises. This was no off-the-record admission, for I had prefaced my questions with the stated purpose of writing a book about Yugoslavia.

Judged by official press accounts the malpractices in economic enterprises range from petty theft to large-scale embezzlement of funds. Financial books are manipulated, payrolls padded, unnecessary materials requisitioned and then sold at a huge profit, and various scarce articles (radios, textiles, etc.) are stolen. In the case of small-scale corruption the regime appears to be helpless. In wholesale merchandising between various enterprises, for example, the men involved in buying, selling and appraising frequently manage an individual rake-off.

Embezzlement was revealed on such a scale in 1952 that the following story was widely told to illustrate in what contempt the lesser thief was held. The alleged source of the story is a man who for a time was confined with some embezzlers. The embezzlers had compared notes as to their respective crimes, and thereafter one of them was fairly regularly baited by the others. At a loss to understand this behavior, the newcomer finally asked why they were piling so much derision upon their fellow prisoner. "The idiot," one of them replied, "he stole only 600,000 dinars!" Seeking to rehabilitate himself, the man who was the object of their contempt began defending himself. "I did the best I could," said he, "after all, men, remember that mine was a small enterprise."

The official organ of the party reported in September, 1952 that material damage from "embezzlement and plunder of public property" in the first six months of 1952 amounted to 340,000,-000 dinars, or roughly double the damage for the corresponding period of 1951.[13] The paper argued, however, that this did not mean that "economic crime" was on the increase, since many offenses discovered in 1952 had taken place in previous years. At the same time, the paper continued, the present state of alertness was not satisfactory, "because damage done to our economy through crime is still great."

A no more vivid portrayal of corruption in Yugoslavia can be presented than by a recitation of some of the reports appearing in the official press. In May, 1952 a group of persons was convicted of damaging the state two million dinars by requisitioning scarce materials over fake signatures, paying low prices and then selling them at several times the cost.[14] While in Belgrade, I learned about impending fraud and embezzlement cases of considerable magnitude in the textile enterprises. More than a month later the press confirmed this information by announcing that "an initial group of sixteen persons, out of a total of forty-eight," would soon be brought to trial for "embezzlement and plunder of public property in the state textile enterprise in Zemun," where "great damage was done to public property in the past two years." [15]

One of the biggest cases of embezzlement reported in 1952

[13] *Borba*, September 4, 1952.
[14] *Politika*, May 30, 1952.
[15] *Borba*, September 4, 1952.

involved the Bor mine and smelting works.[16] In August the "first group of fifteen" was tried and convicted. The principal men involved were the director of the financial section of the mine, the treasurer, the chief of the payroll section at the smelter, and the chief of the bookkeeping section. By "false recapitulation," by getting "special premiums from the treasury," by "making false payrolls," and by pocketing "the salaries of workers who had left Bor," they had embezzled money and industrial ration coupons over a period of four years amounting to "over twenty-five million dinars." In addition to the main culprits, the press reported that there was a whole group of minor thieves.

In one signed piece in the newspaper *Naprijed*,[17] official party organ in Croatia, the following cases of theft, embezzlement, etc. were reported, all in or around Zagreb alone. A "group of criminals" was uncovered in the enterprise "Hidrotehna" which had falsified accounts in the amounts "of 40,000 dinars, 100,000 dinars and 600,000 dinars." In an enterprise transporting goods to the railway station "a group of thieves" was sentenced for having stolen from various enterprises. Likewise, "a group of thieves" was sentenced for having systematically stolen paper from a Zagreb factory since 1948 and sold it at high prices. Similarly, facing the court was "a group of criminals who specialized in the theft of coffee, and who in one instance alone damaged Zanap [distributing enterprise] in the amount of 294,800 dinars."

The same article reported that one Nikola Jankovich was guilty of "various malversations," posing as director of an enterprise that did not exist. Similarly, a Viktor Medved succeeded in getting 760,441 dinars worth of copper wire in the name of an imaginary institution. Another person was able to acquire over 650,000 dinars worth of automobile tires under similar circumstances. The head of the distributing enterprise in Krizhevac embezzled over 300,000 dinars in the first six months of 1952. And a furniture making enterprise in the same city, by selling materials to private individuals, "damaged the state over six million dinars."

In the same article, the writer stated that "the number of

[16] See *Borba,* August 20, 1952; also editorial in Zagreb edition, August 27, 1952.
[17] September 19, 1952.

cases of embezzlement, fraud, shortages of goods and reserves, falsification of goods documents, etc. is relatively large." After reciting the above mentioned cases, the writer concluded: "All these facts speak of numerous cases of crime, which is still plenty widespread in our economic enterprises."

Private Yugoslav sources maintain that there is theft, looting and embezzlement on every hand. They point out also that where the government has caught the culprits it has been largely a matter of accident, despite the regime's ubiquitous secret police and its corps of inspectors. In one instance, for example, the guilty ones who had been receiving money from the government on the basis of one payroll, while paying money out to the workers on the basis of a different payroll, were caught only after this practice had been going on for approximately three years. They might not have been detected even then if it had not been for the fact that one of the men involved became careless, went in for drinking and freely spent thousands of dinars in the course of one evening.

The type of corruption that is almost impossible to detect, according to Yugoslav friends of mine, is the kind that hits the consumer. As an illustration, the operator of a small government-owned beer hall receives a keg of beer which is expected to yield 150 glasses of beer, but he sees to it that he gets 180 glasses and pockets the profit. Similar things happen when individuals are shortchanged on the weight of their groceries, or when a small lumber dispensing enterprise fails to give the consumer full measure. This type of petty corruption is difficult to detect, and the consumer, even if he is aware of it, is reluctant to complain against happenings in a state enterprise for fear of having his motives questioned.

These same private sources also point out that the official press admits that the extent of fraud or embezzlement in certain cases is difficult to determine, often using the word approximate. Considerable credence was given this view when in the case of the Bor mines case *Borba*,[18] reported that experts had spent 700 work hours trying to find out the real situation in the bookkeeping department "but could not get a clear picture." Similarly, a committee that investigated the commercial enterprise "Srem"

[18] August 28, 1952.

found that "the bookkeeping of the enterprise is in such shape that from it one cannot even approach perceiving the number of financial transgressions." [19]

It should be noted that all of this corruption exists in spite of severe penalties (death and long prison terms) which have been meted out to the guilty, and in spite of the regime's insistence that Yugoslavia is now a people's state. How then explain the existence of all sorts of corruption on a wide scale? Yugoslav Communists in their public pronouncements seek to place the blame on "class enemies," "antistate elements," and bitter reactionaries. In the Bor mines case, for example, they referred to those on trial as "former Chetniks and declassed elements." [20]

Such an assertion, of course, is patently absurd. Yugoslav Communists have not entrusted to anyone but their own men positions even remotely approaching the responsibility of those at Bor, one of their biggest enterprises. A non-Communist manager of a small grocery told me that he had to have a party member as cashier. It is utter nonsense to think that the positions of chief of the financial section, the treasurer, the chief bookkeeper and the chief of the payroll section at Bor would be entrusted to "former Chetniks and declassed elements."

Similarly, a group of alleged saboteurs in the textile, leather and food industries of Bosnia-Herzegovina, who were tried and convicted in early 1949, all held important positions. Among them were an assistant minister of industry, the directors of three different factories, the chief director, chief engineer and chief expert of the general directorate of the food industry, and the chief accountant of the general directorate of the chemical industry.[21] It would be difficult to believe that all of these were not party men.

A Yugoslav friend of mine who knows the Communists offered the following explanation, which would seem to make sense. In the United States, he said, you have developed over the decades a tradition of honesty and a scrupulous regard for another person's property. There was a fair amount of it in prewar Yugoslavia, too, he said, manifesting itself in a scrupulous regard

[19] *Politika*, July 5, 1952.
[20] *Borba* (Zagreb edition), August 30, 1952.
[21] *Borba*, April 12, 1949.

for defending the family name. It would have been unthinkable, he added, that sons or daughters of businessmen would engage in wrong doing and thus harm the family name or reputation.

After the Communists came to power, my friend observed, the prewar merchant families were liquidated. Primitives were brought in who had no particular tradition or name to unhold. For the first time these people got a taste of luxury living: a good apartment, bathroom in the house, and other comforts. Their wants multiplied: they wanted good-looking furniture, rugs, a nice dress for the wife, and other things. To get them, all they needed to do was to steal a little here and there, and they did just that. Some, of course, played for much higher stakes.

It must be remembered, too, that the party had attracted many opportunists with highly questionable moral standards. Moreover, many otherwise honest persons simply could not resist temptation when forced to live in dire misery for a number of years. Others, who had been won over to the new regime, became disillusioned, saw no outlook for the future and turned to corruption. When brought to trial for stealing from a special store for high party leaders, one employee of the store reportedly gave this explanation: "I saw food going to ministers, bills of over 30,000 dinars were run up each month, and when they were not paid I was told to tear them up, so why shouldn't I steal?"

For the most part, it seems safe to conclude, the corrupt individuals are the regime's own men, and party leaders are often hard put to know what to do with them. The more serious offenders, of course, receive no mercy. But what to do with the much larger number who are involved in the less serious malpractices poses a more difficult problem.

Note should also be made of the fact that much of the damage to the economy results not, as the Communists insist, from sabotage or evil intent, but rather from ignorance, conflicting orders and bureaucratic red tape. It does not seem to have occurred to them that a complicated bookkeeping system, such as theirs, requires able and trained men, whom for the most part they do not have. To them it seems easier to conceive of failures in terms of sabotage and treason, particularly where non-Communists are concerned.

Capitalist Evils

Not long after economic enterprises had been given a measure of independence through the regime's decentralization program in 1951, the Communist leaders discovered the growth of certain practices long associated with capitalism. One of the most pronounced was the attempt of various enterprises to engage in collusion to set up monopolistic and cartel prices and thus increase their profits. As an illustration, the enterprises from the six republics which were engaged in the buying of raw hides met in the capital city of Slovenia and made an agreement on the division of markets and on purchasing prices.[22] They agreed that no enterprise engaged in the buying of raw hides would do business on the territory of any republic except its own. Moreover, they agreed on a ceiling price to be paid for various types of hides. Since raw hides could not be sold except to these enterprises, the agreement had the effect of keeping buying prices low. Selling prices, on the other hand, were kept high, with resultant profits and high wages for the employees. When these practices were discovered, the enterprises were reminded that "the benefits from the lowering of prices belong to the community," and not just to the employees of a particular enterprise.

In another case, paper mills agreed to make price lists available to each other and, in case of price changes, to give each other thirty days' advance notice.[23] The result was uniform prices through the country. In some other economic pursuits enterprises even sought the assistance of local authorities to exclude competition from outside areas and thus maintain local monopolies. In other instances, enterprises sought to hold up goods so as to create a scarcity and thus increase prices. Sometimes the result was not higher prices, but spoilage and large losses.

The government has lost no time in pointing out that these practices were contrary to its policies and the Marxian principles which it has espoused. It has admitted, however, that detecting some of the evil practices is difficult, for it appears that "very often enterprises make verbal agreements but nothing in writing." [24]

[22] *Borba,* June 15, 1952.
[23] *Ibid.*
[24] *Ibid.*

Enterprises, for their part, are frequently left in a state of confusion by the regime's contradictory decrees. Under the economic decentralization, enterprises were told that they must abide by the market, i.e. they must pay attention to supply and demand. Yet local producers in Sombor, for example, were singled out for public criticism because they refused to deliver their goods to the city trading enterprises at locally prevailing prices, but were selling their goods in Zagreb where much higher market prices prevailed.[25] If by selling for less on the local market, the enterprise should fail to realize a profit, it would then run into the regime's dictum that enterprises must maintain themselves in a state of solvency. Failing this, it might find the National Bank unwilling to extend further credits.

On the other hand, enterprises which competed with one another for foreign markets were quickly brought into line.[26] It did not seem pertinent to Marxian planners that the ability to earn some foreign exchange might have been a life and death matter for a particular enterprise.

In general, enterprises were expected to be solvent, but not too solvent. They could reduce domestic prices provided the aim was not to establish a monopoly. They are expected to operate in accordance with the laws of supply and demand, but be ever on the alert that Communist leaders might condemn them if they take advantage of opportunities which present themselves. They should make a profit, but not too much of a profit. In making a profit they are expected to remember that the benefits are to accrue to the whole community and not to their workers in the form of increased wages.[27] Managements of enterprises have been warned that unless they increase production, attempts to raise wages are really efforts to cheat the community.[28]

Enterprises which have increased their production have also run into difficulties. The main one being that capitalist ogre: overproduction. The regime, while admitting that the previous system of doing things was partly at fault, placed most of the blame on the enterprises, insisting that the goods were of poor quality and hence could not be sold. The party press reported in

[25] *Rijechki list* (Rijeka), November 1, 1950.
[26] *Borba* (Zagreb edition), August 30, 1952.
[27] *Borba*, August 20, 1952.
[28] *Ibid.*, September 1, 1952.

the summer of 1952 that there were "poor quality goods in the retail shops worth about six billion dinars" which "no one will buy." [29] In seven enterprises alone there were "goods amounting close to 509 million dinars that no one will buy."

Understandably, the government does not reveal the full picture of the resulting dislocations. From a reliable source I learned that the factory in Pirot which made *opanke,* a type of peasant shoe, was closing down in the fall of 1952, and the workers were being sent to work in the mines. This factory had around 400 employees. Because the rate of accumulation was sixteen dinars for every dinar of wages, or 1600 per cent, prices were so high that the peasants could not buy the *opanke,* despite their need for footwear. Consequently, the factory's warehouse was full of goods, worth approximately 500,000,000 dinars. In such circumstances the factory could not continue to operate. Although the press made no mention of it, I was able to verify that the Proleter (prewar Boston) shoe factory in Belgrade was forced to close for at least a whole month in 1952, due to overproduction.

In some cases overproduction has resulted in another evil which was not supposed to occur in a Communist state: unemployment. Even enterprises not suffering from overproduction engaged in dismissing some of the less essential workers in order to cut costs and increase profits. At the end of September 1952 *Borba* [30] reported that there were around 4,000 unemployed in the city of Belgrade, certainly an understatement. By June, 1952 approximately 10,000 unemployed persons in Belgrade were receiving aid from the state. [31] Two months earlier a leading cabinet minister had reported that there were 700,000 unemployed persons in Yugoslavia. [32]

For the regime this problem has presented a number of difficulties. It is not easy to find employment for individuals when enterprises throughout the country are seeking to reduce costs. Moreover, many of the unemployed are refusing to accept jobs in the provinces which are being offered to them. They have learned that some of those who had accepted transfers had discovered

[29] *Ibid.,* June 15, 1952.
[30] September 29, 1952.
[31] *Borba,* June 9, 1953.
[32] *New York Times,* February 27, 1953.

upon arrival at their destination that there was no job for them, or that no housing was available. Having given up their residence in Belgrade, or some other city, they were not permitted to return. Understandably, many preferred unemployment rather than the risk of being placed in a similar predicament.

The Future

What has been said in the preceding pages cannot be interpreted to mean that nothing has been achieved toward the industrialization of the country. Dams have been built, factories erected and roads constructed. But whatever the achievements in the field of industry, the result has not been, as a subsequent chapter will show, a raised standard of living. Moreover, it is doubtful if at any time in history, except in the other Communist states, the costs in money, materials and human blood have been so great in proportion to the alleged gains.

The costs have been high. The achievements, even from the Communist point of view, have been small and disappointing. The whole industrialization effort, as we have seen, has been characterized by unreal aims and gross inefficiency. Most disturbing from the point of view of doctrinaire Marxists has been the widespread prevalence of fraud, embezzlement and theft in the government's economic enterprises. Grandiose planning and inefficiency could be explained away in terms of inexperience, ambition and scarcity of technical know-how. But how explain such wanton plunder among those in charge of the economy, most of whom are party members?

Yugoslav Communists explain their economic failures most frequently in terms of the "Soviet system which we inherited." They believe they have found the answer to their difficulties in economic decentralization. Yet decentralization gets away from the "Soviet system" only in part. Certainly the similarities between the Soviet and the Yugoslav economies are more striking than the differences. That neither system commands respect in Yugoslavia is illustrated by the occasionally heard quip: "Save us from Russian organization and Yugoslav decentralization."

In the past the weight of the bureaucracy has been costly. Decentralization, because decisions are in many more hands than heretofore, and in less experienced hands, may actually add to the bureaucratic burden instead of lessening it. The Yugoslav people are aware of this burden; they have a double-edged wise-crack to the effect that "in America every third man has an auto-mobile while in Yugoslavia every third man has a brief case."

The weight of the bureaucracy was brought most forcefully to me when I visited the Rade Konchar (prewar Siemens) plant in Zagreb. The pride and joy of Yugoslav Communists, this plant is frequently the scene of conducted tours for foreign visitors. It is engaged in making electrical equipment, chiefly electric motors and generators. According to the manager, the plant employs ap-proximately 2,900 persons. Of this total, he said, 340 were engi-neers and technicians, while 560 held administrative posts. About 2,000, of whom some 600 were apprentices, were engaged in actual production.

There would seem to be little doubt that this plant is top-heavy with administrative personnel. This is particularly true when we take into account the fact that this plant does not have a sales promotion force, as we might expect to find in capitalist enterprises. Yet, this is supposed to be one of their best-run plants!

In looking at the future one must not, however, discount the impact of significant aid from the West which has been pouring into Yugoslavia. In addition to grants and loans which the re-gime has received, undisclosed quantities of military assistance have been granted. In addition, as noted before, various United Nations agencies have furnished important material and technical assistance. Many Western experts have traveled to Yugoslavia to assist the government, and many Yugoslavs have come to the United States and other Western nations for specialized training in varied fields. It is, therefore, at least in the realm of possibility that the capitalist West may yet succeed in making of the Yugo-slav Communist economy a going concern, as horrible, as shock-ing and as revolting as such a prospect may be to the Yugoslav people.

Chapter 24:

Results in Agriculture

DESPITE the difficulties which they have encountered in industry, Yugoslav Communists have readily admitted that the peasant problem is much more formidable. With three-fourths of the people engaged in agricultural pursuits, the number of individuals involved is much greater. More important, however, is the fact that among the peasantry the concept of private ownership is more firmly entrenched and more meaningful. Even before the Communists came to power, most workers did not have an ownership interest in the places where they worked. To the peasant, on the other hand, ownership was closely identified with his work and his livelihood. The Yugoslav regime, however, remains undeterred in pursuing its basic agricultural policies, policies which have been not only among the least popular but also among the least successful of the government's measures.

Collectivization Unpopular

To Yugoslav peasants in and out of collective farms, the collectivization idea is equally abhorrent. Those who have managed to stay out of collectives will continue to do everything to remain independent. Those who are in collectives, except for rare cases, are getting out wherever they can. The decree permitting withdrawal, it should be remembered, does not make it easy to do so. In most instances the peasant cannot get anything of what he took in, especially livestock, and no more than twenty-five acres of the land which he may have taken in. Moreover, he is forced to assume his share of the collective's debt, although not being able to share in any of its assets.

A variety of reasons lie behind the peasant's hostility toward collectivization. Perhaps the most important is his long-ingrained desire to be master in his own house. He wants to own his land, to manage it as he wishes and to dispense with its produce when and as he sees fit. He does not cherish being told when and how to work his land by men who, in his knowledge, have not put in a serious day's work in their lifetime, and who, in his opinion, know far less than he about farming methods. He does not like the idea of reporting to work at set hours, not even knowing what he will be doing on that particular day. He just does not want to be a "wage slave," which to him is tantamount to a loss of freedom.

Peasants in and out of collectives know that the income of collective farmers has been low. When members of collectives have bought goods and services, however, they have had to pay the collective a high price. Members of one collective, for example, observed that when they used a team of horses to visit friends they had to pay a high rental fee to the collective. While officers of labor co-operatives received relatively high salaries, ordinary members frequently had to seek outside work to make ends meet. This was particularly true when machines were introduced and unemployment created. Most of them remember and look back fondly on better days of the prewar years.

The peasants became particularly embittered when the Tito regime went back on its written promise that they could withdraw from collective farms at the end of three years if they wished to do so. When they saw that withdrawal was impossible, the new feudalism was so repugnant that some peasants simply walked out, leaving everything they had behind them. As one peasant observed: "Men who took all sorts of things—land, livestock, and machinery—into collectives are glad to get out with a patched pair of pants." They preferred losing all and becoming share-croppers among private peasants to staying inside the labor co-operatives. Since most peasants had families, however, such a solution was frequently not feasible.

The fact that they are now permitted to withdraw, although under difficult conditions, has not diminished their hostility toward the labor co-operatives. Of hundreds of peasants with whom I talked, I never found one who said that he was in favor of collectivization. On the other hand, except for rare instances, they were vocal in their opposition. At least 98 per cent of all peasants I talked to expressed unequivocal opposition to the collective idea. "If I have some land, some tools and some cows," observed one peasant, "why should I want to take it into a collective and have someone else tell me what to do and when to do it?" After the decree permitting withdrawals, even the official press has revealed a good deal about the unpopularity of collectivization. In one labor co-operative, for example, when the question was asked as to who wanted to remain in the co-operative, "not a single hand was raised." [1]

Collectivization Unsuccessful

The unpopularity of the collectivization idea has in large measure contributed to the lack of success among the labor co-operatives. Time and again I heard peasants say that men do not work with enthusiasm when the land is not theirs. The following three examples are illustrative of what happens when incentive is lacking. One peasant who raised celery told me of how he had been up at daybreak the previous spring, irrigating and otherwise caring for his crop. He reaped an abundant harvest. "This year," he continued, "we are in a collective. No one works after hours, no one irrigates until the sun is already beating down. I doubt if we shall have any yield, but then no one seems to care."

In another part of the country, an independent peasant told me how he had been up until two o'clock in the morning with his sow who had nine little ones. Without private ownership such concern and care simply did not exist. By contrast, he told me of large losses among new-born pigs at a nearby state farm. The manager (a Communist) had told him that no matter which one of his men he assigned to the night shift, a number of little pigs died of neglect.

In a still different area, local Communist leaders admitted that their stock-raising collective had been a failure and was being disbanded. With tears in his eyes, an older member (a non-Communist) told of the tragedy which had befallen them. Good-

[1] For a number of other revealing examples, see *Politika*, April 24, 1953. Also see letter to the editor, *Borba*, April 30, 1953.

looking buildings had been erected at a high cost, but now they were empty. Most of their sheep had died of disease and lack of proper care, and only a small percentage of the lambs had survived.

A drive through the Yugoslav countryside in summer furnishes a sharp contrast between privately and collectively cultivated crops. The former invariably stood out as superior. Yugoslav Communists have publicly admitted that the collective sector in agriculture has not been able to compete with private peasants in determining market prices, which have risen steadily.[2] Often state and co-operative enterprises simply had little or nothing to sell. Their costs of production have been high, and their productivity has been comparatively low.

The total output of collective farms, even in such rich and productive areas as Vojvodina, has been relatively low. An open recognition of this fact was to be found in 1953 in the speeches of the highest Yugoslav leaders.[3] Even earlier, with a surprising bit of frankness, one of the Central Committee members publicly asked his comrades: "What kind of a co-operative is it which alone consumes all that it produces?"[4] Some Yugoslav Communists have attempted to explain low production in the collectives in terms of the lack of modern equipment—tractors, cultivators, etc. Others have openly recognized that peasants work less land when in collectives than they did when they worked the identical land as independents.[5] Some of them have openly said that "if men will not work with a will, then certainly private holdings will be more profitable than co-operative."[6]

Labor co-operatives were often a failure even before they began to function. They were created by a few party members along with poor peasants, having little land, stock or machinery.[7] In one case thirteen families combined to create a labor co-operative with a total land acreage of less than forty acres. In another instance nine families had thirty-seven acres. Collectives with larger land holdings discovered over several years that the

[2] *Borba,* October 22 and November 15, 1950. Also see *Naprijed,* April 18, 1952.

[3] See speeches by Tito and Kardelj, *Politika,* May 18 and March 29, 1953.

[4] See Bakarich speech, *Naprijed,* April 18, 1952.

[5] *Borba,* November 12, 1950.

[6] Bakarich, *op. cit.*

[7] *Partiski radnik,* April 1, 1949.

percentage of land per member was falling by virtue of the fact that most of the peasants joining them had little or no land.[8] When they, along with other economic enterprises, were put on a profit-and-loss basis, their immediate reaction was not to accept any more applications from poor peasants. Ironically enough, the few peasants who really desired to join collective farms were being turned away.

Collective farms often suffered because members did not look upon them as their own. They were more apt to forget to perform necessary tasks. They showed little interest or care in the upkeep of collective property. Peasants who took good care of their machines did not do so after joining collectives. More often than not they contributed only the minimum work time required in the collective effort. The remainder of their time they devoted to their small household plots. Often they planted the same crop on their individual plots as the collective was engaged in growing,[9] an indication that the collective was not succeeding in meeting the needs of its members even in the produce in which it was specializing.

Collective farms have also suffered from involved and conflicting governmental policies and bureaucratic red tape. One labor co-operative, for example, offered to sell a carload of good onions to the local purchasing enterprise, which did not desire to buy them. Later, an export enterprise in another city agreed to purchase the onions at seven dinars per kilogram. The onions were sorted, packed and loading begun. The local purchasing enterprise, with the assistance of the people's committee, now arrived on the scene, forbade the shipment and bought the onions at six dinars per kilogram. The labor co-operative, however, lost more than the one dinar per kilogram. It had to pay a certain indemnity to the export enterprise to which it had agreed to sell the onions, to say nothing of the extra work involved. The collective lost 15,000 dinars on this carload of onions alone. More important, however, was the admission that: "We have this type of and similar occurrences on all sides." [10]

It is a sad commentary upon Communist policies that nearly

[8] *Borba* (Zagreb edition), August 27, 1952.
[9] *Politika,* May 19, 1949.
[10] Ljubomir Veljkovich, "Za pravilan odnos prema opshtim zemljoradnichkim zadrugama," *Narodna drzhava,* IV (No. 5, 1950), pp. 16–17.

a decade after World War II total agricultural production is still below prewar. The reasons have been indicated, and they are perfectly understandable. Yet the regime's bungling has often resulted in further reducing total production, collective as well as private. Because of improper care, inadequate storage, etc., great losses in farm produce occurred from spoilage. Large losses in livestock have resulted from transportation in railroad cars over considerable distances without provision for feeding or watering. It would be impossible to estimate such losses, but every Yugoslav citizen knows that they have not been small.

No Victory in War on Private Peasant

Regime leaders have admitted in effect that labor co-operatives are spiritually dead.[11] While deploring past employment of force, they have asserted that peasants would not in the future be compelled to form collective farms. Simultaneously, however, they have assessed confiscatory taxes against independent peasants. Some Communists have welcomed such taxation as a means of putting the private peasant out of business immediately. Other regime leaders, while not rejecting confiscatory taxation as a weapon to that end, have clearly implied that the attack should be more gradual and that the one-sided purpose of this weapon should not be made so evident.[12] More recently, it was announced that the whole system of taxing peasants would be changed, in part as a means of forcing them to bring produce to market.[13] Among independent peasants these words are not likely to be cause for rejoicing.

There is no neglecting the fact that the regime's war on the private peasant has inflicted serious damage, but it has not achieved its principal aim, that of driving him into collectives. Influenced in no small measure by what he has seen of labor co-operatives in operation, he has proved more formidable than party leaders had calculated. His initiative to produce independently was destroyed by the regime's policy of compulsory deliveries. Not wishing to give his produce away, he decided to

[11] See Bakarich speech, *Naprijed,* April 18, 1952.
[12] *Ibid.*
[13] See interview with Vukmanovich, *Borba,* June 9, 1953.

work only part of his land. Since confiscatory taxes have replaced compulsory deliveries his lot has not materially improved, although he may be producing a little more.

Independent peasants have suffered severe blows also as a result of other government policies. The army has taken young men away from the farms. Work projects, dam building and other regime ventures have left many peasant areas depleted of manpower. Often a few old women are left to work the farms. A visit to farm areas furnishes dramatic proof of the acute manpower shortage on many farms. Maintenance, too, has been neglected as can be seen from the fact that farm buildings, fences, orchards, vineyards and other physical properties are in a state of disrepair.

Outwardly the peasant seems unmoved. He suffers in silence, but inwardly he is confident of ultimate victory. His attachment to his land is dramatically manifested by the fact that he almost literally takes food from the mouth of his children in order to meet the high tax payments. He lives from one year to the next, desperately hoping for something to happen which will enable him to become master in his own house again.

No matter how the government may alter the collectives it is not likely to attract independent peasants into them. Even if the labor co-operatives could be made to look more attractive, and even if the government made a genuine effort to help the peasant, he would be suspicious and would wonder if it were not a carefully baited trap. Nor is confiscatory taxation apt to force large numbers into collective farms. Many will prefer to see their holdings taken from them, which might not prove such a simple undertaking, rather than sign their properties away.

Where does this leave the government? The Communist regime will never succeed in gaining the peasants' confidence so long as it insists, as it is likely to continue to do, that the "future is in the common working of the soil and not in individual ownership." [14] Its contention in the same breath that it "will never drive men into co-operatives by forceful means" only confirms what the peasant has learned from experience: there is a wide divergence between the regime's professions and its actions. It all adds up to a widespread distrust and a bitter hatred of the government.

[14] See Tito speech, *Borba,* July 28, 1952; also *Politika* May 18, 1953.

The more the regime seeks to achieve collectivization the more it will have the peasant against it.

Under the circumstances, therefore, the government will have to accept a slower tempo in collectivization. It will be forced to continue with improvisations, to seek new methods to improve the efficiency of the collectives, to alter their form in order to make them more attractive. It will seek ways and means of employing the "general-type" co-operative to bring in collectivization via the "back door." At the same time it cannot permit the private peasant to prosper, for this would make him more immune to collectivization, while at the same time causing resentment among collectivized peasants. All this leads to the inescapable conclusion that unless the Communists abandon the collectivization idea, an unlikely occurrence, there would seem to be no end in sight to the war between the regime and the peasant.

Chapter 25:

The Standard of Living

IT CANNOT be denied that the standard of living of the vast majority of Yugoslav workers, peasants and white-collar employees is considerably below that of pre-World War II. In the case of industrial workers, the difference can be approximated with fair accuracy by comparing average wages and the cost of some basic commodities. This is also true of white-collar workers. In the case of the peasant, however, the evidence is of a slightly different character but nonetheless devastating.

For nearly eight years Yugoslav Communists insisted that the standard of living was being raised. In 1953, however, they were to admit that, on the contrary, it had actually gone down. Tito blandly stated that instead of more bread, which he said had been their goal, "there was less." [1] In similar fashion, his close collaborator, Vukmanovich, reported that "purchase funds" had increased, "while on the other hand production of goods for wide consumption remains on the same level." [2]

When in 1950 the Communists were talking about raising the standard of living, the people were relating the following story of a reported conversation between a worker and his peasant friend:

Worker: "Say, John, did you hear that Tito underwent a serious operation?"
Peasant: "No, what kind of an operation?"
Worker: "Double Hernia."
Peasant: "How in the world did he get that?"
Worker: "He was trying to lift the standard of living!"

[1] *Politika,* May 18, 1953.
[2] *Borba,* June 2, 1953.

Spokesmen for the Yugoslav regime, hard pressed for an explanation of their economic status, have sometimes resorted to reminding critical visitors that they inherited a war-devastated country. This is only partially true, and had the regime applied itself to repairing the damage, leaving the people free to produce, Yugoslavia would have recovered rapidly. It should be remembered, by way of comparison, that the country also suffered in World War I, but recovered quickly, and without the assistance of an UNRRA with its millions of dollars. Moreover, foreign loans to prewar Yugoslavia throughout its existence totaled less than one hundred million dollars, while Communist Yugoslavia has received several times that figure during a much shorter period. An uniformed foreign observer may be impressed by the regime's war-devastation argument, but every Yugoslav citizen knows that Communist experimentation has been more ruinous to the economy than the direct consequences of the war.

The Workers

Pre-World War II Yugoslav labor syndicates, although not numerically strong, succeeded in moderately improving the lot of the workers, much to the dislike of the Communist Party. Working underground, the Communists sought to utilize the syndicates for political purposes—to gain recruits for their party and to discredit the Socialists who were in control of the syndicates. Communists did not like to see the syndicates secure advantages for the workers, for this tended to ruin their principal source of recruitment: the poorer dissatisfied workers.

In order to provoke the government to take action against the syndicates, the Communists engaged in such ventures as planting illegal printed matter among syndicate workers. To gain favor with the workers, on the other hand, one of their favorite tactics was always to demand more for them than the syndicates were seeking. When responsible syndicate officers made realistic demands, such as for a 10 per cent wage boost, the Communists would demand a 30, 40 or even a 50 per cent increase. Some of the less politically educated workers were influenced favorably by the Communists, not knowing that these were political tactics and nothing more.

During the enemy occupation of Yugoslavia the workers were about evenly divided between Tito's Partisans and the national movement of Mihailovich. When it was evident that the Allies were on the side of the Partisans, a substantial part of the workers went over to them. Victory seemed to indicate the rightness of the cause, and the workers were confident that the new government would be a workers' regime. Before too much time had elapsed, however, they discovered that all Communist promises were illusory.

When the status of workers is examined today, it is not difficult to perceive why even those workers who were pro-Communist before World War II are now saying to their prewar Socialist friends that the latter's analysis of Communist tactics in the prewar years was absolutely accurate. That the workers should be disillusioned is understandable if we compare their standard of living now with prewar. The figures cited below, I believe, are fairly accurate. Certainly they are not far off, and portray a striking contrast.

Generally speaking, workers today earn five or six times what they earned doing comparable work in prewar years. The following table of some elemental needs illustrates, however, that

Commodity	Prewar Price			Price Summer 1952	How many Times Greater
bread	1½ dinars per Kilogram			30 dinars	20
lard	12 " " "			180 "	15
potatoes	½ "	"	"	30 "	60
beans (dried)	1½ "	"	"	80 "	53
rice	6 "	"	"	250 "	40
meat (pork)	8 "	"	"	200 "	25
meat (beef)	6 "	"	"	170 "	28
butter	22 "	"	"	460 "	20
sugar	12 "	"	"	150 "	12
coffee	42 "	"	"	2000 "	45
milk	1½ "	"	liter	24 "	16
eggs	½ "	"	each	10 "	20
workshirt	36 dinars			2000 "	55
shoes	100 "			2500 "	25
socks	4 "			400 "	100
suit (ordinary)	450 "			9900 "	22
soap	7 dinars per kilogram			170 "	24
washing soda	1 " " "			90 "	90
trolley fare	1½ "			15 "	10
coal	275 " " ton			4000 "	14
wood	100 " " cu. meter			3000 "	30

prices have been multiplied many more times than have wages. That the above comparison is on the conservative side was borne out by a comparison of 1939 and 1950 food prices in the Zagreb area in a somewhat obscure health publication.[3]

One worker pointed out to me that prewar unemployment benefits would equal today's wages in purchasing power. A single man received ten dinars per day, while a married man received five dinars additional for each dependent, up to three. A family with one child could buy the following with fifteen dinars compensation:

Commodity and amount	Price	Price Summer 1952
milk — 1 liter	1½ dinars	24 dinars
bread — 1 kilogram	1½ "	30 "
pork — ½ "	4 "	100 "
sugar — ¼ "	3 "	35 "
lard — ¼ "	3 "	45 "
potatoes — 3 "	1½ "	90 "
	14½ dinars	324 dinars

With an additional child in the family, prewar unemployment benefits would purchase nearly as much as today's wage of a highly skilled worker.

To make matters worse for the workers, the prices of many commodities, including bread, fats, rice, beans, coffee and dairy products had increased noticeably by the summer of 1953. In addition, a number of food items were in scarce supply during the summer of 1953 (e.g. sugar and milk). Moreover, utility rates have skyrocketed in recent years. Rents, which were officially reduced to half of prewar, have more recently been doubled, while wages were simultaneously frozen. Instead of raising the standard of living, surprising as it may seem to some, the Communists are depressing it further. Instead of the familiar, "every year, better and better," the Yugoslav people depict their progress in reverse with: "Every yesteryear, better and better."

During the initial years of the Tito regime an attempt was made to placate workers with Soviet-type awards: labor medals, badges, diplomas, honor titles (Shockworker, Hero of Socialist Labor, Fighter for High Yield, etc.).[4] These, however, found little favor among Yugoslav workers. But workers in industries

[3] *Zdrastvene novine* (Zagreb), June 1, 1953. See table 13.
[4] *Sluzhbeni list,* December 8, 1948.

on the government's high priority list also received increased material benefits, most of which have now been withdrawn.

Toward the end of 1951, in an effort to increase the workers' income without raising his wages, the government inaugurated a system of supplemental grants amounting to 3,000 dinars per child. Nearly half of this was to be paid in cash, the remainder in coupons which entitled the holder to purchase industrial goods at 80 per cent discount. Workers who had any other source of income (e.g. rent, working wife, etc.), or who owned land benefited only in part or not at all from the supplemental grants. Peasants, doctors, lawyers, independent artisans and others were not entitled to any benefits from this source. In mid-1953, however, these grants, described as "unbearable for the economy," were sharply reduced, particularly in the case of families having other sources of income (e.g. farm land).[5]

Workers are keenly aware of their plight. They work long hours, many without pay (e.g. voluntary work, working Sundays "for the party," etc.), yet they cannot buy enough food, to say nothing of the still more expensive textiles. Most telling of all, however, is their awareness that they lived better in the pre-Communist era. To make matters worse, they are convinced that, although they are supposedly living in a workers' state, nearly everyone else lives better than they. They have observed that high regime leaders seem to live well. The same appears to be true of many in the white-collar class. While realizing that the peasant is hard hit, the workers nevertheless believe that he must be eating better than they.

Every worker with whom I was able to talk privately, and who was old enough to remember prewar conditions, told me that workers had lived much better before the war. Workers who once damned prewar private industrialists think differently now. In 1949 a mechanic who had worked in Vlada Ilich's prewar factory said: "All of us workers looked upon Vlada Ilich as a bourgeois and greeted Communism as a liberation. Today the situation is such that if Vlada Ilich appeared all of us would kiss his shoes." In 1952, Vlada Ilich died, and a mammoth turnout of workers appeared at the cemetery to pay their respects. One of

---

[5] *Borba,* July 20 and 21, 1953. Also see Vukmanovich interview, *Borba,* June 9, 1953.

them spoke briefly but glowingly of the departed, who, he said, had been a "real mother" to the workers. As might have been expected, he was rewarded with imprisonment at the hands of Tito's police.

Prewar Communists among railway workers are today bitterly dissatisfied. The same is generally true of the workers in the old mining families. When a non-Communist mining engineer asked one of these miners, "who *was* satisfied with the present regime," he received the following reply: "Only the group of gypsies who get paid for doing nothing but spying." Another miner, who now mines coal but who before the war was working for the French in the Bor copper mines, insists that his whole family could have lived for two months on his prewar monthly salary. Now, he said, "my wife and I alone could not live on my salary if it were not for peasant relatives who help us." "In those days," he continued, "I could buy a good pair of Bata (Czech) shoes for 79 dinars!"

Similar stories could be recounted in other industries and from divergent areas. A cabinetmaker in a small Slovenian town (2,500 population) told me that there were no more than fifty Communists among them, or 2 per cent of the population. "Yet," he continued, "they tell us what to do. We are at their mercy." The net result of Communist rule, he added, has been that "those who were the most enterprising, those who were the most frugal and those who saved the most have had it taken away from them by men who have never had anything and who never tried to have anything."

Typical of the disillusionment among workers was the comment of a seamstress who, as chief of a shop, was doubtless a party member. She had hoped for better times for the workers, she confided to a friend, but instead "times have never been worse for the working class of Yugoslavia." But, as many of my Yugoslav friends have observed, "this is a great school. In fifty years of hard work we could not have taught the worker as much as the Communist Party has taught him in five."

"You may wonder," an intelligent worker volunteered, "why there is no opposition if conditions are so bad, why the people are silent. You people in the West who have not experienced it," he continued, "cannot appreciate the psychological impact of a knock on the door late at night." He told me the oft-heard personal story of how individuals disappeared, never to be heard from again, or only after a number of years. In the early years of the regime, he said, the Communists systematically provoked workers to say what they thought and believed, in order to weed out the potential dissidents. Workers were encouraged to speak up freely in various conferences. The more intelligent ones did, and one by one they disappeared. "They were devoured by the night," he said finally, "and now you understand why workers are silent."

While such dire consequences may not follow criticism today, it is significant that the official press reports that "workers will not discuss at conferences, yet they do that on street corners." The reason given is no less significant: ". . . some Communists, some members of the workers' council and some members of the executive committee of the syndicate organization have the decisive word in interpreting what is Socialistic and what is anti-Socialistic." [6]

Workers find some outlet, however, in surreptitiously telling stories such as the following conversation between Tito and Truman asking each other about their respective countries.

> Tito: "How much does an American worker earn per month?"
> Truman: "About $400."
> Tito: "How much does it cost him to live?"
> Truman: "Approximately $300."
> Tito: "What does he do with the other $100?"
> Truman: "Well, you know we are a democracy, and we don't ask him what he does with it."

With that Truman began asking the questions:

> Truman: "How much do Yugoslav workers earn per month?"
> Tito: "About 7,000 dinars."
> Truman: "And how much do they need to live on?"
> Tito: "About 10,000 dinars."
> Truman: "But where do they get the other 3,000?"
> Tito: "Well, you know we too are a democratic country and we don't ask them where they get it."

Some Communist leaders have admitted that they have kept wages down, but insist that they were forced to do so because col-

[6] *Borba,* March 14, 1953.

lectivized agriculture had not been able to dictate market prices of agricultural produce.[7] Any increase in wages, they reasoned, would have benefited the independent peasant who would have forced prices still higher. In view of the long period of compulsory deliveries when the government determined the vast bulk of all prices, this reasoning evades the real explanation. The simple unadorned fact is that the regime's catastrophically ruinous policies had resulted in a sharp drop in agricultural production, in a country whose average annual prewar yield was great enough to feed the country for three years!

The Peasants

The standard of living among peasants has gone down steadily under Communism. Of hundreds of peasants with whom I talked not a one had any doubts on this score. They were astonished by questions which sought to compare their present standard with prewar. "There just is no comparison," was a frequent exclamation. Amazed that I should ask if they lived better now or before the war, a group of about a dozen peasants seemed well pleased with the answer which one of their number gave me. Said he: "Before the war I worked seasonally at twenty dinars a day and was able to build myself a house. Now I cannot save enough to build a doghouse!"

While occasionally utilizing prices of commodities to illustrate their reduced purchasing power, peasants more often presented a vivid portrayal of their plight by comparing their physical belongings. Time after time, peasants told me how many more pigs, cows, sheep and other animals they had before the war. In and out of collectives the peasants related the same story. One man, now a member of a labor co-operative, told me that they were all better off during the prewar years. "Why," he observed, "instead of two pigs we always had between twenty and thirty."

The system of compulsory deliveries, often exacting more than the farmer's total yield, took from him not only food grains but also livestock, lard, honey, wool, grapes, potatoes and other farm produce. The ridiculously low prices which he received

[7] See Bakarich speech, *Naprijed,* April 18, 1952.

were bad enough. To make matters worse, he was left little or nothing for his own family. When his assessed quota exceeded crop yields, if he chose to stay out of jail, he was forced to sell some sheep, a cow, a farm wagon, or some other property in order to buy the requisite produce at high free market prices from poorer peasants who had not been so heavily assessed.

The whole system of compulsory deliveries was calculated to keep the poor peasant poor and to bring all others down to his level. This was no accident, no result of inexperienced bureaucrats in the people's committees. This was deliberate Communist Party policy, and it did not take the peasants very long to realize it. The policy was not aimed at the well-to-do peasants alone. Those who considered themselves below the average, and who by American standards would have been classed as poor farmers, found themselves treated as "kulaks" and as "enemies of the people."

This indiscriminately hostile Communist Party attitude toward the peasants succeeded in making enemies of nearly all of them. Compulsory deliveries have been abolished, but there is no guarantee that they will not be reintroduced at a future date. In their place have come heavier and heavier taxes, through which the government hopes to keep the peasants at their present low level. Since they have no large-scale outlet for their produce except the government-controlled general-type co-operatives, the regime expects to continue to dictate the prices of the bulk of their produce. In early 1953, for example, the government was paying the peasants sixty-five dollars a ton for wheat, while at the same time importing wheat from Turkey at \$130.00 a ton.[8]

The peasants, however, were apparently selling no more than they had to. In the future, in view of their hostility toward the regime and its policies, they may seek to adjust their production so as to frustrate the government. By planting small amounts of various crops they can come close to being self-sufficient. So long as they can continue to sell produce to direct consumers in order to buy salt, matches and a few other necessities, they can be expected to sell as little as possible to the government, unless the latter pays a fair market price.

How their future actions or those of the government will

[8] *New York Times,* January 1, 1953.

affect their standard of living remains in the realm of speculation. Reduced to a low standard of living, the peasants do not know what the future holds for them. Many who have never been in debt are now way under. Although most of them are not starving, they are often hungry. In most peasant areas the scarcity of clothing is more acutely felt than insufficient food. Peasants in widely scattered areas told me that all of them were virtually naked.

Of luxuries there can be little talk. Tobacco, like all other items, is exceedingly expensive and can be purchased only from the government. Wines, which in the prewar period could be found in the majority of peasant households, are now a luxury. It was scarce even at a wine co-operative which I visited one Sunday. Apologetically, one of the members said to me, "Before the war you could hear champagne corks popping around here all day long on Sundays. Now we don't have a good bottle of ordinary wine from which to offer visitors a drink."

When in the summer of 1952 I visited some peasants in central Serbia, I discovered that one of their number had been a pro-regime Communist. Now working as a day laborer for independent peasants, and sharing their misery, he at one point launched into a seemingly serious, but no doubt mocking praise of Tito, of the progress being made, everything being good, etc.—the general party line. The four or five peasants sitting around laughed out loud at every phrase.

In addition to their personal impoverishment, peasants reported that they had been unable to maintain farm buildings in good repair. Nails, lumber and other necessary items either could not be had at all, or at best at fantastically high prices. Manpower, too, was scarce or nonexistent. Likewise, it has been impossible to replace worn-out furniture and other household goods.

Somewhat characteristic of the peasant's attitude were the responses of two different peasants in their separate chance meetings with a prewar member of parliament. One of the peasants had complained to the deputy in 1929 that their freedom had been taken away, and the deputy had sought unsuccessfully to convince him that such was not the case. When they met in 1950, the peasant was again complaining about the loss of their liberties. The former deputy reminded him that he had insisted that his freedom had been taken away before the war, so why should he complain. Whereupon the peasant retorted: "Let us not engage in jests, this situation is far too serious for that."

Not long after, the same ex-deputy met another peasant who before the war had complained to him of high taxes, and who had pointedly told him that they were all alike, that it really did not matter who ruled. This time when they met, the peasant began with, "What in heaven's name is this? How long can it last? . . ." The ex-deputy reminded him that before the war he had said that it did not matter who ruled. The peasant shook his head, "Oh, how much we have learned since then," he exclaimed.

White-Collar Workers

People who have traditionally been referred to as the white-collar class tend to separate into three fairly distinct groups in Communist Yugoslavia. In the first group are the Communists at the apex of the party hierarchy who hold the more important positions in the bureaucracy. In the second group are the lesser Communists and their sympathizers or onetime camp followers. The last group is made up of teachers, lawyers, doctors, and lower civil servants who never trusted the Communists.

The first group is the smallest and its members continue to live relatively well. Members of the second group, once favored with special stores and other privileges enjoyed by all the party faithful, find it difficult to make ends meet. They must live on a fixed salary which is not high. On the other hand, everything they buy is expensive. Much is expected of them in the form of extra work, assistance with propaganda meetings, volunteer work projects, youth rallies and demonstrations. Many of them are self-sacrificing, loyal and willing to obey party dictates. Many more, however, are disillusioned, dispirited, dejected and demoralized. Once enthusiastic, they are now psychologically exhausted, plodding along, leaving their desks whenever there is a suitable pretext, living almost aimlessly from one day to the next. They have been asked to sacrifice much, but they do not see any signs of a better day. Yet they know it would be treason to betray their real thoughts openly.

The last group—the white-collar workers who never had any illusions about the Communists—suffer material privations similar to those of other citizens. As in the case of other groups in the population, their standard of living has gone down. They are much more cowed, however, than either the peasants or the workers. They need their jobs and yet must fear for them much more than is the case of either the workers or the peasants. This is particularly true of non-Communist teachers, for they know that long range regime policies call for their replacement with loyal party members. In a slightly lesser measure it is also true of civil servants who have been kept in office only because the government has not had a sufficient number of individuals with the necessary specialized training to take over their jobs.

In some ways, however, this group is better off psychologically. They never expected anything good from the Communists. While suffering from material privations, they have received some small comfort from seeing things go as they expected them to. Future developments, they were sure, would permit them to witness the downfall of the Communist edifice. The sizable assistance which the regime has received from the West since its expulsion from the Moscow camp has, however, served to shatter their expectations and to add to their frustrations.

As in the case of industrial workers, the bulk of white-collar employees is faced with high food costs, recently doubled rents, and sharply increased utility rates. Textiles are exhorbitant in cost, particularly the type and variety needed by this group. The fact that one rarely finds a "white collar" in today's Yugoslavia speaks eloquently of the prohibitive clothing costs. Riding a streetcar or a bus with any regularity and indulging in average smoking are both costly luxuries for white-collar employees. Average salaries among white-collar workers have not kept pace with the salaries of workers in most state economic enterprises.

Although it concerns a relatively small group of people, one exception needs to be noted. Actors, musicians, and other artists, as well as the best athletes, are in a category apart. They are on the government payroll and in the past have been able to live in relative comfort. This has been particularly true of the more outstanding personalities, but the less important ones have also been well paid. In spite of the favored treatment which they have received, however, many have chosen freedom when they found themselves outside Yugoslav frontiers. A whole ballet team once refused to return from an official trip to France. Swimmers, polo players, football stars and other athletes have from time to time taken advantage of official trips to remain as exiles in free nations.

Chapter 26:

Medicine, Social Security, Housing

AS IN other endeavors, so in the realm of the social services Communist Party policies have undergone frequent changes.[1] In general these changes came in two phases of development. In the first, new laws, amendments, orders, and directives were calculated to bring about greater uniformity and a more systematic centralization. In the second, the major effort has been directed toward reversing the trend, and moving toward decentralization and more local autonomy.

Party spokesmen, while justifying each succeeding step or change as correct, have conceded that there were many negative results.[2] Understandably, these are rarely specified, but rather alluded to in the abstract verbiage of dialectic jargon. As in other fields, Communists have been forced to change—to improvise for the simple reason that policies and programs have not worked. One reason they did not work in the field of the social services is to be found in the party's predilection to tackle problems without study and with incompetent people. Secondly, the social services have, by and large, rated a low priority under the Communist regime. Except perhaps for certain isolated instances, industrialization, the army, the secret police, party propaganda and other high-priority Communist undertakings have received the bulk of what there was to get. Medicine, housing and social

---

[1] See Nikola Dilber, "Samoupravljanje sluzhbom i sredstvima socialnog osiguranja," *Narodna drzhava*, VI (No. 5–6, 1952), pp. 260–71.
[2] *Ibid.*

security have in considerable measure needed to be satisfied with
the crumbs.

Medicine

Although prewar Yugoslavia had a system of socialized medicine, it was far from adequate to cope with the country's medical
needs. One of the most acute problems involved the high inci-
dence rates of tuberculosis and venereal diseases. This was particularly true of the peasant areas, for the larger proportion of
doctors, nurses, hospitals and clinics were in the cities. Urban
residents, especially in the largest cities, had fairly adequate medical care. Residents of rural areas were not so fortunate. Moreover, they often failed to recognize their ailments or found it in-
convenient to seek medical care.

By the time the Communists had come to power the situation
had worsened considerably. Wartime conditions had brought an
increase in disease, yet medications were more scarce and doctors
were fewer. Many doctors were taken to Germany as prisoners of
war, never to return because of the subsequent Communist seizure of power. Others had been killed by the enemy or they had
fallen in the civil war which raged more or less from 1941 to
1945. During the same time, countless hospitals were destroyed,
looted by the occupier or stripped of their supplies and equipment by adherents of guerrilla bands who were in great need of
medical supplies.

Immediately after liberation, UNRRA, the Red Cross and
other foreign agencies delivered to Yugoslavia considerable medications, laboratory supplies and other necessary equipment. The
Communists had, however, aggravated their problem immeas-
urably by having liquidated many doctors as political enemies.
In nearly all communities, doctors had been active in politics
during the prewar years. Because they were respected by the people, Communist Party functionaries distrusted them, considered
them dangerous, for they were potential leaders around whom
the people might rally.

High postwar illness rates were beyond the comprehension of
many party bosses. In 1946, for example, a group of doctors in
Zagreb narrowly escaped being tried as saboteurs because they

had allegedly certified too many workers as being sick. In view of the mood prevailing in 1946 they would no doubt have been shot had it not occurred to some one to check illness rates in the other major cities and found that Zagreb was no exception.

Medical facilities (hospitals, clinics, medications, etc.) are still below prewar, and the number of doctors, as of 1952, had not reached the 1941 level. At least as late as 1950 many operations (e.g. tonsilectomies) were being performed without any anesthetic. Hospitals and clinics are overcrowded, and waiting rooms are full of sick people. Industrial accidents and industrial diseases have risen sharply. While the government is no doubt making some progress, it appears to be painfully slow.

Although all doctors must put in the requisite number of hours at government clinics and hospitals, they are permitted to practice privately on their own time. Their private earnings, however, are taxed heavily. Not accepting the doctors' reports of their private income, government agents are sent to peer into their offices, which, incidentally, are usually full. They note the number of people in the waiting room, then stand outside to ask patients as they leave how much they paid. On the basis of such surveys, the government estimates the number of patients treated annually and the doctor's total earnings for the year.

Doctors who at the end of the year think that they have paid their taxes are in for a rude awakening. Tax collectors come around with supplementary assessments of several thousand dinars. I personally know of some cases where this has been happening regularly year after year.

The regime's attitude toward doctors has not been helpful. The case of one heart specialist is fairly typical of the government's position. He has had great difficulty in getting necessary medical instruments and apparatus. The government has refused to exchange a sufficient amount of foreign currency for his Yugoslav money in order that he could subscribe to the *Heart Journal,* published in the United States. He has no car at his disposal when it is necessary to make calls, although Communist functionaries parade around in the latest American models. Moreover, he lives on the fifth floor, where he also has his office, in a building whose elevator does not function. As a consequence, heart patients must walk up four flights of stairs!

This and other similar case histories cast some light on the system of values which prevails among Yugoslav Communists. Recently, for example, a woman dentist disconnected the electric power which had operated her drills and other equipment because of the fantastically high electricity rates. She now operates her drills with footpower, and sarcastically refers to it as the "new electrification of the country."

Social Security

The Yugoslav government system of state medicine functions, in reality, under their social security system, which pays for the services to which those under social security are entitled. Doctors are treated as "experts" who furnish advice, but the responsibility for decisions as to what medical services various individuals are entitled to rests with the social security officials. These same officials determine other benefits, such as old-age and unemployment compensation.

Not unlike its prewar counterpart, the present social security system is primarily limited to wage earners and salaried workers. The peasants are excluded, although labor cooperatives are supposed to assume some responsibility for their own members. The free professions, however, have been included, but this has not been without political implications. In the case of clergymen, for example, they are eligible only if they are members of the government-sponsored clergymen's associations. Lawyers, too, are in a similar position, for they must be members in good standing in the regime-sponsored lawyers' guilds.

Until sometime in 1952 the whole social security system was centrally managed and directed. It was financed through the budget of the central government. Because the tendency was to spend "someone else's money" rather freely, the budgeted amounts were expended before the end of the fiscal year, and supplementary grants had to be made.[3] Consequently, the government found that such a situation was impossible and unbearable "from the economic point of view."

In conformity with the general decentralization trend, it was decided to go to the other extreme. In 1952 it was declared that

[3] Dilber, *op. cit.*

social security decisions would be transferred to local assemblies, elected directly in the cities and counties by participants in the social security system.[4] These local assemblies would elect higher governing bodies (assemblies) for each republic. The central government is said to have no right of direct intervention. Only the courts, before whom contested social security cases can be brought, are allegedly able to influence the actions of the social security assemblies.

These assemblies were told that they must find their own sources of revenue, for the central government was no longer going to finance social security activities. It was said, however, that the central government would reduce its taxes on state economic enterprises in the amount which in the past had been set aside for social security. Economic enterprises will now make their social security contributions to local authorities administering the social security program.

There is little likelihood, however, that these assemblies will be free of interference from above. In June of 1953, for example, one of the top leaders in Belgrade asserted that too much money was going into social security.[5] It seems reasonable to conclude, therefore, that the central authorities will continue, if indirectly, to determine the amount of money which is to be spent for social security. Governments of the republics and local people's committees will exercise the more direct supervision over social security activities. More important, perhaps, will be the unifying influence of the Communist hierarchy. Determined not to control matters quite so openly, Communists will no doubt be kept busy in the future as behind-the-scenes co-ordinators.

Housing

The housing situation in Yugoslavia today is considerably worse than in the prewar period. There are several reasons why this should be so. In a few areas the war destroyed many dwellings. In the peasant areas, buildings have continued to deteriorate and peasants, with some exceptions, simply have not been able to procure materials to make needed repairs. It is in the cities, how-

[4] *Ibid.,* pp. 268–69.
[5] See Vukmanovich statement, *Borba,* June 2, 1953.

ever, that the housing problem has been most acute. The main reason being that when the Communists came to power they brought thousands of their camp followers to the cities, where there was no surplus housing.

The Communist leaders, however, were not interested in studying the housing situation. They were content to accept Lenin's statement that there was adequate housing. All that was needed was an appropriate distribution of existing units. One Yugoslav Communist even showed me the citation from Lenin in an effort to convince me that there was no real housing shortage in Belgrade.

Accepting Lenin's thesis, the government housing authorities went into all apartments as well as private homes. Arbitrarily, they decided how many persons should be housed in any one unit or building. Owners had no alternative but to abide by the verdict of the housing authorities, and often they had no choice as to who their tenants were to be. Each owner was told what part of the house he could occupy, the remainder was for rent at government-imposed rates. Apartments as well as private homes were subdivided, making it necessary for several complete strangers to share kitchens, bathrooms and other facilities. It was not unusual for several families to occupy what normally would be a single family unit.

Countless examples similar to the following might be cited. A bureaucrat who had been assigned a room in a doctor's house was transferred to another city, but failed to give up his room. Thereupon the doctor went to the housing authority and succeeded in recovering his room, in which he then set up his office. Then one day three men appeared, proclaimed that they were getting the room back, and began throwing the doctor's things out the window.

For the Communists the housing problem had important political implications. Most of the people residing in the urban areas prior to the arrival of the Communists turned out to be hostile to them. Many of them held no jobs, either because the regime would not employ them or because they were so antiregime as to refuse to work for it in any capacity. Viewing these people as "unproductive" and "antagonistic elements," Communist leaders often dealt harshly with them. Hundreds were resettled to the

periphery of cities in considerably less comfortable quarters.[6]
Many others were forced to leave urban areas entirely without
the government's making any attempt to find other housing for
them.

Antiregime people, however, were not the only ones to suffer.
A shipyard shockworker, in search of housing, found a small
damaged hut, received permission to fix it up and moved in. In
the meantime the ministry of heavy industry began constructing
a large building around him, the walls went up, then the roof. He
sought permission for other quarters and was assigned them.
When he arrived someone else had already moved in, the first to
arrive of three who had been assigned the identical unit. Whereupon the ministry of heavy industry offered to build the man a
little house anywhere in Belgrade, but this proposal was vetoed
by the executive committee of the People's Committee of Belgrade. Since this case was cited by the party press [7] to illustrate
a "heartless attitude" toward a valuable worker, his situation was
no doubt remedied. But one cannot help wondering how many
other and similar hardships received no attention at all.

In some cases, particularly at certain key industrial establishments, the government has erected fairly decent dwellings to
house the workers. In the cities, too, new apartment buildings
have gone up, but party members have told me that they are still
a long way from satisfying housing needs. Moreover, income
from rents has not been sufficient to provide for proper maintenance and depreciation. This was one consideration which led to
the doubling of rents toward the end of 1952.

Some members of the new "ruling class" were responsible for
unusually rapid depreciation of dwelling units. The Yugoslav
press on one occasion reported that some fifty individuals in Belgrade were moved to poorer quarters because they had damaged
their previous places of residence.[8] It seems that some of the new
urban dwellers had, among other things, taken to storing coal in
their rooms and splitting wood on the floors.

[6] *20 Oktobar,* December 3, 1948.
[7] *Borba,* April 7, 1949.
[8] *20 Oktobar,* March 18, 1949.

Chapter 27

Communism for Whom

IT SEEMS appropriate, in view of what has already been said in Part Five, to ask who benefits from the new Communist order in Yugoslavia. It may be assumed that the ruling group, the Communists, are the recipients of certain favors or else they would not be there. It may be interesting to inquire into the nature of these benefits, and to ask if they are shared equally among the members of the ruling elite. It may be pertinent, also, to inquire if anyone else benefits directly or indirectly, and to consider if the negative effects are felt more keenly in some areas than in others.

The First Years of a Privileged Class

Before they came to power, the Communists were more vehement than any other group in their denunciation of the privileges enjoyed by prewar Yugoslav ruling circles. Once in power, however, they systematically created privileges for themselves and their adherents that far exceeded anything known to Yugoslavia in the past. These privileges extended to every phase of life: food, housing, recreation, education, jobs, salaries and even in clashes with the law. In each instance party members had a decided advantage.

Special food stores were established for ministers and other high government functionaries, for army officers, for secret-police employees, for scientific workers and others. Prices were low and goods abundant, although opaque glass windows were utilized in an effort to make this less evident to the general public. The Communist elite was able to obtain certain foods (e.g. chocolate) which the people had not seen for years. They alone could order from abroad items which were unobtainable domestically. Their families had milk when countless small children had none. All this at a time when ordinary citizens were closely rationed, forced to spend much time standing in bread, meat, and other lines to get their rations, and compelled to pay high prices on the open market for certain farm products.

In addition, party members received better and larger housing accommodations. They could travel in better facilities and less expensively. Most of the high bureaucrats rode around in the more expensive models of new American automobiles. They enjoyed priorities at hotels, restaurants and theaters. Whenever they desired to put on banquets, food was always forthcoming from special reserves. They enjoyed longer vacations at less expensive resorts, set aside especially for them. They could get wood and coal cheaply when other people were freezing. Their children had no difficulty in entering the university or selecting the courses of study which they desired, at a time when many brilliant students were being denied entrance.

Party members not only enjoyed job priorities but in addition received better pay for the same type of work. In numerous instances technically trained men received less pay than their privileged "subordinates" who were learning the job. Party members frequently received special bonuses of one type or another. Those who had a record of fighting in Partisan ranks from 1941, for example, were receiving a special monthly supplement, at least as late as 1950, of 6,000 dinars, a sum which was then equivalent to the wage of a highly skilled worker.

Moreover, in clashes with the law or in neglect of one's job, Communists were assumed to have possessed good intentions. Non-Communists, on the other hand, were always presumed to have evil intentions, to be plotting against the new order. The explanation of a party member who wrecked a government car was usually accepted at face value, while a non-Communist driver in a similar situation was suspected of deliberate sabotage, gross negligence, or disrespect and insufficient care for Socialist property. Mistakes in industrial enterprises are likewise scrutinized for motives. In a Belgrade factory, for example, two hundred liters of pure alcohol were lost one night. The man on duty that night was a Communist, and nothing happened. But if he had not been a Communist. . . ?

The above-mentioned privileges are but the main ones enjoyed by the Communists in their first five years of power. Any foreign correspondent who might have written about them would have been labeled "a slanderer," to say the least. Any Yugoslav citizen who might have referred to their existence would, if the authorities knew about it, quite likely land in jail. One man who in a public gathering asked why the special stores existed was bitterly criticized by the Communist leaders at the meeting, and within a few hours (at 2 A.M.) was taken from his home.

Yet an order in October, 1950, abolishing special food stores and other priorities for particular groups, was admission enough of the existence of substantial privileges.[1] Simultaneously, a letter from the party's Central Committee to subsidiary party organizations, explaining and justifying the abolition of certain privileges, merely recorded what all Yugoslav citizens and most foreign observers in Belgrade had long known to be the case.[2]

The 1950 order came at a time when Yugoslavia faced an acute food shortage, only in part due to the drought, and had made a desperate plea for food relief from the United States, which was forthcoming. The principal result of the order was to abolish special food stores and other privileged food supply sources for rank-and-file Communists, as well as to eliminate exclusive vacation resorts which had been available to them. Top party officials, the militia, the secret police and the army continued to enjoy privileged sources of supply.

The immediate impact upon rank-and-file Communists of the order taking away their cherished privileges was anything but pleasant. Ordinary citizens had become accustomed to being discriminated against, and did not become excited about the new order, for they did not trust the Communists in any case. But the rank-and-file Communist, who had just begun putting on weight and had recently become accustomed to the pleasures which these special stores afforded, immediately became a most sensitive man who felt the real meaning of social injustice.

The loss of tangible privileges and the failure of the regime to

---

[1] *Borba,* October 15, 1950.
[2] *Ibid.,* October 17, 1950.

bring about the good life which it had promised have combined to produce bitter dissatisfaction in the Communist rank and file, particularly among the workers. Yet they have had to adapt themselves, for they know that party discipline tolerates no opposition. Some of them found some comfort in the fact that their status accorded them other privileges, however small, which non-Communist members of society did not enjoy.

The Privileged Today

Except for the exclusive stores, Yugoslav Communists, especially those in the upper layers of the hierarchy, continue more or less to enjoy the privileges described above. The best jobs are open only to them, and positions in the bureaucratic hierarchy which they do not now occupy are being turned over to them as fast as their own people can be trained to fill them. The chief of every bureau or office must be a party man. No attempt is made to hide this fact, except perhaps from foreigners. Certainly not from Yugoslavs.

In salary and job classifications, too, Communists occupy a privileged position. An example or two will illustrate how this works. Although the press had announced, during the 1952 readjustment of teachers' salaries, that educational qualifications and experience would be decisive, in practice ways were found to reward the faithful. One young teacher was given credit for seven and one-half years' experience although she had taught no more than two or three years. When asked about this, she told an acquaintance quite frankly that the time she had spent in the hills with the Partisans during the war counted toward her experience.

Similarly, nearly all teachers were placed two salary grades below what the published regulations indicated. Teachers with twenty-three years' experience, for example, were to be placed in group VI at a salary of 15,000 dinars per month. Instead they were put in group VIII at 12,500 dinars. Only those with a special recommendation were put in group VI, and it does not require a particularly perceptive mind to guess who received the outstanding recommendations.

Similar favoritism takes place in government offices. Initially, many key jobs were filled largely by people whose major and often only qualification was political reliability. In their quest for respectability, Communists promulgated rules which require that salaries and positions correspond to education and experience. An application of this rule would put the faithful at a disadvantage. Consequently, special classes were set up in the school of education through which the uneducated leaders could obtain quick degrees.

On the job, Communists have an enviable position. As a general rule, tardiness in arriving to work and leaving their desks during the day or quitting early are overlooked. This is particularly true of informers and those who attend university courses. Sometimes the boss knows that the person concerned is engaged in party work outside the office, other times he just assumes that he has a justifiable excuse. The manager of one enterprise, a non-Communist, told a friend of his that there were five or six people on his payroll who did not work there, and he did not think it wise to ask where they worked or what they did.

Aside from enjoying greater freedom and trust, Communists have other on-the-job advantages. They can, among other things, insult their non-Communist superiors with impunity. A nurse who is a Communist can, for example, tell a non-Communist doctor that he lies, yet no non-Communist hospital employee would dare do that. This type of advantage is also exercised elsewhere. When one housewife recited her reasons for not "volunteering" to spend a weekend picking beans at a state farm, the woman party recruiter turned to her and said: "Only bandits talk that way." After this "there could be no further discussion," said the housewife, "and this is the worst part of our lot. Anyone can judge you in any way, and you dare not say anything."

Communists also receive preferred treatment when it comes to vacations. Not only are their wishes as to the time of vacation given priority but in addition their vacations are of longer duration. Important party men are permitted thirty days; employees who have been commended for their work receive about three weeks; all others two weeks. Discrimination of this type occurs much more frequently among office personnel than it does among workers in mines, plants or factories. By and large, however, the Communists are the ones who benefit whenever exceptions are made or favors extended.

Favoritism was also manifested when students sought entrance into certain fields of study at the university. In the case of medicine, engineering and other professions judged to have a good future, many more students applied than could get in. Admission was in the hands of Communists, and they did not seek to hide the fact that students of proletarian or poor peasant origins were given preference. Other students, in order to stay in school, had to be satisfied with a course of study (e.g. veterinary medicine) in which they had little or no interest. In September of 1953, however, it was announced that qualified students could freely enter any field of study.[3] But there was no explanation as to how some of the resultant problems would be met. The Belgrade Medical School, for example, planned for 360 new students, but 2,032 registered.[4]

Similarly, normal school graduates can, after two years of teaching experience, apply for permission to continue their studies at the university. In the main, only the "reliable" ones receive such permission. In the university, however, they do not necessarily receive the best or even good marks. On the other hand, they seldom fail and nearly always receive better grades than they deserve.

In one instance I discovered that favoritism had been exploited to advantage by a group of young people, ranging from junior-high through high-school age. Ten or fifteen of them decided to form a swimming club and to construct a large raft-like swimming pool on the Sava River in Belgrade. They discovered, however, that such a project would cost nearly a million dinars. Then a bright idea occurred to the boys: they would elect a young UDB (secret police) officer as their president, feeling that the rest would be easy. They were right, the money was forthcoming (approximately three quarters of a million dinars), and they now have their swimming pool, which I visited in the summer of 1952.

Communism and the Masses

The fact that the regime is thoroughly disliked throughout Yugoslavia would seem to indicate that no particular area or

[3] *Borba,* September 22, 1953.
[4] *Politika,* October 2, 1953.

people has been favored. Yet many Yugoslavs are aware that some of them have suffered less than others. And although it may be improper to speak of greater benefits to some areas, it can at least be said that certain areas have suffered less than others from Communist policies.

If it can be said that benefits have accrued as a result of the regime's spending on industrialization, then these benefits have been limited largely to the four smallest republics—Slovenia, Montenegro, Macedonia, and Bosnia-Herzegovina. This is even more true if the spending is calculated on a per-capita basis, for these four republics have less than one-third of the country's total population.

The Communists have made a special effort to improve the status of the Yugoslav regions bordering on Italy and Austria. People living in these areas have, as a consequence, benefited indirectly. Minimum wages, for example, far exceed those in the interior. Even small private pensions (resort hotels) exist in parts of Slovenia (e.g. at Ichichi), although they are not permitted anywhere else in the country.

Some Yugoslavs are inclined to attribute the existence of these pensions to Slovene ingenuity. As additional evidence, they point to the fact that many Slovene peasants are today building new homes, a rare sight in other parts of the nation. When I asked how they were able to get the bricks, I was told that the peasants had banded together and offered to produce lime, in primitive lime kilns, in return for bricks. Government agencies accepted the offer. It is only fair to point out that this would have been impossible in Serbia and Croatia, if for no other reason than the scarcity of wood to fire such kilns.

Yet wherever one travels in Yugoslavia the people insist that they have not gained, that they were better off before the war, that whatever relative advantages may have accrued to some areas the result has not been an improved standard of living. Understandably, the Communist leaders might not agree, although some rank-and-file members admit privately that material conditions are considerably below prewar. Non-Communists also point out that not only has the standard of living gone down, but that in addition the people have been enslaved by a ruthless dictatorship. They are keenly aware that they have never had less political or personal freedom, nor have they ever witnessed such utter disrespect for the human personality. As one Serb who recently succeeded in escaping from Yugoslavia put it: "Everyone can truthfully say that he has never worked so much with less profit, less rest and less peace."

Without minimizing the hardships which other areas have endured, there would seem to be little doubt that the mailed fist of the Communist dictatorship has been felt more severely in Serbia than in any other area of Yugoslavia. There are several reasons why this should be so. Historically, Serbia had a rebellious record, a record of harshness and direct action against tyrants, and the Communists wanted to make sure that this did not happen again. Secondly, during their rise to power, the Communists had little support in Serbia, for Serbia was for Mihailovich. Finally, since prewar Yugoslav governments were closely identified with Serbs and Serbia, the Communists expected to find allies among those elements (especially in Croatia and in Macedonia) who had been dissatisfied with prewar Yugoslavia. Understandably, they did not wish to alienate potential allies unnecessarily.

Although many examples could be cited as evidence of the greater severity of regime actions in Serbia, a few will suffice. It was interesting, for example, that after the Communist rise to power the Croatian hymn was being freely sung in Croatia, while Serbs landed in jail for singing theirs. It was interesting, too, that one of the first men executed in Belgrade by the Communists was the actor, Aca Cvetkovich, for having continued his acting during the German occupation, although many Serbs maintained that his humor and clowning had meant a great deal for the morale of the local populace. By contrast, a Croatian actor, Jozhe Horvat, who continued to dance under the Ustashi and the Germans was in no way penalized. More than that, a film was produced on the basis of his work, *The Flag,* depicting "the new relationship of art to the people."

It may also be significant that when the second nationalization law (1948) was passed late one afternoon, the owners of business establishments in Belgrade found agents waiting for them at the door the next morning, taking even the money in their cash registers and safes. In Zagreb, on the other hand, merchants were given several days in which to make inventory before the government took over. This is not to suggest, however, that in other cities of Croatia and of Serbia the practice may not have varied.

Finally, the Communists have desecrated the most holy place of the Serbs, Vrachar, where Saint Sava was supposedly burned at the stake. At first, the Communist Partisans made it into a stable, but now use it as a garage and a place to store coal and wood. It is unthinkable, on the other hand, that they could have even considered doing anything comparable to Saint Stephen's Cathedral in Zagreb.

Were it necessary, many other examples could be cited to show how the Communists struck harder and more mercilessly in Serbia than in other regions. Among their non-Serb adherents, actual and potential, the Communists make no effort to hide this rather widely-known fact. Among the non-Serb elements who are hostile to them, however, the Communists have welcomed and encouraged rumors to the effect that Serbs were doing pretty well under this regime. In this way they have hoped to deflect popular hostility away from themselves and toward the Serbs, and in some small measure, ironically enough, they have succeeded. In Serbia, on the other hand, they have welcomed and encouraged reports which would convince antiregime Serbs that Croats, Macedonians, or Slovenes, rather than Communists, were responsible for their plight. Here, too, the Communists have had some small measure of success. But the vast majority of Yugoslavs, Croats as well as Serbs, have not been deceived by the arguments of this divide-and-rule philosophy.

PART SIX

YUGOSLAVIA, TITOISM

AND

THE FUTURE

IN JUNE, 1948 the world was electrified with the news of a schism in the camp of international Communism. Yugoslavia's expulsion from membership in the newly created Communist Information Bureau (Cominform) broke the hitherto existing solidarity of the Soviet bloc of nations. The impact of this break upon Yugoslav internal affairs could not at that time be forecast. Since then, however, several years have gone by. The nature of the Tito-Stalin rift has been brought into sharper focus, and the direction of Yugoslav domestic developments has become more evident. In surveying some of the consequences of the break, it seems pertinent to ask not only if a new form of Communism is evolving in Yugoslavia, but also to set forth the principal factors which are likely to play a significant role in the shaping of Yugoslavia's future.

Chapter 28:

Nature of the Break with Moscow

THE fall from grace of Moscow's erstwhile most loyal satellite has been described and analyzed by a number of writers.[1] It is desirable, therefore, to confine this discussion of the nature of Yugoslavia's break with Moscow to a summary of the main factors in the controversy. While there is doubtless much that has not yet been revealed, particularly as to basic Soviet motives, the broad outline of the dispute would seem to be well defined.

World War II Bred Suspicions

Soviet leaders sowed the seeds of distrust in Yugoslavia during World War II. They did so by failing to send any aid to Tito's Partisans, by criticizing Tito's political and military tactics, and by concluding an agreement with the British on spheres of influence in the Balkans, one of whose clauses provided that Yugoslavia would be divided equally into Russian and British spheres of influence.

Tito's fervent pleas in 1941 and 1942 for arms and other supplies evoked from Moscow expressions of encouragement and praise for Partisan activities, as well as regrets that due to "technical difficulties" no help could be sent.[2] To Yugoslav Communist

[1] See Hamilton Fish Armstrong, *Tito and Goliath* (New York, 1951); Adam B. Ulam, *Titoism and the Cominform* (Cambridge, Mass., 1952); Harry Hodgkinson, *Challenge to the Kremlin* (New York, 1952). Also see Vladimir Dedijer, *Tito* (New York, 1953).
[2] See articles by Mosha Pijade, *Borba,* March 22 and 23, 1950.

leaders, however, it soon became evident that the Kremlin was motivated by political rather than technical reasons. Moscow indicated that it did not wish to risk offending its major allies, especially England, by aiding Tito, the bitter enemy of General Mihailovich, leader of the nationalist guerrilla forces. Tito's efforts to discredit the Mihailovich movement were not favorably received in the Kremlin, which directed him to seek to establish a common front with Mihailovich, adding that it was difficult to believe that an ally of England (Mihailovich) was fighting on the side of the Axis Powers.[3]

While it is plausible that the Kremlin in 1941 and 1942 considered it necessary to avoid offending its allies, it seems equally plausible that Moscow's failure to come to Tito's assistance was governed by Soviet resentment of his independent actions. Tito no doubt incurred Soviet displeasure by organizing his guerrilla movement in his own way, and without Moscow's advice or direction. Stalin's criticism of Yugoslav Communist Party tactics adds force to this analysis. The Yugoslavs were criticized for setting up proletarian brigades, for utilizing red stars on Partisan caps, and for establishing people's committees as governing bodies on liberated territory.[4]

The Soviets were apparently worried lest some of Tito's actions create difficulties for them in their relations with the West. They were afraid that the Yugoslav Communists were moving too rapidly. When the latter, a short time after the Teheran Conference, created a provisional government in the name of the National Committee of Liberation, and declared that King Peter II would not be permitted to return to Yugoslavia, Soviet leaders regarded these acts as "a stab in the back to Teheran."[5] As late as September, 1944, according to Tito, Stalin sought to have them permit King Peter's return.[6]

Tito demonstrated his independence by rejecting this advice. Earlier he had made his own arrangements with the West by accepting British and American military missions and by seeking aid from them. Tito's association with the West also helped to

[3] *Ibid.*
[4] Leon Gershkovich, *Dokumenti o razvoju narodne vlasti* (Belgrade, 1948), p. 17.
[5] Vladimir Dedijer, *Dnevnik* (Belgrade, 1950), Vol. III, p. 32.
[6] *Politika,* February 6, 1953.

facilitate the conclusion of the Tito-Shubashich Agreement, which served to endow Tito's postwar government with a certain amount of legality. Such independent behavior could not serve to endear the Yugoslav Communist leaders to the men in the Kremlin.

The Yugoslav Communists, for their part, were seemingly unwilling to believe anything bad about Moscow. If they were possessed of any doubts, they never revealed them until after they were expelled from the Cominform. They heard from Western sources about the spheres of influence arrangement but refused to believe it.[7] While continuing to sing the praises of Moscow, however, they were continually being beset with new difficulties in their dealings with the Soviets.

It is interesting that one of the first things which the Russians attempted after their troops made contact with Tito's forces on Yugoslav territory in 1944 was to put Tito's units under the direct command of the Red army.[8] They had done this with hastily organized Bulgarian guerrilla units which sprang up with the entrance of the Red army into Bulgaria. Rejecting this, Tito argued that whereas Bulgaria was at war with the Allies and could not therefore have an independent army fighting alongside the Allies, the Yugoslav Army was an allied army and hence should not be under any command but its own. The Russians were not easily dissuaded and sought to have their way several times, but Tito held firm.

Although Russian troops moved toward Hungary after the liberation of Belgrade in October, 1944, leaving Yugoslavia, Tito's difficulties with Soviet military authorities were not at an end. As Russian forces moved into Austria, after their conquest of Hungary, the Bulgarian Partisans on their southern flank entered Yugoslavia near the Slovenian city of Maribor. Upon arrival in this border town, they proceeded to loot, to rape and to kill, just as Russian troops had done while on Yugoslav soil. The Yugoslavs promptly called the Russian commander's attention to the matter and asked him to withdraw the Bulgarian units. When he would do nothing, the Yugoslav ambassador in

[7] Dedijer, *Dnevnik,* III, p. 189.
[8] A member of the party's Central Committee is the source of the information concerning their difficulties with the Red army.

Moscow took the matter up personally with Stalin, and the troops were withdrawn.

While not auguring well for the future of Soviet-Yugoslav relations, these quarrels with the Red army, as well as the earlier wartime difficulties, might have been surmountable were it not for the fact that they constituted but the beginning of more far-reaching and more disturbing postwar troubles. If a satisfactory solution had been found to Yugoslav-Soviet postwar relations, the Yugoslav leaders would without doubt have been inclined to forget and forgive past disappointments.

Moscow Aim: Economic Exploitation

Moscow's actions forced the Yugoslav leaders, much against their will, to the conclusion that nothing short of complete domination of the Yugoslav economy would satisfy the Russians. This became strikingly apparent in a number of ways, one of them being the Soviet-sponsored so-called mixed companies. In theory these were to be joint ventures, each nation supplying capital in equal amounts and possessing an equal voice in their operation. In practice, however, the Russians did not want to invest any capital, while insisting upon a predominant voice in their operation. In addition, Soviet leaders wanted to establish mixed companies only in those fields or economic pursuits which interested them. Soviet negotiators were even forced to admit to their Yugoslav counterparts that the produce of mixed companies would be used primarily to meet the needs of the Soviet Union.

That the Russians were little concerned about Yugoslav interests was also demonstrated in the discussions to establish a Soviet-Yugoslav geological society. At first the Soviet representatives made it clear that they did not want any Yugoslav geologists in the society. After assenting to qualified Yugoslav representation, they were adamant in their stand that the reports of the society should go to Moscow. Finally, they conceded that Belgrade could get copies of the reports, or, as one important Yugoslav Communist said to me, "They would tell us only what they wanted us to know."

Although consenting to the formation of two mixed companies in the commercial field, the Yugoslavs in the main rejected the idea of the mixed companies. But Moscow was engaged in simultaneously employing other techniques of economic exploitation. Determined that Yugoslavia should remain basically agricultural and the producer of raw materials,[9] Soviet leaders "often blackmailed" the Yugoslavs into concluding commercial agreements which took from them "the most precious products" [10] at world market prices, which were many times lower than the actual cost of production with semiprimitive Yugoslav methods. In exchange, the Yugoslavs were often forced to purchase articles which they did not need. Everything they bought from Moscow was fantastically expensive, especially if it was procured on a barter basis. One tractor, for example, cost the equivalent of $28,000 worth of copper, while a motorcycle cost the equivalent of $4,000 worth of gypsum.

When the Yugoslavs bought goods or services from Moscow for money they had to be paid for in gold, dollars or other hard currency. Military equipment which Moscow sold to Tito's government, for example, had to be paid for in gold or dollars.[11] To add insult to injury, much of this equipment was old and defective, although newly painted. Gunpowder, sold for hard currency, was delivered in boxes with the reject slips still there, reading: "This powder rejected as unusable." [12]

In essence, therefore, the Russians wanted to determine the course of Yugoslavia's economic development. They wanted her to remain an exporter of raw materials and agricultural products. And they desired to dictate the markets and the prices. Moreover, they sought freedom inside Yugoslavia to explore additional possibilities for economic exploitation. Finally, they expected the Yugoslavs to accept what was sent to them and to pay the prices asked of them. In short, the Soviet Union expected to engage in economic exploitation far more invidious than that of which it has accused the capitalist world.

[9] See Tito speech, *Borba,* December 28, 1948.
[10] *Glas* (Belgrade), May 20, 1949.
[11] *Politika,* December 22, 1949.
[12] *Ibid.*
[13] See Milentije Popovich, "O ekonomskim odnosima izmedju socialistichkih drzhava," *Komunist,* III (July, 1949), pp. 89–146.

Moscow Aim: Political Domination

Economic domination of the type envisaged by Moscow would have been possible only with a Yugoslav Communist Party completely servile to Moscow. In other words, political domination would have to go hand in hand with economic domination. Soviet leaders expected the Yugoslavs to seek and to accept the Kremlin's advice in domestic and foreign political matters. Moscow wanted to shape the internal as well as the external policies of the Balkan states.

Because Stalin did not accord them a special place, but insisted on treating them the same as other satellites, the ego of the Yugoslav leaders was seriously deflated. Tito and his close collaborators believed that they had done more than the other satellite leaders to earn Moscow's respect, yet the Russian master plan seemed to them destined to benefit the more industrialized countries such as Poland and Czechoslovakia. But Moscow's "test of devotion to the cause of proletarian internationalism" was not how much various leaders had done for their own countries, but rather their "attitude toward the Soviet Union." [14] On this score, the Yugoslav leaders, because of a number of independent acts, sometimes contrary to Moscow's expressed wishes, would not rate high.

There can be little doubt that the Soviets expected to have trouble with Tito, but it is equally true that they were confident of being able to deal with him in the event of a showdown. In the guise of military and economic specialists, Soviet agents began to penetrate various branches of the Yugoslav government at an early date. They were gathering information and attempting to discredit Tito. They were at work, too, in the Yugoslav Communist Party, endeavoring to build up an anti-Titoist wing which they hoped would gain control of the party and in the process eliminate the "Tito clique."

It is unclear at what time the Soviets sought to undermine Tito's leadership in the party, but the process had certainly begun by early 1946. Fortunately for him, Tito's agents were on the alert and succeeded in frustrating Soviet designs. Soviet agents

[14] *For a Lasting Peace for a People's Democracy!* (Bucharest), December 5, 1948.

and their Yugoslav assistants were rounded up before they could do any damage. Having failed to achieve their aim, Soviet leaders in early 1948 resorted to a series of sharply critical private letters in an effort to bring Tito to heel and to discredit him in the eyes of important Yugoslav Communists. When Tito's close collaborators remained loyal, Soviet leaders prepared to have the top Yugoslav leaders condemned by the various Communist Parties which were members of the Cominform. But the Yugoslavs refused to attend the meeting which had been called for this purpose, and were promptly excommunicated from the Cominform.

Ideological Considerations

It seems amply evident from what has been said above that ideological differences between Belgrade and Moscow were not basic to the controversy. Ideological arguments, however, have been employed in support of both positions. Moscow has insisted that the conflict is entirely ideological, that the "Tito clique" has betrayed Marxism and has sold out to the imperialistic West. For the Kremlin such a stand is entirely logical. For years Soviet leaders have set themselves up as the final arbiters of what is Marxian and what is un-Marxian. It mattered not that Tito and others might disagree, for that very disagreement constituted proof of heresy.

In the months immediately following their expulsion from the Cominform, the Yugoslav Communists did not resort to ideological arguments in defense of their position. They pointed out that the Soviet arguments were really false, that Yugoslavia was true to the Marxian cause. Almost simultaneously, they began in gradual fashion to detail the facts concerning their difficulties with the Russians: the wartime disagreements and the Soviet efforts to dominate Yugoslavia economically and politically.

As time went by, however, the Yugoslav Marxists have attempted to buttress their position with ideological arguments.[15] They have discovered many unpleasant things about the Soviet Union. They have found that it is not the utopia they once

[15] Milovan Djilas, "Lenjin o odnosima medju socialistichkim drzhavama," *Komunist,* III (September, 1949), pp. 1–53.

thought it was. The multitude of things which they now find wrong with the Soviet Union, they attribute to Stalin's "revisionism" of Marxism-Leninism.[16] Soviet actions toward Yugoslavia, Soviet slave-labor camps, the ubiquitous Soviet secret police, the rigid Soviet bureaucracy, the tendency to attribute all important inventions and other achievements to Russians—all these, and many more, according to Yugoslav Marxists, are the result not of Marxism but of Stalin's departure from Marxist-Leninist teachings.

[16] See Tito's report to the party's Sixth Congress, *Borba,* November 4, 1952.

Chapter 29:

Towards a New Communism?

IT NEEDS to be reiterated that the Soviet-Yugoslav break did not come about because of any lack of conviction in the correctness of the Marxian doctrine on the part of the Yugoslav leaders. More than that, Marxist theoreticians in Yugoslavia have since the break been diligent in affirming their loyalty and devotion to the Communist cause. By contending that Soviet leaders have gone down the path of "revisionism," the Yugoslav Communists have set themselves up as true defenders of the faith.

On the other hand, they have been equally quick to criticize the ideas which characterize Western democracy and to deny that Yugoslavia has been moving toward any acceptance of them. Insofar as their ideological pronouncements are concerned, therefore, there is nothing to indicate that their basic political beliefs have changed. Concrete situations and actual problems, however, may dictate changes in tactics, which in turn would require theoretical elaboration and justification.

As a study of Yugoslav Communism, past and present, this book does not pretend to predict the future. Predictions even for the short run are hazardous. Yet some projection into the future of current trends would seem desirable and useful. In considering the prospects for the future in the realms of politics, economics and human rights, I have attempted to limit myself to primary questions and to avoid generalizations on secondary matters or generalizations which are not strongly supported by the facts.

Political Prospects for the Future

So long as the Yugoslav Communists can manage to hold on to power the basic political decisions will continue to be made by the Central Committee of the League (formerly party) of Yugoslav Communists. This is the one overpowering fact about future political prospects in Yugoslavia. All else is subordinate. It matters not what other organizations (e.g. the People's Front, now renamed the Socialist Alliance of the Working People of Yugoslavia) may be brought to the fore or what elaborately devised governmental machinery may be erected. Behind whatever political façade the party may create, its small tightly knit group of leaders will continue to be the sole repository of effective political power.

In the exercise of their powers, however, the Communists may strive to remain in the background, to the extent that this is feasible. They may even permit nonparty people to participate in minor unimportant decisions, provided, of course, that the results are not contrary to basic Communist policy. All decisions of any consequence will be made by the Communists alone, although the well-known Communist practice of having these decisions rubber-stamped by various people's assemblies, in order to convey the impression of popular participation, will doubtless be continued.

The Yugoslav leaders now rarely refer to their regime as a "dictatorship of the proletariat" or even as a "people's democracy." Rather, they seem to prefer the term "socialist democracy." But whatever they call it, the fact remains that the Yugoslav regime is a Communist dictatorship. The men who run it know that they are unpopular, but as a member of the Central Committee said to a friend of mine, "that does not matter, for we are strong enough."

Under these circumstances, therefore, it would be naive to assume that the Yugoslav leaders would submit to a free election at any time in the foreseeable future. They cannot permit other political parties or competing political programs. To do so would mean political suicide, and the Yugoslav Communists know it. This is not to say that they will not attempt to create the impression of free elections, or that they could not permit individual candidates opposed to the official line. So long as they control the secret police, and so long as they count the ballots, the Communists could go a long ways in creating the form of free elections without endowing them with any substance.

The so-called political reforms of the past two years, like those in the economy, fall in the category of administrative reorganization. Both were primarily the result of a necessity to find a way out of the ever-present chaos, the increasing apathy among the people and the general sense of failure to be found everywhere—all of which have been generated by the regime's actions and policies. That the future will bring new "reforms" in both the economic and political spheres can be taken for granted.

The Future of Human Rights

In the matter of human rights, as in the case of politics, forms and realities are not apt to coincide. The exercise of the commonly known human rights will be possible to the extent that such actions do not imperil the political dictatorship. And it is the dictatorship which determines what acts may endanger it. In short, Yugoslav citizens will enjoy those rights which the regime believes it safe to extend to them. Since the right which they most desire is that of being able to throw the regime out of office, there is little likelihood that Yugoslav citizens will be satisfied with whatever rights may be extended to them in the near future.

There can be no talk of freedom of speech, of the press, of association or of religion so long as Communists are in power. This is not to say that the regime will not from time to time permit divergent views on certain subjects to appear in the controlled press. They have already had debates on such subjects as "Art for Art's Sake," but it would seem a safe bet that no criticism of substantive Communist policies or basic aims would be permitted. Yugoslav citizens may be allowed some discretion in debating how to build a Marxist society, but they will not be conceded the right to question the wisdom of Marxism, much less to advocate capitalism or other ideas prevalent in the West.

As a feeling of resignation and futility permeates Yugoslav society, which seems inevitable if the prospects of a general war against the Communist camp diminish, the Yugoslav regime will with considerable safety be able to let people grumble and complain. More and more they will be able to keep the secret police in the background, concentrating on the few who may be considered really dangerous. No organized opposition is likely to be permitted, however, even though it be nothing more than a discussion group. Nor is there much of a prospect for Yugoslav citizens to be allowed to leave their country freely, unless, of course, the regime perceives that they would have few places to go, even if permitted to do so.

The regime's fundamental policy of seeking to wipe out religion will without doubt continue, although an outward appearance of toleration may be sedulously cultivated. There may be fewer interferences with religious worship, but the systematic and deliberate campaign to destroy the religious idea in the minds of the young will continue at least as long as the Yugoslav leaders seek to establish a Communist society.

Yugoslav citizens who may be unwilling to reconcile themselves to the regime will continue to feel the ever-present hand of the secret police. Techniques have been refined, however, so that brutality and violence are far less in evidence. Moreover, friends of the West are rarely condemned as such any longer. Rather, they are accused of being pro-Soviet or pro-Cominform! A well-known Belgrade engineer, Peter Ristich, was sentenced in early 1953 to twelve-years' imprisonment as an alleged Soviet spy, although his friendship for the West and his detestation of all things Communist is thoroughly known there. He was arrested, along with five other friends of the West, in the early summer of 1952 for having given visiting French newspapermen unfavorable information about conditions in Yugoslavia. This was his real crime!

One item in the Yugoslav press, reporting the sentencing of two men to five and three years, respectively, for spreading "unfriendly propaganda," tended to confirm unofficial reports that friends of the West were being condemned as Cominformists. The paper cited one of the cases as a "clear example of how the remnants of reaction have found themselves . . . on the Cominform line." [1]

[1] *Politika,* January 10, 1953.

The Future of the Economy

The key to the future of the Yugoslav economy under the Communists is to be found in the words collectivism, change and experimentation. Unless the Yugoslav Communists abandon Marxism, they are certain to adhere to the collectivist approach. A change in tempo and the employment of new methods, particularly in agriculture, would seem to be a fairly certain outlook. Few, if any, concessions to private enterprise can be expected.

In view of how the economy has functioned in the past, innovations, reforms and general experimentation can be expected. In their search for workable solutions to economic problems, Yugoslav Communists will doubtless continue to improvise and to resort to trial and error methods. In doing so, it is not out of the realm of probability that some workable formulas might be devised. But it is hardly conceivable that inefficiency, corruption and popular hostility could be eliminated in the near future.

Moreover, the much heralded decentralization of the economy has given rise to new and seemingly unexpected problems. One of the most serious, if one is to judge by the official press, is "localism" or "particularism." What was meant by these terms was far from clear at the outset, but gradually a more precise meaning has emerged. At least two distinct but related aspects are involved. First, a local selfishness, manifesting itself in an emphasis on local instead of national problems, a disinclination to exploit local resources (e.g. timber) which would reduce the comparative wealth of the area and a tendency to point to a more rapid industrialization in other areas, seemingly as an indication of favoritism.[2] The second aspect of particularism is the tendency in local areas and in local enterprises to reject outside interference in their affairs.[3] Ironically enough, interpreting the so-called decentralization to mean local initiative and independent local decisions has been labeled particularism and therefore wrong. Admittedly, even some local Communists had become "the bearers of erroneous concepts." They had apparently found nothing wrong, for example, in an enterprise deciding to give its

[2] *Politika,* September 30 and October 1, 1953; *Borba,* August 12, 1953.
[3] *Borba,* September 29, 1953; *Politika,* October 2, 1953.

night shift workers their supper and a liter of wine free.[4] These developments add force to the contention that a planned economy, if it is to prevent its component parts from working at cross purposes, will have to accept a substantial amount of centralized direction and guidance.

Despite all of these and other difficulties with which the Titoists continue to be confronted, it must not be forgotten that Western assistance to the Tito regime has been considerable. With this aid it may be possible for the Communists to work out Yugoslavia's economic destinies. Without it they would have failed long ago.

Titoism: Halfway House to Freedom?

When the Soviet-Yugoslav break came most Americans applauded it, for it signified a rift in the Soviet camp. We saw the break almost solely in terms of a split in the Soviet bloc, a thing we desired and approved. In our thinking there was a tendency to identify the voice of Tito with the voice of the Yugoslav people. We assumed that they would welcome the break just as enthusiastically as we had done, and that as a consequence Tito would become a popular hero.

The general Yugoslav reaction, however, was much more cautious than ours. They welcomed the break, not so much as a split in the Soviet camp as a first step toward the collapse of Communist power everywhere. Immediately following the break some of Tito's bitter enemies greeted me with, "Long Live Tito," explaining that what they really meant was "hooray for the _____, for he has kicked out the first stone from under the Communist edifice." Most Yugoslav citizens were afraid to be optimistic, yet they hoped that the rift with Moscow would be a half step—a halfway house to freedom.

In the years since the Moscow-Belgrade quarrel the Yugoslav people have seen their cautious hopes diminish. On the one hand, they have witnessed a strengthening of the Tito regime, and on the other, they have not seen that regime change in its fundamentals. "It's still Communism," was a frequent remark which I heard. Yet for many of them hope springs eternal. They

[4] *Ibid.*

are confident that in the long run Communism, Titoist as well as Stalinist, will fall. In the short run, however, I did not find one person in a hundred, except for party men, who was hopeful that things would materially improve.

Are the Yugoslav people better off, it might be asked, than those in the Soviet satellite countries? My answer would be unquestionably yes. They are not exploited economically by a foreign power, nor is there the same degree of tenseness which is to be found in the satellites. Both of these circumstances, however, have resulted more from aid and association with the West than from any particular effort on the part of the Yugoslav Communists.

The Yugoslav people realize that despite their difficulties they are for the time being better off than their compatriots in the satellite states. Even if they could be assured that their present advantage would continue, which is an impossibility, no one could expect them to be more than temporarily satisfied. After all, if a person is suffering from a chronic disease, it is small comfort to be told that his case is milder than those of similarly afflicted persons elsewhere in the world.

Chapter 30:

Keys to the Future: World Politics

UNQUESTIONABLY, the future of Yugoslavia will in no small measure be shaped by the ebb and flow of world politics. More specifically, it will depend upon the status of the controversy between the Soviet Union and the West, and the extent to which political leaders in the Western world, especially those in the United States, view the Yugoslav regime as a potentially useful ally. These factors will dictate the type and amount of assistance which the Yugoslav government will receive. And there can be little doubt that Western policies toward the regime will have considerable bearing upon its political future domestically.

Western Aid

Following Tito's excommunication from the Cominform family the Western Powers decided to extend limited assistance to his regime. In doing so, they were motivated by two primary considerations. This was the first split in what had seemed a monolithic Communist empire, and consequently a hopeful indication that other defections would materialize, enhancing the prospect of stopping the menace of Soviet expansionism without war. Second, and equally compelling, was the fact that the defenses of the Western world in the summer of 1948 were woefully weak. Tito's assistance to the Communist uprising in Greece and his threatening presence on the Trieste frontier had taxed Western defenses to no small degree. His break with the

Cominform would not only have the effect of subtracting the Yugoslav armed forces from Stalin's total, but would in addition, it was hoped, lead to early solutions in Greece and in Trieste.

While these were two overriding considerations supporting the policy then adopted by the West, the decision to extend assistance to Tito was not made without some misgivings. Those who were responsible for shaping foreign policies in Western capitals, and particularly their representatives in Belgrade, were fully cognizant of the danger that aid from the West might have the effect of solidifying a regime that was bitterly hated by at least 85 per cent of the people. Yet they were also sure that the Cominform stooges in the Yugoslav Communist Party constituted the only force which was then in a position to benefit from any immediate struggle for power.

What of the successes or failures of the decision to extend limited aid to Tito, in view of the two predominant reasons which motivated it? The prospect that the Tito heresy would spread has so far proved to be a forlorn hope. A Soviet reign of terror wiped out potential dissidents in the satellite states. It is now self-evident that dissension within the Communist empire, if and when it comes, will arise from reasons which will be far more overpowering than the fact that with Western assistance Tito managed to hang on to his political life.

On the basis of the second consideration, however, Western policy was amply vindicated. The rebellion in Greece was liquidated. The question of Trieste, while remaining unsettled, was removed from the serious crisis category. And while it may be difficult to ascertain how important were Tito's forces in the Kremlin's plans in 1948, their removal from the Moscow camp enabled the West to forge its defenses with far fewer worries than would otherwise have been the case.

As Western defenses were built up, however, Tito's value to the cause of the free world diminished rapidly, and the second principal reason on which the policy of assistance was based became, like the first, no longer valid. Yet even after the initially critical period in the Western defense buildup had passed, economic assistance to Tito's regime was not only continued but also increased. In addition, military supplies in not inconsequential quantities have been delivered to his government.

Understandably, continued and increased assistance could have been justified in terms of the defense of a common heritage if Tito's Yugoslavia had been a part of the free world. Western policy makers, cognizant of the nature of the Tito regime, were aware that extending increased assistance to it could not be justified alone on the basically negative argument that Tito's forces had been denied to the Kremlin camp. Consequently, they decided that Tito's army would make a positive and significant contribution to the defense of the free world in case of Soviet or Soviet-directed aggression. But how sound was this view? How good an ally is Tito's Yugoslavia?

How Good an Ally?

It is not easy to assess the contribution which any nation would make in a conflict with the Soviet bloc. There are many factors, known and unknown, which would need to be taken into account. Moreover, conclusions would have to remain tentative. Yet, in view of the decision of the Western Powers to gamble on Yugoslavia, it would seem imperative that certain disturbing conditions, no matter how unpleasant they may seem to defense planners, be examined. These conditions, by and large, cast serious doubts on the wisdom of the risk which the Western Powers have undertaken.

The Yugoslav army, although untried, is seemingly well trained and, thanks to assistance from the West, has become fairly well equipped. In case of war, however, it would require a steady stream of supplies and new equipment. Yet, as everyone knows, an effective fighting force needs more than men and guns. There must be a will to fight, not only among soldiers but also among the population in general.

On the question of morale Tito's Yugoslavia would rate extremely low. While the people are strongly anti-Soviet, their hostility toward Communism is closely identified with the Tito regime. It must be remembered that the bulk of Yugoslavia's soldiers are recruited from that group in the population which is most universally hostile to the regime: the peasants. In my talks with hundreds of Yugoslavs from all walks of life, none except the Communists (who make up no more than 5 per cent of the population) believed that the army would really fight, unless there was a hope that in the process Yugoslavia, too, would be liberated from Communism.

The attitude of countless Yugoslavs was expressed in phrases such as the following: "Sure we will fight if you assure us that we too will be free . . . if you are here to take command . . . if the American flag is here. . . . Give us hope of liberation from tyranny and we will all fight. . . . Under Tito's command? Never. . . . Fight for what? To preserve this bloody tyrant and his gang? . . . Would you really expect us to help in the liberation of other peoples from Communism, while being content to remain its slaves?"

In substance, therefore, the problem of whether the Yugoslavs would make a fair contribution to the cause of the free world against Soviet aggression rests squarely, it seems to me, upon whether they would view such a conflict as a fight for their liberation too. Most of them are of the opinion that a war between the Soviet Union and the West would also result in their being liberated from Tito's Communism. Imbued with such a belief, the people could be expected to revolt against Tito's regime, and it is not at all likely that they would wait until the end of hostilities before doing so.

In either case the West faces a dilemma. If the prospects of the Yugoslav army's fighting are not bright then Tito is a poor military risk. If, on the other hand, the chances of the army's fighting are good, it will be because of a hope and an expectancy of freedom. But in such an eventuality Tito would become a political liability of the worst sort. Aware of these factors, Tito's government could be expected to resist entering any conflict. If forced to do so, however, the regime's first thoughts and actions would no doubt be turned toward a ruthless extermination of pro-Western elements suspected of desiring or assisting a popular revolution. As Tito's potential allies, the leaders of the Western Powers should think this through, and decide if this is really the way they would want to reward friendship and loyalty.

One other disturbing problem merits attention: the officer corps. Unlike the ordinary soldiers, the officers are Communists, at least all of those holding command positions of any importance. This means that there is a political-ideological chasm between officers and enlisted men. Far more important, however, is the officer corps' loyalty to Tito. All those known to have, or even suspected of having, Cominformist sympathies were purged. But no one knows how many may have escaped detection. No one knows how many of Tito's officers who are today publicly criticizing the Soviet Union are doing so on orders from Moscow. Nearly every non-Communist Yugoslav with whom I talked was convinced that the officer corps was at heart pro-Soviet.

A number of men who had served in Tito's army told me that they had doubts about the loyalty of the officer corps should a Soviet attack materialize. As one reservist put it: "We really do not know what our officers, convinced Marxists that they are, would do in a conflict with other Marxist nations whose center and overwhelming power is the Soviet Union." Another pointed out that the Communist officers know full well that if they should be captured fighting against Cominform forces, they would not be treated as ordinary prisoners of war but as traitors—as betrayers of the Communist ideology. And a veteran of World War II observed: "If the Yugoslav Communists could betray the nation in the name of the USSR and World Communism in the period 1939–1941, there is no reason to believe that the bulk of them might not do it again at some time in the future."

Moreover, methods which the Titoists have used in their efforts to ferret out officers with Cominformist sympathies cannot be expected to contribute to the building of an effective and united officer corps. Suspicions are created among officers by provocateurs in what are supposed to be tests of reliability. Among honorable men this type of testing is repugnant. Among Yugoslav Communist officers, where ideological division under present circumstances is to be expected, it serves to create suspicion and uncertainty.

If the various factors discussed above are taken into account, it would be difficult to escape the conclusion that the military contribution which Yugoslavia would make to the free world under Communist leadership is *at best* uncertain. Can the risks which the Western Powers have undertaken be justified under these circumstances? Is this type of policy, it may be asked, likely to inspire confidence in the West among enslaved peoples?

Yugoslav Foreign Policy

Since their split from the Soviet bloc, Yugoslav Communist leaders have stressed independence as a cardinal point in their foreign policy. They have rejected every suggestion that their international relations would in any way be determined by anyone but themselves. The foreign policy which they have formulated seems, in broad outline, to have taken shape. While it cannot now be predicted how future world events may serve to change their foreign policy, it would seem at this writing to be an essentially three-fold policy.

First of all, the fondest hope of the Yugoslav Communists is to be able to rejoin the ranks of international Communism, under changed circumstances of course. But this must await long-term developments. These include a significant change in the leadership and policies of the Soviet Union, the defection of China, and the capture of power by Communists in other countries. Yugoslav leaders insist that sooner or later the defection of China is a certainty. They also believe that sooner or later Communism will be victorious in other countries (e.g. in Western Europe). To the Yugoslav Communists these expected developments spell one thing—the rise of a strong bloc of Communist nations which will be independent of Moscow.

The existence of such an independent Communist force, they are convinced, will force the Soviet Union to come back into the Marxian fold from which it has strayed. Inevitable changes in the Soviet leadership, especially after Stalin's death, will, they hope, hasten the downfall of the Marxist "revisionism" which has prevailed in the Soviet Union. When that happy time arrives, they believe, relations between states ruled by Communists will be on the basis of equality. It will be remembered that one of the most persistent Yugoslav arguments against the Soviet Union has been that the latter has tried to impose its will on other Communist-ruled nations and to treat them as inferiors.

This aspect of Yugoslav foreign policy concerns the long run, and Yugoslav Communists are realistic enough to know that their hopes and expectations may prove illusory. The second and third aspects of their foreign policy are designed to meet their more immediate requirements and to provide for an alternative should their hopes of returning to the Communist camp prove ill founded.

Yugoslav Communist leaders are convinced, I am sure, that their uneasy and indefinite alliance with the West is of a temporary nature. Sooner or later there will be a parting of the ways. In the meantime, however, they are seeking to get all they can from the West, at as little cost as possible and without compromising their convictions as Communists. By acting as if the West needed them more than they needed the West, Yugoslav Communist rulers have succeeded in obtaining considerable Western assistance, including military equipment and supplies.

The tactics which they have employed are interesting. In essence, they have tried to strike a balance between seeming to do what the West desired and a truculent independence which served advance notice on Western leaders that no concessions to Western ideas would be considered, let alone granted. They moved toward the signing of a Balkan Pact with Greece and Turkey, for example, with considerable hesitation and after having asserted a number of times that they would sign no pacts. Although of questionable value to the free world's arrangements to meet the threat of Soviet aggression, the pact has been utilized by the Yugoslav regime to "prove" that relations with the West have not been one-sided. For the time being the West is supposed to be satisfied, but the Yugoslav leaders know, as do those in the West, that an end will come to assistance from the West. At that point, if not before, the Yugoslav leaders expect a parting of the ways.

Anticipating the time when their uneasy relationship with the West will come to an end, and pending favorable developments in the camp of international Communism—or perhaps even failing them—the Yugoslav leaders have evolved a third phase of their foreign policy. Their aim has been to develop mutually satisfactory relations with socialist circles and other noncapitalist forces outside the Soviet bloc. They have sought to curry favor with Western European and Asian socialists, as well as with the non-socialist rulers in such newly founded states as India and Burma, men who are not particularly concerned about Yugoslavia's anticapitalist doctrines and policies. They have sponsored all sorts of visits to Yugoslavia—at the Yugoslav taxpayer's expense—by a variety of individuals and delegations representing European and Asian socialists and other anti-Soviet leftists whom they hoped to impress.

It can be argued with considerable logic, I believe, that while the Yugoslav Communists prefer and hope for the ultimate victory of the Marxian idea along their own preconceived lines, their systematic efforts to establish cordial relations with political forces not identified with either side in the present international struggle indicate that they have doubts about the ultimate victory of World Communism. Consequently, they are taking these steps as the best protection available against the day when the Communist empire might collapse, and the anti-Communist tide threaten to sweep them out of existence.

Western Policy and the Future

Admittedly, the Western policy of assisting the Tito regime was from the beginning a calculated risk, but a risk which a realistic survey of the world situation demanded at that time. Much has happened in the intervening years since the Tito-Stalin split in 1948 to change that appraisal. When and in what ways the policies of the Western Powers toward the Yugoslav Communists may be altered is a matter of conjecture. Perhaps even before these words appear in print the Western Powers will have revised their estimates of Yugoslav defense capabilities and probabilities, and will have adjusted their policies accordingly. Perhaps they will have exerted pressure upon the Yugoslav rulers to modify some of their basic policies so as to make them less repugnant to the Yugoslav populace.

Whatever the Western Powers might seek to accomplish, they are certain to find the Yugoslav Communist rulers tough negotiators, whose moral standards are no different from those of other Communists. It should be recalled that they are the same individuals who, like the other Communists in Eastern Europe, accepted solemn pledges about free and unfettered elections, about guaranteeing freedom and protecting human rights, only to disregard these pledges with utter contempt. They are people without scruples. Is there any reason to believe that they would honor new commitments any more faithfully than those they undertook so solemnly in the past?

For the Western Powers, and especially for the United States, assistance to Communist Yugoslavia has posed an important moral question. The vast majority of Yugoslavs are sincere and loyal friends of the West, yet the policies of the Western Powers in World War II played a significant part in their enslavement. But surprisingly enough, rancor and bitterness are in large part submerged and subdued, for the Yugoslav people hope and expect the West to redeem itself.

Realizing that the regime has been in desperate need of Western aid, the Yugoslav people have not been able to understand why the Western Powers, especially the United States, have given so freely without seeking some concessions for those who are the true friends of the West, of freedom and of democracy. As time passes, it will be more difficult for Western leaders to evade the moral question. Sooner or later someone in a position of responsibility must ask: "How can we justify contributing to an *indefinite* enslavement of those people?"

Chapter 31:

Keys to the Future: the Yugoslav People

FOR the time being the vast majority of the Yugoslav people have no voice in shaping their future destinies. They are at once the prisoners of a stern domestic dictatorship and of the struggle between the Soviet Union and the West. Their experiences, within the confines of this imprisonment, will certainly influence Yugoslavia's future once she is free again. One cannot now predict the exact nature of this influence, but with the passage of time the new generation will take on an added importance. Consequently, youth is destined to become an important key to the future.

The present rulers, the Communists, also have a role to play. In a sense they are also prisoners of the game of international politics. They are by no means agreed as to the ultimate wisdom of their independent stand toward the Soviet Union. Nor do they regard their present foreign relations as anything more than temporary. Moreover, they are beset with thorny domestic problems, trying to lead an unwilling people down the path toward a Communist society.

Continuing Crisis in Communist Ranks

The inevitable stresses and strains to which the League of Yugoslav Communists is subjected will make for a continuing, although perhaps somewhat subdued, crisis within party ranks. This crisis is at once ideological and practical. On the ideological side it encompasses the twin attractions—both dangerous to the party's present position—the pro-Cominform-Soviet philosophy and the democratic ideas of the West. On the practical side there is an awareness that the regime's policies have been far from successful. Yet the Communists dare not think of failure and the consequences which it would bring.

That pro-Soviet elements in Yugoslav Communist ranks are important cannot be denied, although it is impossible to assess their strength with accuracy. In talking to foreigners, Yugoslav leaders have sought to minimize the number of Cominform adherents and to discount the attractiveness of Cominform propaganda. To their own members, however, they have publicly said that "the USSR and the ideology which dominates that country" constitute the main threat, and that Cominformists are "the main present danger to socialist Yugoslavia." [1]

Pro-Cominform sympathies among Yugoslav Communists have been manifest in several ways, but the Tito regime has attempted to hide this fact. Non-Communist Yugoslav intellectuals, who best know how the Communist mind works, believe that most Yugoslav Communists are still favorably inclined toward Moscow. They argue that this is certainly true of the party intellectuals, who realize that in the long run they will either stand or fall with the USSR. An independent existence between two hostile camps they consider precarious and at best temporary. Their only ultimate hope, they reason, is the camp of international Communism.

When I asked some of my acqaintances if they had anything but logical arguments to support their beliefs, they were quick to respond. Several pointed out that their beliefs were reinforced by the constant disappearance of Communists, "and the disappearance of men you would least suspect of being pro-Cominform." One man told me that in his office the only two Communists had disappeared. Later on he was told to take them off the payroll because they had received prison sentences exceeding six months.

A worker in Zagreb told me that among older party members he has heard such remarks as "this isn't it"; "this is not what

[1] *Borba*, June 27, 1952.

we expected," etc. He noted that many of these party men had become apathetic and had almost completely withdrawn from active participation. Peasants have told me that local Communists whom they know have said: "This is no good . . . how can we build socialism without Russia and against the whole world!" Moreover, these same peasants noted that local Communists had been happy about victories of North Korean and Chinese Communist troops.

It must be remembered that observations such as the above are not readily apparent, for the regime is ruthless toward pro-Cominform elements. Yet new evidence of pro-Cominform activity is being uncovered continually, and in the most unexpected places. One of these was the special school for diplomats and journalists, which was established after the break with Moscow. In 1952 the school was abolished, in part at least, because it was discovered that a large number of the students, some observers insist a sizable majority, were pro-Cominform. It should be emphasized that the students were handpicked for loyalty and other qualifications, and that the Tito regime expected to staff the Yugoslav foreign service with them. Theoretically, there should not have been a Cominformist in the lot, let alone such a large number. What then can be said of pro-Cominform sympathies among less rigidly screened Communists?

Yugoslav Communists with whom I talked insisted that the pro-Cominformists were small in number and that they were principally people with whom they always had trouble. They were ambitious, dissatisfied individuals who had not achieved the recognition to which they believed they were entitled. Some of them were men who had engaged in fraud or other malpractices. To cover up their wrongs or personal disappointments they made it known that they approved of the Cominform resolution which had excommunicated the Yugoslav leaders.

What loyal Titoists fail to mention is that the Cominform now directs its Yugoslav followers to disguise their views, keep their jobs and work from the inside. A few hidden Soviet supporters have been discovered in important positions, but it is admitted that ferreting out such individuals is not an easy task. An editor of the newspaper *Politika,* after he had been drinking heavily at a party of Yugoslav Communists, said to the only American at the party, "You and I are enemies, but we understand each other. Except for one other person here, they are all fools. . . . Do you think that I believe all that nonsense I write in *Politika!*" Yet he remains undetected. Interestingly enough, *Politika,* as late as February 6, 1953, complained about the reprinting and use in schools of pro-Soviet pedagogical materials. Under the circumstances now prevailing in Yugoslavia, it hardly needs be said, suspicion knows no bounds, with no assurance that the right persons will be apprehended.

Communists are often accused of being pro-Cominform simply because they evidence dissatisfaction with the way things are developing. The Titoists see in every dissatisfied Communist a potential Russian agent, and as a preventive measure he is turned in and accused of being sympathetic to the Cominform. How many such suspects are held for shorter or longer periods of time can only be speculated about. There is some reason to believe that the number has not been small. One minor incident will illustrate the nature of the detailed inquiry which Tito's secret police have sought to make into pro-Cominform sympathies among party members.

A man who was imprisoned with two Cominform suspects reported that one told him that he was about 50 per cent rehabilitated, while the other said that he was roughly 75 per cent rehabilitated. Curious to discover the nature of a rehabilitation that could be expressed in percentages, he ventured after a time to inquire of what it consisted. They told him that they were asked to submit the names of all their party comrades with whom they talked about the Cominform resolution when it was brought forth in 1948, and that up to that time they had been willing to submit 50 and 75 per cent of the names, respectively. It was obvious that these in turn would be questioned.

Regime leaders contend that since 1948 some 14,000 party members have been sent to prison for pro-Cominform activities,[2] but there is no reason to trust this figure. In any case it does not include the large number of suspects who have been held for questioning. It should be noted, moreover, that no figures have

[2] See Rankovich's report to the Sixth Party Congress, *Politika,* November 7, 1952.

been published on death sentences, although they have not been insignificant.

The Titoists know that a Cominformist is unscrupulous, that he is prepared for anything. Hence they deal harshly with him. Once a Communist disappears as a Cominformist he seems to leave no trace behind him. From time to time those who recant are released, but they are forbidden to talk about their experiences, except to say that they have seen the error of their ways and to praise the authorities for helping them to become rehabilitated. I know one Yugoslav Communist, a veteran of the Partisan war, who, although arrested and held for only a few days, carried marks on his body for several months. He was warned that if he told anyone about the beatings he had received he would never return. There would seem to be considerable evidence that those who are rearrested are never heard from again.

The Cominform threat to Tito's party is accompanied by a scarcely less aggravating menace: the corrupting nature of Western ideas. Closer contacts with the West, following the Cominform excommunication, have brought with them "foreign ideas" which are "harmful and counterrevolutionary." [3] In an overwhelmingly pro-Western population, a number of Communists, particularly the newer recruits, moved toward an easy acceptance of certain bourgeois notions. Party leaders have recognized the serious nature of this threat to their ideological position and are actively engaged in combating it.

Following a meeting of the party's Central Committee in June, 1953, a concerted drive against Western, especially American influence, was begun. [4] A campaign against "trashy" literature, comic strips and romance adventure stories was launched in the interests of Marxian purity. Singing groups that gathered in cafés were depicted as "going backward." Magazines and newspapers that had utilized a fair amount of material furnished by the United States Information Center were closed down; others were told that this should be warning enough. The growing tendency of individuals to use "mister" instead of "comrade" in addressing one another also came under attack. Finally, and perhaps most important of all, a purge of party members who

[3] See Tito's report to the Sixth Party Congress, *Borba*, November 4, 1952.
[4] See *Borba*, June 2 and 27, 1953; also *New York Times*, July 6, 1953.

had succumbed to bourgeois and nationalistic influences was begun.[5]

Some Yugoslav leaders have hinted, however, that they may be fighting a losing battle. On the one hand, the really militant Communist is apt to be pro-Soviet. To him certain recent innovations in Yugoslav internal affairs are contrary to his ideological training. There is a conflict between what he had learned and what he is now told must be done. This inner conflict occasionally manifests itself in the form of a letter to the editor. When one troubled Communist inquired why religious objects, such as ikons and small silver crosses, were being sold in a government store, he was told that the most important thing was economic solvency of the enterprise. His reaction was to write a bitter letter to the party organ, *Borba,*[6] in which he asserted that "crosses and ikons have a bad influence on our youth and we will have more harm than good from their sale," and called for an end to this "trade." Enterprises should be solvent, he said, "but not at any price." Another party member took strong exception to the printing of a church calendar in the newspaper for Pioneers in Slovenia.[7]

To this type of militant Communist Tito seems to be moving away from Marxism, and he is not easily satisfied with the official pronouncements. On the other hand, Tito is saddled with many party members who are not militant enough. Many of them joined the party after it was firmly in power. Marxism with them is only skin-deep; they learned the requisite Marxian phrases from party courses and small handbooks. Many of them belong to the party not to struggle for the realization of a Communist society but to get an extra room, more firewood and other privileges. Where prewar Communists risked arrest to read and spread the Communist press, today's Communists, by contrast, receive it by mail and many of them do not bother to look at it. In some instances they read only the sports' news.

Many of these Communists viewed the party's seizure of political power as an end in itself. They do not perceive the continuing need for an agitated ideological struggle. They have

[5] See speech by Petar Stambolich, *Politika,* June 27, 1953.
[6] Zagreb edition, September 2, 1952.
[7] See letters to the editor, *Borba,* January 3, 1953.

ceased being politically active; they do not come to party meetings, nor do they pay dues. Moreover, many of them who have made visits to the West, in connection with the aid which has been extended to the Tito regime, have become convinced that the West is not so decadent as they had been led to believe. Even the impact of Western films upon many Communists who have not traveled in Western countries has not been insignificant.

Party policies have in no small degree also contributed to this "unfavorable" situation. After the order declaring that enterprises must be solvent, for example, many government publishing firms threw Marxist writings aside. In order to insure profits, they began translating and publishing works of Western writers, many of whom are considered bourgeois by ideological Marxists. Similarly, the decree permitting withdrawals from collective farms caused no end of confusion and disillusionment among the party rank and file. Frequently, they were at a loss what to do. If they retained their former iron-clad methods of control they were condemned. If, on the other hand, they let up too much, particularly where the "class enemy" was concerned, they were damned for not being vigilant enough.

These and other experiences, together with the lack of apparent successes in the economy, have made for a less vigilant and increasingly apathetic Communist. Many of them have consented to having their children baptized, although usually in secret. Some have gone to mass. Others have rationalized the observance of the *Slava* (patron saint's day) on the ground that the people observe it, and they did not wish to "separate themselves from the people." [8] In some areas, which the official press labels "backward," many Communists have even celebrated Christmas in recent years.[9]

It is this type of apathetic member whose purge was begun in the summer of 1953, for party leaders declared that there would "be no room in the League of Communists for men who run away from duties and obligations." [10] In their determination to combat Western influence and to purge party members, the Yugoslav Communists seemed distinctly on the defensive. They

[8] *Borba,* February 27, 1953.
[9] *Ibid.,* January 23, 1953.
[10] See Stambolich speech, *Politika,* June 27, 1953.

were angry. They were provocative in the celebration of their state holidays; always trying to prove that they had not surrendered to the bourgeois and reactionary West.[11]

The campaign against Western influence exploded in all its ignominious fury in October, 1953. Using the United States-British decision to turn over the occupation of Trieste's Zone A to Italy as a pretext, Tito's organized "goon squads" made a shambles of the United States Information Centers in Belgrade and Zagreb. On the premises of the former, an American diplomat, William B. King, was severely beaten. It seems significant that the full fury of these assaults upon property and personnel (both American and local) was primarily directed against the American information centers rather than against the embassy proper. British reading rooms suffered a similar fate.

Ironically enough, it appears at this writing (October, 1953) that Tito has for the time being more effectively cut off the Yugoslav people from contacts with the West than was the case during the most hostile anti-American campaigns of his Cominform period. Yugoslavs who ventured to enter the information centers were freely beaten and otherwise terrorized. American books and information bulletins were snatched from their hands and burned in the streets. In the press, over the radio and in signs painted on the sidewalks, American and British information centers were characterized as places where only traitors would go.[12]

The suddenness of the violence tended to obscure the fact that the anti-Western, particularly anti-American, campaign had steadily been gaining momentum during the summer of 1953. The Trieste issue simply offered a convenient pretext for organized direct action, in which Communists seemingly feel so much at home.

Yugoslav Communists and the Future

The Yugoslav Communists face an uncertain future. They are far from united. The bulk of the rank and file will go whichever direction today's leadership or that of another day takes them. Among the governing elite, however, there is considerable

[11] For example see letter to *Borba*, April 30, 1953.
[12] For example see *Politika*, October 14, 1953.

uncertainty as to future developments. Some are certainly pro-Soviet. Some are cognizant of failure and would gladly leave the party, but with blood on their hands they have nowhere to go. Those most loyal to Tito are interested in the maintenance of political power above all else. They dare not think of failure. They are only too well aware of the dreaded personal consequences to themselves should the regime be replaced by a democratic order.

Fearing that the West may be giving some consideration to the possibilities of a democratic government's replacing his regime, Tito and his cohorts have surreptitiously purveyed a carefully calculated propaganda line that chaos would result if the regime should fall or be replaced. Since it is impossible for any democratic alternative to make itself known, either in the form of organizations, political parties, or individual leaders, the Titoists and their stooges have had considerable success among Western representatives by simply asking the question: who would replace the present government; who is there that could lead the country? While further reference will be made to this question in the section to follow, it is of interest here because the Titoists have found it necessary or useful as a political propaganda weapon.

While the Titoists dare not think of losing political power, practical experience may force them to the conclusion that building a Communist society according to the Marxian formula is an impossibility. If they are forced to this conclusion, and the various changes in the economy would seem to be indicative of such a possibility, if not a probability, their main concern will be the retention of political power. Under such circumstances they might let their system degenerate into a type of bastard dictatorship where ideological purity and ultimate economic objectives are considerably less important than maintaining political power.

During the electoral campaign of 1953, for example, Tito's listeners could hardly believe their ears when they heard him proclaim: ". . . I and all my collaborators hated it [the system of compulsory crop deliveries] from the bottom of our hearts." [13] If this could happen, observed one Yugoslav citizen, "this man"

---

[13] *Politika,* September 28, 1953.

could one day announce: "We are abolishing socialism . . . we always hated it from the bottom of our hearts."

Yet the tightly knit group at the apex of the Communist hierarchy, fearing negative reports and their consequences, may find it necessary to continue talking to the rank-and-file Communists about striving for ultimate objectives long after it has become convinced of the utter futility of pursuing them. Having become accustomed to good houses and automobiles, the privileged who are full may even find it difficult to believe the hungry.

It would be naive to assume that the Soviet Union and its agents would not seek to make the most of a situation favorable to them. If Tito's economic reforms signify an abandonment of hope in the victory of Marxism, or if they seem to make more remote the day of victory, Soviet arguments that the Tito regime has betrayed Marxism will have an increased impact upon a significant core of Yugoslav Communists. The possibility of a revolt against Tito by the pro-Soviet elements within his own party should not be minimized. Should it fail to materialize, however, it would nevertheless be erroneous to minimize the negative effects of the presence of dissatisfied elements within the Yugoslav regime upon the program and policies of that regime.

A pro-Cominform revolt against Tito might, ironically enough, be supported by some Yugoslavs who have suffered untold hardships and who so hate the Tito regime that they would accept added suffering if this would also bring about Tito's downfall. They would jump from the proverbial pan into the fire if they could drag Tito with them. There is some reason to believe that the Titoists fear a Soviet attempt to overthrow them through a movement whose avowed purpose was restoration of the monarchy, popular revolution and democracy.

Many Yugoslav anti-Communists who passionately desire freedom and democracy are seriously concerned about the present state of affairs. It is beginning to look to them as if liberation from Communism might come about sooner to those nations which are satellites of the Soviet Union than those which assert their independence. They are frankly afraid that should Soviet power collapse, at a time when the West is allied with Tito, their own hopes of liberation would be dimmed. To them that is not a pleasant prospect.

What Do the People Want?

Whatever the people want, one thing is certain: they do not want Communism in any form. While a precise estimate of popular opposition to the regime may be difficult to arrive at, it is certainly over 80 per cent, and more likely around 90. When in 1950 I returned from two and one-half years service in Yugoslavia, I estimated popular opposition to the Tito regime to be around 85 per cent, an estimate in which my foreign service colleagues concurred. After a renewed visit of several months in the summer and autumn of 1952, I was convinced that the more accurate figure would be 90 per cent. My Yugoslav friends whose judgment I trust and who know the situation intimately insisted that even this figure was too low.

My independent investigations revealed that the Yugoslavs whose judgment I valued seldom exaggerated the extent of popular hostility. In my conversations with countless peasants, for example, I did not find one in a hundred who was for the regime or who had anything good to say for it. Although I talked to far fewer workers, the result was not essentially different. Many a worker said to me, in slightly varied form: "Yes, I was for a broad people's democracy, I fought with the Partisans, but I did not fight for this!" Men who know the attitude of workers confirmed my findings. Among white-collar employees, except for party members, the situation is not much different. The manager of a small store in a city on the Adriatic said to me: "During the war ninety per cent of us were for the Partisans. Today ninety per cent of us are against." The attitude of youth, because of its particular importance for the future, is accorded separate treatment in the section to follow.

To naive Westerners Tito's propagandists have sought to convey the impression that the regime was popular. To the more sophisticated observers, however, they have sought to explain popular hostility in terms of mistakes and arrogance on the part of untrained local officials. They have tried to convey the impression, also to their own people, that Tito was personally popular, that he would rectify injustices if he only knew about them. To add force to this doctrine, a few selected persons have been permitted to carry their appeals to him. By the very nature of their cases, Tito has invariably been able to rule in their favor. Hence, they could go back to their communities singing his praises.

But the people have not been fooled by these tactics. I did not find a single Yugoslav who subscribed to this doctrine. While I sought to put the question in the most objective and dispassionate terms, Yugoslavs would rarely take me seriously. Some said, "Of course he is popular [in the sense of notorious] by his crimes!" Others observed, "Yes, he is more popular [again in the sense of notorious] in that his mother is cursed more often." One Yugoslav told me that the people know that orders come down from the top. Moreover, he said, "local officials are really 'little Titos who frequently invoke Tito's authority in support of their acts and their decisions." When anyone invokes laws or the constitution in protest, local officials fall back on Tito's speeches and other pronouncements to support their position.

It is well to recall, in this connection, the remarks of Tito himself, made at an earlier date. Not only was he aware of a "mistrust toward the people's authority," but he also realized that those at the top could not escape blame. "Men tell me," he said, "that this mistrust is only toward the people's authority at the bottom. I do not believe this, for we at the top are responsible for weaknesses at the bottom." [14]

What then do the Yugoslav people want? Given a free choice, few would want to return to prewar arrangements. Yet nearly every one would gladly go back to them in preference to their present regime. They would do so for two primary reasons. By contrast with life under Communism, they enjoyed relative material prosperity and relative freedom in the prewar years. I found individuals who had been most critical of prewar regimes now saying that they had not been so bad.

This attitude was particularly noticeable among ordinary people. In Croatia, for example, where prewar regimes and the Karageorgevich dynasty had not been popular, I found peasants talking about the "golden age" when referring to prewar Yugoslavia. A Croatian worker assured me that prewar opposition to the monarchy was limited to "a few politicians." When I asked his attitude toward exiled King Peter II, he replied with firmness: "What the hell, he would be a free citizen and would let me work

[14] *Borba,* November 27, 1948.

as I pleased!" The "worst part of this regime," he continued, "is that you are not the master of anything. You do not dare object or complain."

I found this reaction to be quite typical. The people were not inclined to argue much about monarchy or other political forms so long as these would provide them a semblance of freedom and some opportunity to seek material betterment through ways of their own choosing. For the most part, all of them desire a government along democratic lines, but not in the sense in which the Communists define the term democracy. They want freedom and not a police-state dictatorship. They want political differences debated and personal rights respected. They abhor a secret police and its surveillance of their activities. They do not want the state to interfere in the realm of religion or the home. Above all, they do not want to be regimented politically or economically. They desire to be masters of their own destinies to the utmost extent possible.

On the major political objectives the people seem to be pretty well agreed. But since no organized opposition is possible, they are unable to develop their ideas in more concrete form. Serbs, Croats and Slovenes with whom I talked were fairly well agreed that the future organization should be along federal lines, but not the fake type of federalism practiced by the Communists. While they conceded that monarchy may be necessary to a transition period, there was skepticism about it as the ultimate form, particularly among Croats. It would all depend, said one of them, upon whether the monarchy would follow British practice of being above politics. The first concern of all, as one Serb pointed out, is political freedom. "After that we shall find a solution. We were always more concerned about freedom from tyranny than with the sanctity of the monarchy," he added, "and you can see that from the number of monarchs we assassinated." A former Croat politician expressed similar sentiments when he said: "In freedom, men of stature will arise among Serbs as well as among Croats."

The Titoists, as previously indicated, have sought to purvey the doctrine that all would be chaos if the present regime fell. Who would lead the country, they have asked cleverly, as if to boast that they have killed off all potential non-Communist leaders. Certainly the Titoists did kill countless potential leaders, but they did not kill them all.

There are still many former members of parliament, leaders of prewar political parties, and members of other prewar governmental bodies who are respected by their fellow citizens more than ever before. Even former politicians who are today in exile are greatly respected, and news of their activities eagerly followed, principally perhaps because they believe that the exiled leaders have dedicated themselves to their liberation. In thinking about this problem, it may be well to recall that with the imminent collapse of Germany and Italy in World War II there were no clearly discernible leaders in those countries, yet they arose. And Italy, it should be remembered, had been under the Fascist heel for twenty years.

Youth and the Future

Communist governments have staked everything on youth and on the generations to come, and in this respect Tito's regime is no exception. Regardless of one's political philosophy, the importance of the new Yugoslav generation to the country's future cannot be overestimated. It is not difficult to ascertain the general attitude of Yugoslavia's youth, but because of the impact of other factors (e.g. world politics) it would be hazardous to speculate on the course which it will follow. It is possible, however, to portray the views and the outlook of youth, and to set forth the principal reasons for its basic attitudes.

Initially, in 1945, there was willingly or unwillingly a fair amount of enthusiasm for the regime among young people. Great promises for the future were held out to them. They were to be the masters of their destiny, which was to be one of freedom, abundance and happiness. They were to participate in the building of a better and more just society.

At the outset young people of gymnasium age (11–19) received the greatest attention from the regime. In the first phase, youth homes, youth restaurants, a place to play chess, a place to dance, and facilities for other youth activities were established. In this way youth was in part removed from family influence, while at the same time becoming one of the main actors in the regime's propaganda manifestations. Young people, by and large, liked this phase. The second phase, however, was different. More and more young people were asked to accept duties. They were given the job, for example, of informing the secret police on such matters as who visited with their parents, what was said by whom, etc. Despite being forbidden to do so, most young people told their parents about these assignments, and family loyalty on the whole prevailed. As the dire effects of the regime's policies upon their respective families became increasingly evident, parental loyalty was reinforced among young people.

It is doubtful if the regime ever had the support of a majority of the youth. For a time it was impossible to tell which way the large but undecided sector of youth would move. Now it is clear that they have moved away from and into passive opposition to the regime. In addition, many of those who were once enthusiastic supporters have become disillusioned. And few new recruits have been won over in the meantime.

In general, therefore, it can be said that the regime's support among youth has dwindled constantly. This has become particularly evident within the past few years. In 1950, for example, gymnasium teachers told me that, while the regime had not won the youth, they could not predict what the future would bring. In 1952, on the other hand, they were definite in asserting that the regime had completely lost the support of the youth. One teacher told me that he was "uncertain" about 5 per cent of his students. All the others, he said, are against. Teachers in different cities told a similar story. "Two or three years ago," said one of them, "there was a sprinkling of proregime students in my classes. Now I don't know if any exist. Certainly there is no manifestation of it."

University professors and other responsible persons who knew something about the attitude of youth told essentially the same story. A professor of economics, for example, said that when he read to his class from a speech by one of the Politbureau members assertions to the effect that economic conditions were better than prewar, his students laughed. One able observer believed that the regime may still command support of about 25 per cent of the youth. There are many young people who are away from home, he pointed out, and these receive stipends from the government and are in other ways held in line by Communist Party pressure. "Peasant youth," he added, "is all against."

Some observers referred to the new generation as the "lost generation." "They have been subjected to everything bad," said one, "they saw corpses, they witnessed indiscriminate killings, they have experienced lies, deception, and all types of propaganda." Among the principal crimes of the regime according to one teacher, was its "corruption of children and of youth." The children "have learned to lie, to evade, to respect no moral standards." One university student seemed to subscribe to the doctrine of the lost generation when he said: "Youth for the most part is undecided, disoriented. There are few real Communists among them—men who are convinced in the rightness of their ideology. . . . There are sympathizers and opportunists. . . . Most of us will grow up convinced in nothing."

Young people with whom I had an opportunity to associate exhibited considerable reluctance to talk freely. Fear may have played a part, as well as shyness, but the lack of practice in free expression was without doubt also a reason. While some young people expressed only a guarded opposition to the regime, and some preferred to remain noncommittal, the complete absence of enthusiasm for the regime seemed significant to me. Moreover, actions often spoke louder than words in depicting the attitude of youth.

Youth opposition to the regime was manifest in several ways. One of the most noticeable, as pointed out in an earlier section, was the failure of more and more young people to turn out for government-sponsored "voluntary" work projects, political conferences and propaganda demonstrations. Even young people who promised to turn out often failed to do so. In one division of Belgrade University, for example, some four hundred students signed up for "voluntary" work in the summer of 1952, but when the time of departure arrived only seventy responded. Many of those who are mobilized in propaganda demonstrations make light of their participation. In the spring of 1952, the party made an all-out effort to organize protest demonstrations in response to the United States-British decision giving Italy some voice in the administration of Trieste (Zone A). In response to the statements of Communist leaders at these rallies some of the students shouted: *"Tako je Mile"* ("That's right Mile"), evoking considerable laughter among their companions. The man's name was not Mile; this was the Yugoslav equivalent of "Tell it to Sweeney!"

In a number of other ways, too, youth seeks to show its independence, its rebellion against party imposed conformity. Frequently, they affect mannerisms from American movies or attempt to pattern their clothes (e.g. "zoot suits") in a way that is calculated to irritate party purists. They seek to emulate the latest American jazz adaptations, and dance patterns (e.g. "jitterbugging"). Many go to church out of caprice. They show their contempt for the premilitary training which they are required to undergo by going to football (soccer) matches between the civilian team (Red Star) and the military team (Partisan), cheering the former and heaping abuse on the latter. This was carried to such a point that the Communist press was forced to take note of it publicly and to condemn the practice.

One of the most effective manifestations of the attitude of university youth is the practice of postponing the final examination, and thus putting off the dreaded day when with diploma the graduate is handed an order to proceed to his job in some uncertain place. In early 1952 the official press reported that there were 12,000 university students (about one-fifth of Yugoslavia's university population) who had completed their work, qualifying for the final examination, but who had refrained from trying for their diplomas.[15] According to official figures, the number of such students increased markedly with and after the school year 1949–50.[16] The situation became so aggravating that the official press devoted considerable notice to it and asked for effective remedies.

When I talked to Communist youth leaders about this problem, however, they insisted that their press had "really overplayed the story." Yet, in view of the press stories, one is led to wonder if the official figures really told the whole story.

Student motives for putting off the final examination no doubt varied. Some who had left their peasant areas or their small provincial towns for the first time, had found life in the

[15] *Politika,* March 29, 1952.
[16] *Ibid.,* June 9, 1952.

larger cities much more enjoyable, and had little desire to leave for unknown assignments. In order to remain a while longer, they changed courses of study, took odd jobs, and argued that they were unprepared for the final examination. In the case of some it was a matter of calculated political opposition. On the other hand, one professor told me that a fair proportion of these students had come into the university primarily on qualifications of political reliability. "They are really not competent for any skilled job," he added, "and they do not relish the thought of failing in their examinations and becoming common laborers."

Whatever the motives, this attitude on the part of university youth constitutes a telling commentary on the failure of the regime to evoke enthusiasm among young people. If university students had great hopes for the future, if they believed regime propaganda about the new vistas that are supposedly ahead for them, one would think that they would be eager to complete their university work and to get on with the building of the new society. If one is to judge by what competent Yugoslav observers tell him, by what he hears from young people and by observing their actions, he cannot escape the conclusion that youth enthusiasm for the regime has been constantly on the wane.

A number of reasons explain the failure of the Tito regime to win youth over to its side. First, there are the broken promises and the evidences of failure, which have had a demoralizing effect. Much was promised and, as one shrewd peasant said to me, "He who tells a lie will not be believed when later he tells the truth." Even a "three-year-old child knows," he continued, "that if once or twice you promise him candy and you fail to deliver, you are not to be trusted or believed."

Despite all the professions about freedom, youth knows that there is little real freedom or democracy. Young people became aware from the outset that they could not express views on public questions if they did not conform to the party line. On the other hand, while not being able to do things they wished to do, they were asked to do things for which they had no enthusiasm. They were asked to become informers. They were required to work on summer youth projects, and threatened with expulsion from school if they failed, although constantly referring to these projects as voluntary. Students found these projects hard going from the physical point of view because the food was not adequate for difficult physical labor. And the daily political indoctrination came to be resented. In the meantime, the government's "economy drive" resulted in many students' losing their scholarship stipends, which for a time had been fairly liberal.

Moreover, other discrepancies between the regime's professions and its practices had their disillusioning effect. This in turn raised youth's estimate of their non-Communist parents, teachers and clergymen. Early Communist brutality against unenthusiastic and so-called reactionary students turned many a youngster into an opponent of the regime. As the Titoists violated the most basic moral principles, more and more young people had their belief in religion and in the moral precepts which they learned at home and from non-Communist teachers considerably reinforced. Youngsters who saw their parents disappear into the night did not easily forget.

The violence of the regime's collectivization drive against the peasants, the compulsory deliveries of grain, the sentences at hard labor for those who failed or were unable to deliver the required amounts—all these turned the peasant youth against the regime. When I asked one peasant student who had just finished a year at the university in Belgrade to explain the "large-scale" student dissatisfaction about which he had told me, he replied that it stemmed in large part from the fact that the students' parents had suffered under the regime. "Some parents were killed, some have been imprisoned, subjected to compulsory crop deliveries and heavy taxation." The general impoverishment of the peasant, he noted, has meant that the peasant could not afford to buy clothes for his children and he has in other ways found it difficult to send them to school.

Some students who otherwise might have been favorably inclined toward the regime were repelled by the methods and attitudes of crude and narrow youth leaders. Many of these youth leaders came from small provincial towns. They came to Belgrade, Zagreb or other larger cities, and as sons of important Communists, they were highly recommended by their respective provincial party organizations. Students from the larger cities, including Communists, being on a higher cultural level, found the provincial boys with their narrow views quite unbearable.

But these sons of important Communists had to be given significant jobs in working with youth. These half-literate leaders had a
tough time with youth that had learned to dance, to dress a certain way, to use fingernail polish, and to behave in other ways
which were strange to the backward village.

Finally, the break with the Kremlin in 1948 showed youth
that all was not well in the Communist camp. Yugoslav propaganda had established Moscow as politically and ideologically
infallible. Youth had been led to expect great successes because
Russia was "helping" them. The break shattered all this. As time
passed, it became more and more evident that the bright promises
and glorious expectations were illusory.

With the continuation of the struggle between the Soviet
Union and the West, and with the increased penetration of Western ideas among those who are already disillusioned, more and
more Yugoslav young people doubt the permanence of the Tito
regime. Is it any wonder then that youth does not wish to be
attached to something that it considers temporary?

Yugoslav youth, despite all of the corrupting influences of a
Communist dictatorship, offers at this writing a hopeful symbol
to the free world. As a key to the future of the Yugoslav people's
traditional aspirations to freedom and democracy, Yugoslavia's
new generation merits confidence. But the members of that generation know full well that they alone cannot be the masters of
their destiny. Their hopes and their fears are centered in the
West, and particularly in the United States. They know that the
actions or inactions of the free world will in large part determine
their fate.

Bibliographical Note

ALTHOUGH this book is based upon Yugoslav sources and upon the author's experiences in Tito's Yugoslavia, it seems desirable to append a brief bibliographical note which would also include some English-language works that have been published since Tito's rise to power. Only a few selected titles are included, however, and no attempt has been made to select articles from the growing periodical literature on Yugoslavia, much of it, unfortunately, being shallow, sketchy and misleading.

1. For general background information on various phases of Yugoslavia's past the best single work is Robert J. Kerner, ed., *Yugoslavia* (Berkeley, 1949).

2. On the World War II period and the Communist seizure of power, a number of works by the Communists themselves are invaluable. Among these is Vladimir Dedijer's three-volume diary, *Dnevnik,* (Belgrade, 1945, 1946 and 1950, respectively). Parts of Dedijer's diary have appeared in English, and his official biography of the Yugoslav dictator, *Tito* (New York, 1953) contains many extracts from the diary's pages. Equally valuable is Leon Gershkovich's, *Dokumenti o razvoju narodne vlasti,* "Documents Concerning the Development of the People's Authority" (Belgrade, 1948), which is widely used as a textbook in Yugoslav schools, universities and special indoctrination courses. The collected speeches, articles and orders of Josip Broz Tito, under the title, *Borba za oslobodjenje Jugoslavije, 1941–1945,* "The Struggle for the Liberation of Yugoslavia, 1941–1945" (Belgrade, 1947) contain significant materials. Also of value are the volumes of collected documents whose publication was begun in Belgrade in 1949 by the Military-Historical Institute of the Yugoslav Army (Vojno-istoriski institut Jugoslovenske armije), *Zbornik dokumenata i podataka o narodno-oslobodilachkom ratu Jugoslovenskih naroda.* Unfortunately, one cannot assume that all significant documents have been included. And the practice of omitting parts of reproduced documents, notably German, makes many of these documents of little value. Finally, the official record of the Mihailovich trial, *The Trial of Dragoljub-Drazha Mihailovich* (Belgrade, 1946) is interesting both for its contents as well as for its omissions.

The writings of members of British military missions in Yugoslavia during World War II shed a good deal of light on the Communist revolution. Among these are: Stephen Clissold, *Whirlwind: An Account of Marshal Tito's Rise to Power* (London, 1949); Jasper Rootham, *Miss Fire: The Chronicle of a British Mission to Mihailovich, 1943–1944* (London, 1946); Fitzroy Maclean, *Eastern Approaches* (London, 1949). Two accounts published in this country also contain significant information. They are: David Martin, *Ally Betrayed; The Uncensored Story of Tito and Mihailovich* (New York, 1946), and Constantine Fotitch, *The War We Lost; Yugoslavia's Tragedy and the Failure of the West* (New York, 1948).

3. For a study of Tito's Yugoslavia it is imperative that one dig deeply and critically into Yugoslav publications. These are many and varied, and obviously only a few can be mentioned here. Perhaps the most important single source is the Yugoslav press, particularly the national organ of the Communist League (Party), *Borba,* although the party organs in each of the republics should not be overlooked (e.g. *Naprijed* in Croatia and *Partiski radnik* in Serbia). Of almost equal importance are the official organs of the Socialist Alliance of the Working People of Yugoslavia, notably the national organ, *Politika.* Particularly revealing of the Communists' long-term ideological campaign are the newspapers designed for youth. The most important of these is *Omladina* (Youth), official organ of the People's Youth of Yugoslavia. Student papers at various universities (e.g. *Narodni student,* Belgrade; *Studentski list,* Zagreb) also contain pertinent materials.

Also useful are various periodical publications. Some of the more important are: the bimonthly organ of the party's Central Committee, *Komunist;* the monthly publication of the Central Committee of the national youth organization, *Narodna omladina* (People's Youth); and the bi-monthlies, *Arhiv za pravne i drushtvene nauke* (Archive for Legal and Social Sciences) and *Narodni pravnik* (People's Jurist). The English-language quarterly, *New Yugoslav Law: Bulletin on Legislation in the Federal People's Republic of Yugoslavia,* contains important but selected materials for those who do not read Serbo-Croatian. Because of frequent political and economic changes in Yugoslavia, however, these periodicals cannot always be relied upon to depict accurately the current state of affairs.

The collected articles, speeches, interviews and other statements of Josip Broz Tito, under the title, *Izgradnja nove Jugoslavije,* "The Building of the New Yugoslavia" (Belgrade, 1947) are interesting for the first years of Tito's regime.

The records of the various party congresses, especially the principal reports (printed in the press and often separately), are a must for students of Tito's Yugoslavia. The proceedings of parliament, *Stenografske beleshke* (Stenographic Notes), as well as the government's official gazette (*Sluzhbeni list*) are also helpful as sources of laws, decrees and other official acts which impinge upon every phase of Yugoslav life.

There have been few book-length studies in English of Yugoslavia under Communist rule, and far fewer deserve mention. Particularly perceptive of the internal workings of Tito's regime is Josef Korbel's, *Tito's Communism* (Denver, 1951). Also discerning, but lacking Korbel's intimate firsthand experiences, is Reuban H. Markham, *Tito's Imperial Communism* (Chapel Hill, 1947). On the other hand, Robert St. John's, *The Silent People Speak* (New York, 1948) is almost totally uncritical and unperceiving. In the same category is Louis Adamic's, *The Eagle and the Roots* (Garden City, 1952), which idolizes Tito or his associates on almost every page.

4. The Yugoslav press and other Yugoslav publications are replete with materials on the foreign relations of the Tito regime. These are chiefly in the form of speeches and other pronouncements of the Yugoslav leaders. One of their more important recent exposes in English, prepared principally for Western consumption, is Vladimir Dedijer's, *Tito* (New York, 1953).

Perhaps the best account of Tito's foreign relations is to be found in Hamilton Fish Armstrong's, *Tito and Goliath* (New York, 1951). Also valuable is Adam B. Ulam, *Titoism and the Cominform* (Cambridge, 1952). Harry Hodgkinson, *Challenge to the Kremlin* (New York, 1952) is interesting for its broad philosophical discussion of the various implications in Tito's challenge to Moscow. Also interesting is Leigh White's, *Balkan Caesar: Tito versus Stalin* (New York, 1951). Important documentary materials are to be found in *Soviet-Yugoslav Dispute: Text of the Published Correspondence* (London, 1948).

Index

[For subject index, see analytical Table of Contents]